Famous
Conversions
THE CHRISTIAN EXPERIENCE

Edited by

Hugh T. Kerr
and
John M. Mulder

William B. Eerdmans Publishing Company
Grand Rapids, Michigan

Copyright © 1983 by Wm. B. Eerdmans Publishing Company
255 Jefferson Ave. S.E., Grand Rapids, Michigan 49503

First published 1983 as *Conversions: The Christian Experience*

Reprinted 1996

Library of Congress Cataloging-in-Publication Data
Main entry under title:

Famous conversions: the Christian experience.

1. Converts—Addresses, essays, lectures. 2. Conversion—
Addresses, essays, lectures. I. Kerr, Hugh T.
(Hugh Thomson), 1909- . II. Mulder, John M., 1946- .
BV4930.C63 1983 248.2′4 83-5660
ISBN 0-8028-4065-5

CONTENTS

ACKNOWLEDGMENTS

Several people have assisted us in valuable ways in the preparation of this book, and we would like to record our gratitude to them. The library staffs of Princeton Theological Seminary, Louisville Presbyterian Theological Seminary, and Western Theological Seminary helped us secure the texts of these conversion accounts and provided us with congenial surroundings for our work. Elizabeth W. Meirs assisted us at an early stage of our work with the correspondence, and Virginia Marcum and especially Ava Melton were invaluable in making sense of the tangled problems of permissions. The editorial staff of Eerdmans has been helpful and cooperative in bringing this book to publication. While the present work is a joint undertaking, it became a communal endeavor, and we appreciate the tolerance but even more the support and enthusiasm that these people and our colleagues provided to us. We hope that in some small way this survey of the church's witnesses might be a means of recovering what the Apostles' Creed means by the "communion of saints."

HUGH T. KERR
JOHN M. MULDER

INTRODUCTION

The English word "conversion" suggests the act of "turning around," moving from one place to another. The turning process can be physical, spiritual, emotional, theological, or moral. It is this physical-spiritual combination that lies behind the original Hebrew and Greek vocabulary in the Old and New Testaments.

The word conversion does not often appear in the Bible, but certain synonyms such as "repentance," "regeneration," and "being born again," occur almost everywhere and with great frequency throughout the Scriptures. The notion of "turning" can be variously stated, as for example "to turn," "to return," "to turn to," "to turn away from, "to turn toward," or "to turn around." To be converted is like making a "U-turn." It is "starting at square one again" or "back to the drawing board."

Conversion, however it may be described, involves a complete change from one life-style to another. It may require abandoning an aimless and unsatisfying perspective in exchange for a new and promising incentive to live a more meaningful life. Sometimes the fact and experience of conversion are related to the search for intellectual truth or the longing for moral purity and goodness. At other times, and these make up the more graphic accounts of dramatic conversions, deep emotional earthquakes erupt out of the past, shatter the present, and make way for a new tomorrow.

I

In the Hebrew Scriptures, conversion is often associated with the divine challenge to the people of Israel to return from their false worship to the true faith of the Holy One, "the Father of Abraham, Isaac, and Jacob." Especially in the prophetic literature, the perverse Israelites were confronted by the eloquence of Isaiah, Jeremiah, Ezekiel, and others who urged them to forsake their idolatry and immorality, and to turn toward the merciful God who created them, provided for them, and led them out of bondage into the new life of the promised land.

Let the wicked forsake his way,
　and the unrighteous man his thoughts;
let him return to the Lord, that he
　may have mercy on him,
　and to our God, for he will abundantly pardon.
(Isa. 55:7; cf. Ezek. 18-30, 32; Hos. 14:2)

Elsewhere in the Old Testament, and particularly in the so-called penitential Psalms, the longing for conversion grows out of a deep sense of sin, suffering, and frustration. Here we cannot be sure whether the Psalmist speaks as an individual or for the people as a whole. But a profound sense of oppression and alienation, whether personal or corporate, pervades these lyrical expressions of religious faith. The stab of conscience, the shame of inward uncleanness, the remorse for sin, and the sensation of being lost and alone—all these agonies of soul are coupled with prayers for mercy, forgiveness, and a new chance to begin all over again.

Create in me a clean heart, O God,
　and put a new and right spirit within me.
Cast me not away from thy presence,
　and take not thy holy spirit from me.
Restore to me the joy of thy salvation,
　and uphold me with a willing spirit.
(Ps. 51:10-12; cf. Ps. 6, 32, 38, 102, 130, 143)

There are also accounts of individual conversion experiences in the Old Testament, and indeed most of the pivotal figures, such as Abraham, Moses, Jacob, Samuel, and the prophets, were summoned by an insistent God in such a way that they could only describe their call as an abrupt right-about-face. The dramatic episode of the prophet Isaiah is typical:

I saw the Lord sitting upon a throne, high and lifted up; and his train filled the temple . . . and the house was filled with smoke. And I said: "Woe is me! For I am lost; for I am a man of unclean lips . . . for my eyes have seen the King, the Lord of hosts!"
(Isa. 6:1-8)

The basic elements in this incident tend to be repeated in almost every Old Testament conversion experience. There is the flashing vision of truth, the conviction of sin and unworthiness, the joy of forgiveness and absolution, and the ready acceptance of a new life of mission and service.

II

In the New Testament, conversion and all its cognate terms, such as repentance and new life, are directly related to the person and message of the Christ figure. Jesus began his public ministry by announcing that "the kingdom of God is at hand; repent, and believe in the gospel" (Mark 1:15). And his final words to his disciples commissioned them to convert the world: "Go therefore and make disciples of all nations" (Matt. 28:19).

The conversion experience summons up almost endless figures of speech in the New Testament writings. It can be a transfer out of darkness into light (I Pet. 2:9), a spiritual rebirth or being born again (John 3:3), a restoration from impurity (Titus 2:14), a translation from death to life (John 5:24), a turning away from Satan to God (Acts 26:18), a totally new creation (II Cor. 5:17), a getting rid of an old and acquiring a new humanity (Col. 3:9), a dying to self but rising again in Christ (Rom. 6:2-8).

The classic case of Christian conversion is, of course, that of the apostle Paul (Acts 9:1-19; 22:1-21; 26:1-23). The experience was dramatic, decisive, and determinative. Paul was never the same again, and in many ways the apostolic incident parallels Isaiah's prophetic vision. But the New Testament does not suggest a single stereotype for an authentic conversion experience. Nicodemus, for example, who provokes the dialogue with Jesus about what it means to be born again (John 3), is himself an ambiguous illustration of conversion. We don't really know whether Jesus persuaded Nicodemus or not. All we know is that later on he turned up at the time of Jesus' burial and entombment and gave some assistance (John 19:38).

The New Testament balances the sudden conversion of Paul with the more gentle and subtler changes wrought in people like Zacchaeus (Luke 19:1-10), Matthew (Matt. 9:9; cf. Mark 2:13; Luke 5:27), Lydia (Acts 16:14), and Timothy (Acts 16), to say nothing of all those nameless souls who are lumped together as converts, saints, and martyrs in the book of the Acts, the Pauline epistles, and the letter to the Hebrews.

If a new kind of life is what conversion implies in the New Testament, the consequence of the Christian conversion experience is a new sense of mission. The disciple as follower becomes the apostle, one sent out to proclaim the good news of the gospel. In the early apostolic church, conversion is seldom described as an experience to glory in as if it were sufficient in itself as sheer emotional ecstasy. Conversion in the authentic Christian sense implies a commission to tell others and to follow in the footsteps of a Master whose commitment took him to the cross. That is one reason why Christians in the New Testament are such busy people. They are out to convert everyone and to turn the world upside down. So we read of Paul and Barnabas, in a typical description of their many travels, that they "passed through both Phoenicia and Samaria, reporting the conversion of the Gentiles, and they gave great joy to all the brethren" (Acts 15:3; cf. 17:6).

III

While a conversion experience may be for the convert the most real and significant event in his or her life, it is almost always difficult to interpret or explain to others. The reason is simply that conversion involves complex questions of theology, psychology, and sociology.

Theologically, it is not easy to say how the experience of conversion begins. Do human misery and the longing for a better life prompt the conversion quest? Or, does God's grace within the human soul initiate the process? No doubt the human and the divine interact, but the paradox remains.

Psychologically, conversion can be readily related to, say, the crisis of adolescent identity or to the sense of moral and personal failure and the therapeutic need for acceptance. But while psychology can illuminate the dark places of the human spirit, it cannot explain the convert's assurance of being born again or that God has turned life upside down and inside out.

Sociologically, conversion can be put in the context of culture and history. Paul's conversion is not the same as Augustine's, and Pascal's testimony is not that of C. S. Lewis. Not only do times and seasons color the conversion experience, but certain historical and cultural factors seem to be especially propitious for mass revivals, group conversions on a large scale, and evangelistic preaching calling for public decisions.

The Middle Ages illustrates very clearly how historical and sociological factors relate to conversion experiences. From the time of Augustine to the eve of the Protestant Reformation, personal conversion reports appear only infrequently. There are at least two cultural reasons for this medieval silence.

From the time of Constantine through the European expansion of Christendom and into the period of the Crusades, vast geographical areas and countless individuals became Christian. But it is an extremely delicate exercise to distinguish between authentic conversions and political conquests by might and sword.

Yet there is a second reason for the medieval gap. Monks in monasteries, aristocrats, and royal patrons might have possessed hand-copied manuscripts and dictated to scribes and secretaries. But we must remember that Gutenberg's Bible was not printed until 1456. If one purpose for recording a personal conversion experience would be to persuade and convince others, many in the Middle Ages who might have given evidence of their faith were mostly restricted to oral rather than literary communication.

In any case, to recognize that there are not only theological but psychological, historical, and sociological factors involved in conversion underscores the mystery of the relation between human questing and divine initiative. Those who have recorded their innermost thoughts and feelings about conversion also often confess to being puzzled by what happened, how, and why.

IV

This mysterious quality invariably accompanies the various ways the church has understood conversion throughout history and the different kinds of experiences that Christians themselves have described. To speak of "types" of conversion may do an injustice to the converted person, for each individual experience may well contain unique features. Even so, several common themes seem to emerge in the variety of Christian conversion accounts. Three may be noted here.

First, conversion is sometimes a dramatic and clearly identifiable experience, such as Paul's confrontation with Christ on the Damascus road. But it can also be a long and extended process, sometimes with no clear beginning and no clear end. In his classic discussion, *The Varieties of Religious Experience* (1902), William James described this as the difference between the "once-born" and "twice-born" individual. The "once-born" person is one of those fortunate people whose lives are not marked by radical breaks or deep crises; rather, they seem to go "from strength to strength," with confidence in God's sustaining love and trust in God's forgiveness and guidance. In the words of Horace Bushnell, an apologist for "Christian nurture," they seem to be people who never remember a time when they were not Christians.

The "twice-born" are those whose lives can be described as a series of signposts—of new directions taken, of ends and new beginnings, and specifically of a definite and certain experience of conversion at a particular moment. Many of the conversion accounts in this book are examples of this second type, in part because the stories of the life-long conversions of the "once-born" cannot be easily summarized or described. We may be tempted to accord spiritual superiority to the "twice-born," but throughout its history the church has always welcomed both kinds of Christians into fellowship—rejoicing in the joy of the new convert while, at the same time, sustaining the life of those who grow in grace day by day.

Second, the Christian church has also wrestled to understand the nature of the conversion experience and its importance within the church itself. Some Christians have argued that God's grace is so great and mysterious, and human sin so pervasive, that one cannot talk about a definite moment for becoming a Christian; such a claim, they insist, would be arrogant and would limit God. Others insist that God's love is so powerful that it breaks through at specific times in human life to bring certainty of forgiveness. Some even maintain that an individual can become perfect through a recreation of the Holy Spirit. Each of these arguments emerges from different understandings of the church itself.

Is the church a body of "visible saints," as the New England Puritans assumed—people who have had a definite conversion and can narrate it publicly to others? Or is the church a combination of the "twice-born" *and* the "once-born"—both confessing Jesus Christ as Savior, but experiencing God's grace in different ways? These questions, and several other more complicated versions of them, have marked the history of Christianity and demonstrate the complexity of the nature of conversion itself.

It is also true, as several of the following accounts make clear, that conversions sometimes cross church and denominational lines. For all kinds of reasons, a particular creed or communion may be abandoned in favor of another. When vigorous and perhaps underhanded attempts are made to woo converts from one church to another, we castigate the process as unjustifiable "proselytizing." No doubt, examples of forced conversions can be found in Christian history at home and abroad. But, happily, there is little proselytizing among the churches today. Usually, when a person moves from one denomination to another, it is for personal, rather than pressured, reasons.

This also reminds us that conversion is an inclusive term and that Christian experiences come in many forms and varieties. As several of the personal accounts that follow clearly indicate, conversion is not necessarily limited to a radical shift from unbelief or doubt to Christian faith. Those who move, for example, from one branch of Christianity to another were obviously already Christian even if the new commitment also represents the renewing, as well as the widening and deepening, of Christian experience.

In addition, we include a few whose conversion experience seems more in the nature of vocational decision rather than emotional experience. And, although we do not raise the issue here, history sometimes shows us converted Christians who later lost the initial radiance of their experience.

Third, as the following accounts demonstrate, there is a remarkable, even exhilarating, variety in the way people describe their conversions. For some, it is obviously a highly emotional experience, shattering the very depths of their beings and reaching into the inner recesses of the human psyche. For other people, it seems to have been a much more intellectual matter—a recognition of the truth of Christianity and its doctrines without a deep emotional crisis. Sometimes the experience is primarily moral, leading the individual from a life that is seen as sinful or wrong into a pattern of behavior and a vision of existence that emphasizes obedience, discipline, social justice. But at other times the experience seems to be aesthetic rather than moral—a glimpse of the beauty of Holiness and a new way of perceiving the world and one's place in it. Some emphasize the power of God and their surrender to God's amazing grace, while others stress the decision they made to accept the forgiveness that was offered to them in Jesus Christ.

Given this variety, how can conversions be judged and evaluated? Many would insist that such judgment must be left to God. Even after Jesus told Nicodemus that he must be born again, he cautioned that "the wind blows where it wills, and you hear the sound of it, but you do not know whence it comes or whither it goes; so it is with every one who is born of the Spirit" (John 3:8). Conversion is a mystery of God, and the varieties of conversion experiences testify to that divine initiative seeking out those who are lost, finding them, and bringing them home.

And yet, on the basis of the Bible and the history of the Christian church, it is clear that faith must not be understood as merely an experience—even a conversion experience. Jesus admonished his followers, "Not everyone who says to me, 'Lord, Lord,' shall enter the kingdom of heaven, but he who does the will of my Father who is in heaven" (Matt. 7:21).

Christianity is a way of life in which our thoughts and deeds and experiences are infused and transformed by the mystery of the love of God, a way of life witnessing to the love and forgiveness revealed in Christ Jesus. "You will know them by their fruits" (Matt. 7:16).

V

The conversion accounts included in this volume have been selected as *representative* of the wide variety of recorded experiences. Rather than attempting to "type" each one, the entries are simply listed in more or less chronological sequence. Each is introduced with a brief preface to set the author and the account in context, and in many instances the texts have been shortened and digested in the interests of uniformity.

The literary style and format of the original texts have been retained, including quaint and obsolete expressions as well as the masculinist language that many contemporary readers may find offensive and unacceptable. Many today, including the editors, wish to be more inclusive in our language, especially language about God, creation, and human nature. But that is a literary responsibility for today and tomorrow rather than an impossible assignment to rewrite the historical annals and classic texts of the past.

Extensive and diverse as the selections may appear, they still fall short of a full-scale roll-call. But that, of course, is impossible. As the writer of the epistle to the Hebrews noted, "time would fail" to tell of all Christ's faithful witnesses (Heb. 11:32). If true in New Testament times, how much more so today!

Even so, some names that obviously belong here had to be ignored either because there is no written personal record available, or the account is so short and ambiguous as to lack significant detail. For example, Francis of Assisi, according to his contemporaries and his later biographers, definitely did have a conversion experience. It was probably associated with one of three events: a heavenly voice that told him to restore and rebuild churches, a head-on confrontation with extreme poverty in Rome, or his identification with a leper begging alms. Biographers of Francis have written at great length about the legends of the Saint, but the Little Friar wrote nothing about his experience, and it seems only proper to respect his reticence.

Thomas Aquinas, the foremost medieval theologian and the "doctor" of modern Catholicism, stopped writing his massive *Summa Theologiae* when he was in sight of the end. Apparently he experienced a mystical vision of some kind, for when a colleague asked why he didn't continue, Thomas replied: "I cannot go on. . . . All that I have written seems to me like so much straw compared to what I have seen and what has been revealed to me." But beyond that we simply don't know what happened.

Martin Luther, the great reformer, was struck to the ground by a lightning bolt and cried in terror: "St. Anne, help me! I will become a monk." Later on, Luther was to write scathingly of both saints and monks, but of this experience he tells us very little. A year before his death, as he looked back on his tempestuous career, he prepared a "Preface" to his writings and alluded to a breakthrough for him on the doctrine of justification. It emerged from reflection on the Pauline text: "the righteousness of God is revealed through faith for faith; as it is written, 'He who through faith is righteous shall live' " (Rom. 1:17). Historians raise questions about the accuracy of the details, but as he remembered it, Luther wrote: "Here I felt that I was altogether born again and had entered paradise itself through open gates."

Dwight L. Moody, who spent most of his revivalistic and preaching career calling for conversions and urging sinners to repent, himself left no extended account of his own experience. His application for church membership in Boston was deferred because of the vagueness of his beliefs. But shortly thereafter something must have happened even though all he could write about was his joy to be alive. "I thought the old sun shone a good deal brighter than it ever had before—I thought that it was just smiling upon me; and as I walked out upon Boston Common and heard the birds singing in the trees, I thought they were all singing a song to me. . . . It seemed to me that I was in love with all creation."

Today, Billy Graham falls into the same category. He tells us that at the age of sixteen, an evangelist in a tent meeting "had an almost embarrassing way of describing your sins and shortcomings," and in that meeting "something began to speak to my heart." Later he wrote that when he began his ministry of evangelism, he "had not read a single book on the subject of conversion." But his teenage experience, he said, was still vivid and "the brilliance and wonder" of the encounter remained.

During the great century of the so-called foreign missionary movement, hundreds of converts to Christianity in every land under the sun added their names, famous and obscure, to the Christian inventory. For example, Toyohiko Kagawa, the Tokyo slum reformer, wrote many best-sellers in his day that were widely translated, but he tells us almost nothing about his conversion. It was simply, so he says, an outcry: "O God, make me like Christ!" That was it, and it is enough. Illegitimate, half blind, always sick, the little orphaned Japanese became as much like Jesus as anyone before or after his time.

In India, the high-caste Sadhu Sundar Singh confessed his Christian faith as the result of a vision he received shortly after he had poured kerosene on a Bible and burned it. With precise notation, he wrote: "At 4:30 a.m. [Dec. 18, 1904] I saw . . . a great light. I thought the place was on fire. . . . I saw the form of the Lord Jesus Christ. It had such an appearance of glory and love." The Sadhu (holy man) became something of an ascetic, adopted a simple life-style, communed alone with wild beasts at night, and was last seen making for Tibet, off-limits for Christians. In his day, Singh's books were translated and distributed in the hundreds of thousands, but he never made much of his own conversion.

At the center of this Christian missionary movement in its more expansive years stood the tall, elegant, and eloquent John R. Mott. An American emissary at home everywhere in the world, Mott's evangelism was inspired with his own enthusiasm and irrepressible optimism. At age thirteen, he wrote later, a Quaker evangelist "led my father, two of my sisters, and me to Christ." As a Cornell University student, he came to the point where he was able "with Thomas to say to Christ with intellectual honesty, 'My Lord and my God.'" In his own Methodist tradition, it was a sort of "second blessing," but he never wrote about it in any detail.

It would be intriguing to include, just to mention two more possibilities, Søren Kierkegaard and T. S. Eliot. Different in so many ways, both have deeply influenced later generations, one as the father of existentialism, and the other by way of new modes and moods of poetry. The melancholy Dane sought all his life to define what it means to be a Christian, and Eliot in his mature years, quietly and without show, joined the Church of England, a symbol of his Christian commitment.

There is only one ambiguous note in Kierkegaard's *Journals,* entered with the exact moment—"*May 19* [1838]. *Half-past ten in the morning. There is an indescribable joy.* . . ." But we don't know whether it was joy at the prospect of returning to his father's house for a reconciliation, or whether the reference is more subtle, his spiritual joy at returning to his heavenly Father's true home.

Raised as a Unitarian in America and hating dramatic public conversions, T. S. Eliot arranged for a private baptism. Shortly thereafter he made his first confession and said that "the recognition of the reality of Sin is a New Life." Like Kierkegaard, Eliot's own person must be discovered behind his writing, and the best account of his conversion is between the lines of his poem *Ash Wednesday,* with the penitent turning and turning on the winding stairway. The image suggests the classic turning away from sin toward God.

Such tantalizing but terse accounts only make us wish for more. Alas, some who might have taught us by revealing their inmost experiences have chosen rather to remain silent about themselves.

Happily, there are so many others, as these representative selections indicate. And whether famous or not, the important thing for any Christian is not only to record what it means to be converted but to have one's own name "written in the Lamb's book of life" (Rev. 21:27).

*"Jesus answered him, 'Truly, truly, I say to you,
unless one is born anew,
he cannot see the kingdom of God.'"*
(John 3:3)

*"The wind blows where it wills,
and you hear the sound of it,
but you do not know whence it comes
or whither it goes;
so it is with every one who is born of the Spirit."*
(John 3:8)

The Apostle Paul

The dramatic experience of Paul on the road to Damascus still constitutes for many the prototype and model of Christian conversion. It is true, of course, that not all authentic conversions follow the Pauline pattern. Yet there remains something normative in this early apostolic account.

Scholars and psychologists seem fascinated by Paul's conversion, and they try to interpret what it meant and why it happened as it did. Obviously, Paul regarded his experience as of monumental and life-changing importance. There are three more or less parallel accounts of the episode in the book of the Acts, and Paul made passing references to the event on other occasions (e.g., Gal. 1:15-16; I Cor. 9:1; 15:8; II Cor. 4:6).

Before his conversion, Paul was known as a relentless persecutor of the new disciples of Jesus. On many occasions in his letters, Paul enumerates his credentials as a good Jew, a Pharisee in fact (cf. Rom. 11:1; II Cor. 11:22; Phil. 3:5). Paul wants to emphasize this side of his preconversion life simply because, in sharp contrast, his postconversion mission is to be an apostle of Jesus Christ whom he had persecuted. The radical difference of *before* and *after* links Paul's experience with so many later converts, even though their experiences may not have been as sudden or dramatic.

It is possible when interpreting Paul's conversion, or any other for that matter, to so dwell on the details or the discrepancies as to miss the main point. The essential ingredient in the three accounts in Acts, linking all three to a common confrontation, is the question and answer exchange. "Why do you persecute me?" ... "Who are you?" ... "I am Jesus." Perhaps, then, with this in mind, we can say that the Pauline experience is after all the common experience of all converts.

As with so many crucial biblical passages, an examination of various translations and versions can be helpful. For visual as well as comparative reasons, the three accounts are given in parallel columns. From the Revised Standard Version of the Bible, copyrighted 1946, 1952 © 1971, 1973.

1

Acts 9:3-19

Now as he journeyed he approached Damascus, and suddenly a light from heaven flashed about him. And he fell to the ground and heard a voice saying to him, "Saul, Saul, why do you persecute me?" And he said, "Who are you, Lord?" And he said, "I am Jesus, whom you are persecuting; but rise and enter the city, and you will be told what you are to do." The men who were traveling with him stood speechless, hearing the voice but seeing no one. Saul arose from the ground; and when his eyes were opened, he could see nothing; so they led him by the hand and brought him into Damascus. And for three days he was without sight, and neither ate nor drank.

Now there was a disciple at Damascus named Anani'as. The Lord said to him in a vision, "Anani'as." And he said, "Here I am, Lord." And the Lord said to him, "Rise and go to the street called Straight, and inquire in the house of Judas for a man of Tarsus named Saul; for behold, he is praying, and he has seen a man named Anani'as come in and lay his hands on him so that he might regain his sight." But Anani'as answered, "Lord, I have heard from many about this man, how much evil he has done to thy saints at Jerusalem; and here he has authority from the chief priests to bind all who call upon thy name." But the Lord said to him, "Go, for he is a chosen instrument of mine to carry my name before the Gentiles and kings and the sons of Israel; for I will show him how much he must suffer for the sake of my name." So Anani'as departed and entered the house. And laying his hands on him he said, "Brother Saul, the Lord Jesus who appeared to you on the road by which you came, has sent me that you may regain your sight and be filled with the Holy Spirit." And immediately something like scales fell from his eyes and he regained his sight. Then he rose and was baptized, and took food and was strengthened.

Acts 22:6-16

"As I made my journey and drew near to Damascus, about noon a great light from heaven suddenly shone about me. And I fell to the ground and heard a voice saying to me, 'Saul, Saul, why do you persecute me?' And I answered, 'Who are you, Lord?' And he said to me, 'I am Jesus of Nazareth whom you are persecuting.' Now those who were with me saw the light but did not hear the voice of the one who was speaking to me. And I said, 'What shall I do, Lord?' And the Lord said to me, 'Rise, and go into Damascus, and there you will be told all that is appointed for you to do.' And when I could not see because of the brightness of that light, I was led by the hand by those who were with me, and came into Damascus.

"And one Anani'as, a devout man according to the law, well spoken of by all the Jews who lived there, came to me, and standing by me said to me, 'Brother Saul, receive your sight.' And in that very hour I received my sight and saw him. And he said, 'The God of our fathers appointed you to know his will, to see the Just One and to hear a voice from his mouth; for you will be a witness for him to all men of what you have seen and heard. And now why do you wait? Rise and be baptized, and wash away your sins, calling on his name.' "

Acts 26:12-18

"Thus I journeyed to Damascus with the authority and commission of the chief priests. At midday, O king, I saw on the way a light from heaven, brighter than the sun, shining round me and those who journeyed with me. And when we had all fallen to the ground, I heard a voice saying to me in the Hebrew language, 'Saul, Saul, why do you persecute me? It hurts you to kick against the goads.' And I said, 'Who are you, Lord?' And the Lord said, 'I am Jesus whom you are persecuting. But rise and stand upon your feet; for I have appeared to you for this purpose, to appoint you to serve and bear witness to the things in which you have seen me and to those in which I will appear to you, delivering you from the people and from the Gentiles—to whom I send you to open their eyes, that they may turn from darkness to light and from the power of Satan to God, that they may receive forgiveness of sins and a place among those who are sanctified by faith in me.' "

Constantine

(ca. 280–337)

In the history of Christianity, few conversions rival Constantine's for its impact on the church and all of Western culture. Converted in his youth, he united the Roman empire under his rule and gave protection to the beleaguered band of early Christians. Constantine declared Christianity to be the official religion of the empire, thus beginning the Christianization of Europe and the shift of Christian power away from its origins in the Middle East to Europe and subsequently elsewhere throughout the world.

This union of church and state became the dominant pattern in Western church history — at least until the eighteenth century — and today it is often described as Constantinian Christianity. In short, Constantine's conversion marked a revolutionary turning point for Christianity.

The enduring effects of this conversion are fairly obvious; the conversion itself is difficult to describe. We have no account by Constantine himself, but Eusebius (260? – 340?), known as the "first" church historian, recorded an early version in his *Ecclesiastical History*. Another description appears in *The Life of Constantine the Great*, which is supposed to have been written later by Eusebius. The second account emphasizes the powerful vision revealed to Constantine, and this dimension of the story was probably picked up from a very brief narrative of Constantine's conversion by Lactantius, a Christian tutor in Constantine's family. Reprinted here are the two versions by Eusebius.

Despite the differences, it is clear that Constantine was converted in A.D. 312 and that his victory over Maxentius at the Milvian Bridge ended a Roman civil war and assured Constantine's control over the Roman empire. But the variations in the texts raise difficult problems. Was there a vision? Was Constantine's conversion a genuine religious experience or a matter of astute political policy? What influenced him to accept Christianity? Did he become a full Christian at once or did he accept Christianity as only one of many forms of worship of an all-powerful deity?

An account from Constantine himself would probably not answer these questions, for they are tied to the mystery of the conversion experience itself. It may have been good politics to give the empire a common religion, but there was no compelling reason why it had to be Christianity. Yet Constantine became a Christian; with that the history of the world changed, and the church today still lives with the results of Constantine's decision for Christ.

Excerpted from Eusebius, *The Ecclesiastical History,* IX, 9, 1-12, and *The Life of Constantine the Great,* I, xxvi-xxxix, in *Nicene and Post-Nicene Fathers of the Christian Church,* 2nd series, ed. Philip Schaff and Henry Wace (New York, 1890; Grand Rapids: Eerdmans, 1952), I: 363-64, 489-93.

When Constantine, whom we have already mentioned as an emperor, born of an emperor, a pious son of a most pious and prudent father, and Licinius, second to him,—two God-beloved emperors, honored alike for their intelligence and their piety,—being stirred up against the two most impious tyrants by God, the absolute Ruler and Saviour of all, engaged in formal war against them, with God as their ally, Maxentius was defeated at Rome by Constantine in a remarkable manner, and the tyrant of the East did not long survive him, but met a most shameful death at the hand of Licinius, who had not yet become insane. Constantine, who was the superior both in dignity and imperial rank, first took compassion upon those who were oppressed at Rome, and having invoked in prayer the God of heaven, and his Word, and Jesus Christ himself, the Saviour of all, as his aid, advanced with his whole army, proposing to restore to the Romans their ancestral liberty. But Maxentius, putting confidence rather in the arts of sorcery than in the devotion of his subjects, did not dare to go forth beyond the gates of the city, but fortified every place and district and town which was enslaved by him, in the neighborhood of Rome and in all Italy, with an immense multitude of troops and with innumerable bands of soldiers. But the emperor, relying upon the assistance of God, attacked the first, second, and third army of the tyrant, and conquered them all; and having advanced through the greater part of Italy, was already very near Rome. Then, that he might not be compelled to wage war with the Romans for the sake of the tyrant, God himself drew the latter, as if bound in chains, some distance without the gates, and confirmed those threats against the impious which had been anciently inscribed in sacred books,—disbelieved, indeed, by most as a myth, but believed by the faithful,—confirmed them, in a word, by the deed itself to all, both believers and unbelievers, that saw the wonder with their eyes. Thus, as in the time of Moses himself and of the ancient God-beloved race of Hebrews, "he cast Pharaoh's chariots and host into the sea, and overwhelmed his chosen charioteers in the Red Sea, and covered them with the flood," in the same way Maxentius also with his soldiers and body-guards "went down into the depths like a stone," when he fled before the power of God which was with Constantine, and passed through the river which lay in his way, over which he formed a bridge with his boats, and thus prepared the means of his own destruction. In regard to him one might say, "he digged a pit and

opened it and fell into the hole which he had made; his labor shall turn
upon his own head, and his unrighteousness shall fall upon his own crown."
Thus, then, the bridge over the river being broken, the passageway settled
down, and immediately the boats with the men disappeared in the depths,
and that most impious one himself first of all, then the shield-bearers who
were with him, as the divine oracles foretold, "sank like lead in the mighty
waters"; so that those who obtained the victory from God, if not in words,
at least in deeds, like Moses, the great servant of God, and those who were
with him, fittingly sang as they had sung against the impious tyrant of old,
saying, "Let us sing unto the Lord, for he hath gloriously glorified himself;
horse and rider hath he thrown into the sea; a helper and a protector hath
he become for my salvation;" and "Who is like unto thee, O Lord; among
the gods, who is like unto thee? glorious in holiness, marvelous in glory,
doing wonders." These and the like praises Constantine, by his very deeds,
sang to God, the universal Ruler, and Author of his victory, as he entered
Rome in triumph. Immediately all the members of the senate and the other
most celebrated men, with the whole Roman people, together with children
and women, received him as their deliverer, their saviour, and their benefactor, with shining eyes and with their whole souls, with shouts of gladness and unbounded joy. But he, as one possessed of inborn piety toward
God, did not exult in the shouts, nor was he elated by the praises; but
perceiving that his aid was from God, he immediately commanded that a
trophy of the Saviour's passion be put in the hand of his own statue. And
when he had placed it, with the saving sign of the cross in its right hand,
in the most public place in Rome, he commanded that the following inscription should be engraved upon it in the Roman tongue: "By this salutary
sign, the true proof of bravery, I have saved and freed your city from the
yoke of the tyrant; and moreover, having set at liberty both the senate and
the people of Rome, I have restored them to their ancient distinction and
splendor." And after this both Constantine himself and with him the Emperor Licinius, who had not yet been seized by that madness into which he
later fell, praising God as the author of all their blessings, with one will
and mind drew up a full and most complete decree in behalf of the Christians, and sent an account of the wonderful things done for them by God,
and of the victory over the tyrant, together with a copy of the decree itself,
to Maximinus, who still ruled over the nations of the East and pretended
friendship toward them. But he, like a tyrant, was greatly pained by what
he learned; but not wishing to seem to yield to others, nor, on the other
hand, to suppress that which was commanded, for fear of those who enjoined it, as if on his own authority, he addressed, under compulsion, to
the governors under him this first communication in behalf of the Christians,
falsely inventing things against himself which had never been done by him.

*   *   *

Thus then the God of all, the Supreme Governor of the whole universe, by his own will appointed Constantine, the descendant of so renowned a parent, to be prince and sovereign: so that, while others have been raised to this distinction by the election of their fellow-men, he is the only one to whose elevation no mortal may boast of having contributed.

While ... he regarded the entire world as one immense body, and perceived that the head of it all, the royal city of the Roman empire, was bowed down by the weight of a tyrannous oppression; at first he had left the task of liberation to those who governed the other divisions of the empire, as being his superiors in point of age. But when none of these proved able to afford relief, and those who had attempted it had experienced a disastrous termination of their enterprise, he said that life was without enjoyment to him as long as he saw the imperial city thus afflicted, and prepared himself for the overthrowal of the tyranny.

Being convinced, however, that he needed some more powerful aid than his military forces could afford him, on account of the wicked and magical enchantments which were so diligently practiced by the tyrant, he sought Divine assistance, deeming the possession of arms and a numerous soldiery of secondary importance, but believing the co-operating power of Deity invincible and not to be shaken. He considered, therefore, on what God he might rely for protection and assistance. While engaged in this enquiry, the thought occurred to him, that, of the many emperors who had preceded him, those who had rested their hopes in a multitude of gods, and served them with sacrifices and offerings, had in the first place been deceived by flattering predictions, and oracles which promised them all prosperity, and at last had met with an unhappy end, while not one of their gods had stood by to warn them of the impending wrath of heaven; while one alone who had pursued an entirely opposite course, who had condemned their error, and honored the one Supreme God during his whole life, had found him to be the Saviour and Protector of his empire, and the Giver of every good thing. Reflecting on this, and well weighing the fact that they who had trusted in many gods had also fallen by manifold forms of death, without leaving behind them either family or offspring, stock, name, or memorial among men: while the God of his father had given to him, on the other hand, manifestations of his power and very many tokens: and considering farther that those who had already taken arms against the tyrant, and had marched to the battle-field under the protection of a multitude of gods, had met with a dishonorable end (for one of them had shamefully retreated from the contest without a blow, and the other, being slain in the midst of his own troops, became, as it were, the mere sport of death); reviewing, I say, all these considerations, he judged it to be folly indeed to join in the idle worship of those who were no gods, and, after such convincing evidence, to err from the truth; and therefore felt it incumbent on him to honor his father's God alone.

Accordingly he called on him with earnest prayer and supplications that he would reveal to him who he was, and stretch forth his right hand to help him in his present difficulties. And while he was thus praying with fervent entreaty, a most marvelous sign appeared to him from heaven, the account of which it might have been hard to believe had it been related by any other person. But since the victorious emperor himself long afterwards declared it to the writer of this history, when he was honored with his acquaintance and society, and confirmed his statement by an oath, who could hesitate to accredit the relation, especially since the testimony of after-time has established its truth? He said that about noon, when the day was already beginning to decline, he saw with his own eyes the trophy of a cross of light in the heavens, above the sun, and bearing the inscription, CONQUER BY THIS [In Hoc Signo]. At this sight he himself was struck with amazement, and his whole army also, which followed him on this expedition, and witnessed the miracle.

He said, moreover, that he doubted within himself what the import of this apparition could be. And while he continued to ponder and reason on its meaning, night suddenly came on; then in his sleep the Christ of God appeared to him with the same sign which he had seen in the heavens, and commanded him to make a likeness of that sign which he had seen in the heavens, and to use it as a safeguard in all engagements with his enemies.

At dawn of day he arose, and communicated the marvel to his friends: and then, calling together the workers in gold and precious stones, he sat in the midst of them, and described to them the figure of the sign he had seen, bidding them represent it in gold and precious stones. And this representation I myself have had an opportunity of seeing.

Now it was made in the following manner. A long spear, overlaid with gold, formed the figure of the cross by means of a transverse bar laid over it. On the top of the whole was fixed a wreath of gold and precious stones; and within this, the symbol of the Saviour's name, two letters indicating the name of Christ by means of its initial characters, the letter P being intersected by X in its centre: and these letters the emperor was in the habit of wearing on his helmet at a later period. From the cross-bar of the spear was suspended a cloth, a royal piece, covered with a profuse embroidery of most brilliant precious stones; and which, being also richly interlaced with gold, presented an indescribable degree of beauty to the beholder. This banner was of a square form, and the upright staff, whose lower section was of great length, bore a golden half-length portrait of the pious emperor and his children on its upper part, beneath the trophy of the cross, and immediately above the embroidered banner.

The emperor constantly made use of this sign of salvation as a safeguard against every adverse and hostile power, and commanded that others similar to it should be carried at the head of all his armies.

These things were done shortly afterwards. But at the time above specified, being struck with amazement at the extraordinary vision, and resolving to worship no other God save Him who had appeared to him, he sent for those who were acquainted with the mysteries of His doctrines, and enquired who that God was, and what was intended by the sign of the vision he had seen.

They affirmed that He was God, the only begotten Son of the one and only God: that the sign which had appeared was the symbol of immortality, and the trophy of that victory over death which He had gained in time past when sojourning on earth. They taught him also the causes of His advent, and explained to him the true account of His incarnation. Thus he was instructed in these matters, and was impressed with wonder at the divine manifestation which had been presented to his sight. Comparing, therefore, the heavenly vision with the interpretation given, he found his judgment confirmed; and, in the persuasion that the knowledge of these things had been imparted to him by Divine teaching, he determined thenceforth to devote himself to the reading of the Inspired writings.

Moreover, he made the priests of God his counselors, and deemed it incumbent on him to honor the God who had appeared to him with all devotion. And after this, being fortified by well-grounded hopes in Him, he hastened to quench the threatening fire of tyranny. . . .

And already he was approaching very near Rome itself, when, to save him from the necessity of fighting with all the Romans for the tyrant's sake, God himself drew the tyrant, as it were by secret cords, a long way outside the gates. And now those miracles recorded in Holy Writ, which God of old wrought against the ungodly (discredited by most as fables, yet believed by the faithful), did he in every deed confirm to all alike, believers and unbelievers, who were eye-witnesses of the wonders. For as once in the days of Moses and the Hebrew nation, who were worshipers of God, "Pharaoh's chariots and his host hath he cast into the sea, and his chosen chariot-captains are drowned in the Red Sea,"—so at this time Maxentius, and the soldiers and guards with him, "went down into the depths like stone," when, in his flight before the divinely-aided forces of Constantine, he essayed to cross the river which lay in his way, over which, making a strong bridge of boats, he had framed an engine of destruction, really against himself, but in the hope of ensnaring thereby him who was beloved by God. For his God stood by the one to protect him, while the other, godless, proved to be the miserable contriver of these secret devices to his own ruin. So that one might well say, "He hath made a pit, and digged it, and is fallen into the ditch which he made. His mischief shall return upon his own head, and his violence shall come down upon his own pate." Thus, in the present instance, under divine direction, the machine erected on the bridge, with the ambuscade concealed therein, giving way unexpectedly before the appointed time, the bridge began to sink, and the boats with the men in them went bodily to the bottom. And first the wretch himself, then his armed attendants and guards, even as the sacred oracles had before described, "sank as lead in the mighty waters." So that they who thus obtained victory from God might well, if not in the same words, yet in fact in the same spirit as the people of his great servant Moses, sing and speak as they did concerning the impious tyrant of old: "Let us sing unto the Lord, for he hath been glorified exceedingly: the horse and his rider hath he thrown into the sea. He is become my helper and my shield unto salvation." And again, "Who is like unto thee, O Lord, among the gods? who is like thee, glorious in holiness, marvelous in praises, doing wonders?"

Having then at this time sung these and such-like praises to God, the Ruler of all and the Author of victory, after the example of his great servant Moses, Constantine entered the imperial city in triumph. And here the whole body of the senate, and others of rank and distinction in the city, freed as it were from the restraint of a prison, along with the whole Roman populace, their countenances expressive of the gladness of their hearts, received him with acclamations and abounding joy; men, women, and children, with countless multitudes of servants, greeting him as deliverer, preserver, and benefactor, with incessant shouts. But he, being possessed of inward piety toward God, was neither rendered arrogant by these plaudits, nor uplifted by the praises he heard; but, being sensible that he had received help from God, he immediately rendered a thanksgiving to him as the Author of his victory.

Augustine
(354–430)

Like the apostle Paul, with whom he had so much in common, Augustine's career as churchman and theologian began with a sudden, dramatic conversion. With both men, the experience became determinative for all their subsequent life and thought, and, in later years, each frequently reminisced about his conversion experience, indicating its enduring and normative influence.

Born in 354 in Tagaste, North Africa, Augustine was the last and the greatest of the so-called early church "Fathers." He also had one foot in the early Middle Ages, so that both patristic and medieval theology were combined in his own system. But "system" is hardly the right word for Augustine's theology. He was, especially in his youthful years, an eclectic sampler of various schools of philosophy, religion, and morality. Even after his conversion and during his prolific writing career, Augustine moved from topic to topic in an endless succession of seemingly unrelated works. His two most important theological foci were sin and grace, and the conflict which these two set up in his own experience, as in his conversion, provided a trademark for nearly everything he did or wrote.

It is tempting to interpret Augustine psychologically at this point, for just as his theology seems to combine opposing ideas, so does his personality. His father, Patricius, was not a religious man and seemed mostly untroubled by moral questions; but Augustine's mother, Monnica, was a Christian of rare devotion. Perhaps Augustine was himself the mixture of the sensual father and the Christian mother.

After some years of studying in various centers, and a long-standing relationship with a nameless mistress, by whom a son, Adeodatus, was born, Monnica and a few friends persuaded Augustine to go to Milan to study with the great Ambrose. It was while in Milan, in the year 386 and in the company of a friend, Alypius, that Augustine experienced his moving conversion. He had been agonizing, as had Paul, about the power of sin and the failure of his will. "I do not do the good I want, but the evil I do not want is what I do. . . . Wretched man that I am!" (Rom. 7:19, 24).

Augustine's own description of the event needs no further commentary. It was included in one of the world's great devotional classics, the *Confessions*. Although written more than ten years later, we can be reasonably certain, because of its intensity, that Augustine remembered the experience vividly, even to the details.

The text is taken from Augustine: Confessions and Enchiridion, trans. and ed. Albert C. Outler, vol. VII of the Library of Christian Classics (London: SCM Press; Philadelphia: Westminster Press, 1955). Reprinted by permission.

There was a little garden belonging to our lodging, of which we had the use—as of the whole house—for the master, our landlord, did not live there. The tempest in my breast hurried me out into this garden, where no one might interrupt the fiery struggle in which I was engaged with myself, until it came to the outcome that thou knewest though I did not. But I was mad for health, and dying for life; knowing what evil thing I was, but not knowing what good thing I was so shortly to become.

I fled into the garden, with Alypius following step by step; for I had no secret in which he did not share, and how could he leave me in such distress? We sat down, as far from the house as possible. I was greatly disturbed in spirit, angry at myself with a turbulent indignation because I had not entered thy will and covenant, O my God, while all my bones cried out to me to enter, extolling it to the skies. The way therein is not by ships or chariots or feet—indeed it was not as far as I had come from the house to the place where we were seated. For to go along that road and indeed to reach the goal is nothing else but the will to go. But it must be a strong and single will, not staggering and swaying about this way and that—a changeable, twisting, fluctuating will, wrestling with itself while one part falls as another rises. . . .

Now when deep reflection had drawn up out of the secret depths of my soul all my misery and had heaped it up before the sight of my heart, there arose a mighty storm, accompanied by a mighty rain of tears. That I might give way full to my tears and lamentations, I stole away from Alypius, for it seemed to me that solitude was more appropriate for the business of weeping. I went far enough away that I could feel that even his presence was no restraint upon me. This was the way I felt at the time, and he realized it. I suppose I had said something before I started up and he noticed that the sound of my voice was choked with weeping. And so he stayed alone, where we had been sitting together, greatly astonished. I flung myself down under a fig tree—how I know not—and gave free course to my tears. The streams of my eyes gushed out an acceptable sacrifice to thee. And, not indeed in these words, but to this effect, I cried to thee: "And thou, O Lord, how long? How long, O Lord? Wilt thou be angry forever? Oh, remember not against us our former iniquities."[1] For I felt that I was still enthralled by them. I sent up these sorrowful cries: "How

---

[1] Cf. Ps. 6:3; 79:8.

long, how long? Tomorrow and tomorrow? Why not now? Why not this very hour make an end to my uncleanness?"

I was saying these things and weeping in the most bitter contrition of my heart, when suddenly I heard the voice of a boy or a girl—I know not which—coming from the neighboring house, chanting over and over again, "Pick it up, read it; pick it up, read it."[2] Immediately I ceased weeping and began most earnestly to think whether it was usual for children in some kind of game to sing such a song, but I could not remember ever having heard the like. So, damming the torrent of my tears, I got to my feet, for I could not but think that this was a divine command to open the Bible and read the first passage I should light upon. For I had heard[3] how Anthony, accidentally coming into church while the gospel was being read, received the admonition as if what was read had been addressed to him: "Go and sell what you have and give it to the poor, and you shall have treasure in heaven; and come and follow me."[4] By such an oracle he was forthwith converted to thee.

So I quickly returned to the bench where Alypius was sitting, for there I had put down the apostle's book when I had left there. I snatched it up, opened it, and in silence read the paragraph on which my eyes first fell: "Not in rioting and drunkenness, not in chambering and wantonness, not in strife and envying, but put on the Lord Jesus Christ, and make no provision for the flesh to fulfill the lusts thereof."[5] I wanted to read no further, nor did I need to. For instantly, as the sentence ended, there was infused in my heart something like the light of full certainty and all the gloom of doubt vanished away.

Closing the book, then, and putting my finger or something else for a mark I began—now with a tranquil countenance—to tell it all to Alypius. And he in turn disclosed to me what had been going on in himself, of which I knew nothing. He asked to see what I had read. I showed him, and he looked on even further than I had read. I had not known what followed. But indeed it was this, "Him that is weak in the faith, receive."[6] This he applied to himself, and told me so. By these words of warning he was strengthened, and by exercising his good resolution and purpose—all very much in keeping with his character, in which, in these respects, he was always far different from and better than I—he joined me in full commitment without any restless hesitation.

Then we went in to my mother, and told her what happened, to her great joy. We explained to her how it had occurred—and she leaped for joy triumphant; and she blessed thee, who art "able to do exceedingly

---

[2] This is the famous *Tolle, lege; tolle, lege.*
[3] Doubtless from Ponticianus, in their earlier conversation.
[4] Matt. 19:21.
[5] Rom. 13:13.
[6] Rom. 14:1.

abundantly above all that we ask or think."[7] For she saw that thou hadst granted her far more than she had ever asked for in all her pitiful and doleful lamentations. For thou didst so convert me to thee that I sought neither a wife nor any other of this world's hopes, but set my feet on that rule of faith which so many years before thou hadst showed her in her dream about me. And so thou didst turn her grief into gladness more plentiful than she had ventured to desire, and dearer and purer than the desire she used to cherish of having grandchildren of my flesh.

[7] Eph. 3:20.

Ignatius Loyola
(1491?–1556)

St. Ignatius Loyola was a contemporary of both Martin Luther and John Calvin, and like them he sought to reform the church. But unlike them, Loyola was completely devoted to the Roman Catholic Church, and his impact and the influence of the order he founded, the Jesuits, have decisively shaped the history of both Catholicism and Protestantism.

Born into a family of Spanish nobility, Loyola decided to become a soldier, and the discipline of military life affected him deeply. In 1521 he was seriously injured in the siege of Pamplona by the French, and he retreated to the castle of Loyola to recover. There he began reading devotional literature on the life of Christ and the saints, and he was converted. When his health permitted, he made a pilgrimage to Montserrat where he conducted an all-night vigil before the altar of the Virgin Mary and hung up his sword. He then spent a year at Manresa near Montserrat, where he had several mystical experiences of Jesus Christ. These formed the basis of what later became the *Spiritual Exercises*, Loyola's most famous work and the manual for the Jesuit order. It is widely used even today, especially for spiritual retreats.

After a pilgrimage from Manresa to Rome, Loyola began his studies, first in Spain and then in Paris. In 1534 he laid the foundation for the Society of Jesus, or Jesuits, with six companions, including Francis Xavier. In 1540 the Pope commissioned the new order; the Jesuits were placed under the direct control of the Pope himself, and the priests took a special vow of papal loyalty.

The Jesuits were not founded to combat Protestantism, but they did become the vanguard of the papacy in the Counter-Reformation. Effective in reducing abuses within the Roman Church, they were also successful in winning back whole areas of Europe in allegiance to Rome. Throughout their history the Jesuits have been noted for their extensive missionary work, especially in some of the most difficult areas of the world, as well as for their contributions to scholarship and education. Since Vatican II, they have been significantly involved in improving ecumenical relations between Protestants and Catholics.

The following account of Loyola's confession was dictated by him, and characteristically he referred to himself in the third person, suggesting his modesty and self-denial. His piety was demanding and disciplined, and as a soldier of God, he continually required "more" of himself and of others. His motto: "For the greater glory of God."

St. Ignatius' Own Story, as Told to Luis González de Cámara, trans. William J. Young, S.J. (Chicago, 1956), 7-12. Copyright by Henry Regnery Co.

U p to his twenty-sixth year he was a man given over to the vanities of the world, and took a special delight in the exercise of arms, with a great and vain desire of winning glory. He was in a fortress which the French were attacking, and although the others were of the opinion that they should surrender on terms of having their lives spared, as they clearly saw there was no possibility of a defense, he gave so many reasons to the governor that he persuaded him to carry on the defense against the judgment of the officers, who found some strength in his spirit and courage. On the day on which they expected the attack to take place, he made his confession to one of his companions in arms. After the assault had been going on for some time, a cannon ball struck him in the leg, crushing its bones, and because it passed between his legs it also seriously wounded the other.

With his fall, the others in the fortress surrendered to the French, who took possession, and treated the wounded man with great kindliness and courtesy. After twelve or fifteen days in Pamplona they bore him in a litter to his own country. Here he found himself in a very serious condition. The doctors and surgeons whom he had called from all parts were of the opinion that the leg should be operated on again and the bones reset, either because they had been poorly set in the first place, or because the jogging of the journey had displaced them so that they would not heal. Again he went through this butchery, in which as in all the others that he had suffered he uttered no word, nor gave any sign of pain other than clenching his fists.

His condition grew worse. Besides being unable to eat he showed other symptoms which are usually a sign of approaching death. The feast of St. John drew near, and as the doctors had very little hope of his recovery, they advised him to make his confession. He received the last sacraments on the eve of the feast of Sts. Peter and Paul, and the doctors told him that if he showed no improvement by midnight, he could consider himself as good as dead. The patient had some devotion to St. Peter, and so our Lord wished that his improvement should begin that very midnight. So rapid was his recovery that within a few days he was thought to be out of danger of death.

When the bones knit, one below the knee remained astride another, which caused a shortening of the leg. The bones so raised caused a protuberance that was not pleasant to the sight. The sick man was not able to put up with this, because he had made up his mind to seek his fortune in the world. He thought the protuberance was going to be unsightly and asked the surgeons whether it could not be cut away. They told him that it could be cut away, but that the pain would be greater than all he had already suffered, because it was now healed and it would take some time to cut it off. He determined, nevertheless, to undergo this martyrdom to gratify his own inclinations. His elder brother was quite alarmed and declared that he would not have the courage to undergo such pain. But the wounded man put up with it with his usual patience.

After the superfluous flesh and the bone were cut away, means were employed for preventing the one leg from remaining shorter than the other. Many ointments were applied and devices employed for keeping the leg continually stretched which caused him many days of martyrdom. But it was our Lord Who restored his health. In everything else he was quite well, but he was not able to stand upon that leg, and so had to remain in bed. He had been much given to reading worldly books of fiction and knight errantry, and feeling well enough to read he asked for some of these books to help while away the time. In that house, however, they could find none of those he was accustomed to read, and so they gave him a Life of Christ and a book of the Lives of the Saints in Spanish.

By the frequent reading of these books he conceived some affection for what he found there narrated. Pausing in his reading, he gave himself up to thinking over what he had read. At other times he dwelt on the things of the world which formerly had occupied his thoughts. Of the many vain things that presented themselves to him, one took such possession of his heart that without realizing it he could spend two, three, or even four hours on end thinking of it, fancying what he would have to do in the service of a certain lady, of the means he would take to reach the country where she was living, of the verses, the promises he would make her, the deeds of gallantry he would do in her service. He was so enamored with all this that he did not see how impossible it would all be, because the lady was of no ordinary rank; neither countess, nor duchess, but of a nobility much higher than any of these.

Nevertheless, our Lord came to his assistance, for He saw to it that these thoughts were succeeded by others which sprang from the things he was reading. In reading the Life of our Lord and the Lives of the Saints, he paused to think and reason with himself. "Suppose that I should do what St. Francis did, what St. Dominic did?" He thus let his thoughts run over many things that seemed good to him, always putting before himself things that were difficult and important which seemed to him easy to accomplish when he proposed them. But all his thought was to tell himself, "St. Dominic did this, therefore, I must do it. St. Francis did this; therefore, I must do it." These thoughts also lasted a good while. And then other things taking their place, the worldly thoughts above mentioned came upon him and remained a long time with him. This succession of diverse thoughts was of long duration, and they were either of worldly achievements which he desired to accomplish, or those of God which took hold of his imagination to such an extent, that worn out with the struggle, he turned them all aside and gave his attention to other things.

There was, however, this difference. When he was thinking of the things of the world he was filled with delight, but when afterwards he dismissed them from weariness, he was dry and dissatisfied. And when he thought of going barefoot to Jerusalem and of eating nothing but herbs and performing the other rigors he saw that the saints had performed, he was consoled, not only when he entertained these thoughts, but even after dismissing them he remained cheerful and satisfied. But he paid no attention to this, nor did he stop to weigh the difference until one day his eyes were opened a little and he began to wonder at the difference and to reflect on it, learning from experience that one kind of thoughts left him sad and the other cheerful. Thus, step by step, he came to recognize the difference between the two spirits that moved him, the one being from the evil spirit, the other from God.

He acquired no little light from this reading and began to think more seriously of his past life and the great need he had of doing penance for it. It was during this reading that these desires of imitating the saints came to him, but with no further thought of circumstances than of promising to do with God's grace what they had done. What he desired most of all to do, as soon as he was restored to health, was to go to Jerusalem, as above stated, undertaking all the disciplines and abstinences which a generous soul on fire with the love of God is wont to desire.

The thoughts of the past were soon forgotten in the presence of these holy desires, which were confirmed by the following vision. One night, as he lay awake, he saw clearly the likeness of our Lady with the holy Child Jesus, at the sight of which he received most abundant consolation for a considerable interval of time. He felt so great a disgust with his past life, especially with its offenses of the flesh, that he thought all such images which had formerly occupied his mind were wiped out. And from that hour until August of 1553, when this is being written, he never again consented to the least suggestion of the flesh. This effect would seem to indicate that the vision was from God, although he never ventured to affirm it positively, or claim that it was anything more than he had said it was. But his brother and other members of the family easily recognized the change that had taken place in the interior of his soul from what they saw in his outward manner.

Without a care in the world he went on with his reading and his good resolutions. All the time he spent with the members of the household he devoted to the things of God, and in this way brought profit to their souls. He took great delight in the books he was reading, and the thought came to him to select some short but important passages from the Life of Christ and the Lives of the Saints. And so he began to write very carefully in a book, as he had already begun to move a little about the house. The words of Christ he wrote in red ink and those of our Lady in blue, on polished and lined paper in a good hand, for he was an excellent penman. Part of his time he spent in writing, part in prayer. It was his greatest consolation to gaze upon the heavens and the stars, which he often did, and for long stretches at a time, because when doing so he felt within himself a powerful urge to be serving our Lord. He gave much time to thinking about his resolve, desiring to be entirely well so that he could begin his journey.

Teresa of Ávila
(1515–1582)

Teresa of Ávila, or St. Teresa of Jesus, was a Spanish mystic and reformer who combined a life of intense piety with significant practical accomplishments. She was one of ten children in a family of Spanish nobility and was considered the "most beloved of them all." Her mother died when she was thirteen, and approximately three years later Teresa entered an Augustinian convent where she lived for a year and a half. In 1536 she joined the Carmelite convent in Ávila but soon fell desperately ill. At one point she went into a coma and was presumed dead; although she recovered, she suffered paralysis in her legs for three years.

During her first two decades as a Carmelite nun, Teresa experienced not only poor health but also profound religious struggles, describing this period as "nearly twenty years on that stormy sea." Never abandoning the practice of prayer, she began to realize that she was "sometimes being addressed by interior voices," and she saw "certain visions" and experienced revelations. The account of her conversion comes after her twenty-year struggle, and it indicates the new peace she received.

With this sense of assurance, Teresa launched a reform of the Carmelite order, and with St. John of the Cross, another famous Spanish mystic, she assisted in establishing reformed Carmelite monasteries for monks as well. She corresponded widely, and her letters reveal a woman of great administrative skill, shrewd judgment, and a good sense of humor. Her highly disciplined practice of what she called "mental prayer" continued and ultimately led in 1572 to a "spiritual marriage" in which she said her soul remained absorbed in God.

Her greatest devotional writing is The Interior Castle, but she is also noted for The Way of Perfection (a manual for her nuns) and her autobiographical writings, Life and Book of Foundations. She was canonized in 1662, and in 1870 she was one of the first two women to be named a Doctor of the Church. Her consuming passion to see Christ symbolizes how, in her own life, she united the spiritual and the physical, contemplation and achievement.

Excerpted from The Life of the Holy Mother Teresa of Jesus in The Complete Works of Saint Teresa of Jesus, trans. and ed. E. Allison Peers (London and New York, 1944), I: 54-57. Reprinted by permission of Andrews and MacMeel, Inc.

By this time my soul was growing weary, and, though it desired to rest, the miserable habits which now enslaved it would not allow it to do so. It happened that, entering the oratory one day, I saw an image which had been procured for a certain festival that was observed in the house and had been taken there to be kept for that purpose. It represented Christ sorely wounded; and so conducive was it to devotion that when I looked at it I was deeply moved to see Him thus, so well did it picture what He suffered for us. So great was my distress when I thought how ill I had repaid Him for those wounds that I felt as if my heart were breaking, and I threw myself down beside Him, shedding floods of tears and begging Him to give me strength once for all so that I might not offend Him.

I had a great devotion to the glorious Magdalen and often thought of her conversion, especially when I communicated, for, knowing that the Lord was certainly within me then, I would place myself at His feet, thinking that my tears would not be rejected. I did not know what I was saying; but in allowing me to shed those tears He was very gracious to me, since I so soon forgot my grief; and I used to commend myself to that glorious Saint so that she might obtain pardon for me.

But on this last occasion when I saw that image of which I am speaking, I think I must have made greater progress, because I had quite lost trust in myself and was placing all my confidence in God. I believe I told Him then that I would not rise from that spot until He had granted me what I was beseeching of Him. And I feel sure that this did me good, for from that time onward I began to improve. My method of prayer was this. As I could not reason with my mind, I would try to make pictures of Christ inwardly; and I used to think I felt better when I dwelt on those parts of His life when He was most often alone. It seemed to me that His being alone and afflicted, like a person in need, made it possible for me to approach Him. I had many simple thoughts of this kind. I was particularly attached to the prayer in the Garden, where I would go to keep Him company. I would think of the sweat and of the affliction He endured there. I wished I could have wiped that grievous sweat from His face, but I remember that I never dared to resolve to do so, for the gravity of my sins stood in the way. I used to remain with Him there for as long as my thoughts permitted it: I had many thoughts which tormented me.

For many years, on most nights before I fell asleep, when I would commend myself to God so as to sleep well, I used to think for a little of that scene—the prayer in the Garden—and this even before I was a nun, for I was told that many indulgences could be gained by so doing; and I feel sure that my soul gained a great deal in this way, because I began to practise prayer without knowing what it was, and the very habitualness of the custom prevented me from abandoning it, just as I never omitted making the sign of the Cross before going to sleep.

To return now to what I was saying about the torture caused me by

my thoughts: this method of praying in which the mind makes no reflections means that the soul must either gain a great deal or lose itself—I
mean by its attention going astray. If it advances, it goes a long way, because
it is moved by love. But those who arrive thus far will do so only at great
cost to themselves, save when the Lord is pleased to call them very speedily
to the Prayer of Quiet, as He has called a few people whom I know. It is
a good thing for those who follow this method to have a book at hand, so
that they may quickly recollect themselves. It used also to help me to look
at a field, or water, or flowers. These reminded me of the Creator—I mean,
they awakened me, helped me to recollect myself and thus served me as
a book; they reminded me, too, of my ingratitude and sins. But when it
came to heavenly things, or to any sublime subject, my mind was so stupid
that I could never imagine them at all, until the Lord showed them to me
in another way.

I had so little ability for picturing things in my mind that if I did not
actually see a thing I could not use my imagination, as other people do,
who can make pictures to themselves and so become recollected. Of Christ
as Man I could only think: however much I read about His beauty and
however often I looked at pictures of Him, I could never form any picture
of Him myself. I was like a person who is blind, or in the dark: he may be
talking to someone, and know that he is with him, because he is quite sure
he is there—I mean, he understands and believes he is there—but he
cannot see him. Thus it was with me when I thought of Our Lord. It was
for this reason that I was so fond of pictures. Unhappy are those who
through their own fault lose this blessing! It really looks as if they do not
love the Lord, for if they loved Him they would delight in looking at
pictures of Him, just as they take pleasure in seeing pictures of anyone
else whom they love.

It was at this time that I was given the *Confessions of Saint Augustine,*
and I think the Lord must have ordained this, for I did not ask for the book
nor had I ever seen it. I have a great affection for Saint Augustine, because
the convent in which I had lived before becoming a nun belonged to his
Order, and also because he had been a sinner. I used to find a great deal
of comfort in reading about the lives of saints who had been sinners before
the Lord brought them back to Himself. As He had forgiven them I thought
that He might do the same for me. There was only one thing that troubled
me, and this I have already mentioned: namely that, after the Lord had
once called them, they did not fall again, whereas I had fallen so often that
I was distressed by it. But when I thought of His love for me, I would take
heart once more, for I never doubted His mercy, though I often doubted
myself.

Oh, God help me! How amazed I am when I think how hard my
heart was despite all the help I had received from Him! It really frightens
me to remember how little I could do by myself and how I was so tied and

bound that I could not resolve to give myself wholly to God. When I started to read the *Confessions,* I seemed to see myself in them and I began to commend myself often to that glorious Saint. When I got as far as his conversion and read how he heard that voice in the garden, it seemed exactly as if the Lord were speaking in that way to me, or so my heart felt. I remained for a long time dissolved in tears, in great distress and affliction. Dear God, what a soul suffers and what torments it endures when it loses its freedom to be its own master! I am astonished now that I was able to live in such a state of torment. God be praised, Who gave me life to forsake such utter death!

I believe my soul gained great strength from the Divine Majesty: He must have heard my cries and had compassion on all my tears. I began to long to spend more time with Him, and to drive away occasions of sin, for, once they had gone, I would feel a new love for His Majesty. I knew that, so far as I could tell, I loved Him, but I did not know, as I should have done, what true love of God really means. I think I had not yet quite prepared myself to want to serve Him when His Majesty began to grant me favours again. It really seems that the Lord found a way to make me desire to receive what others strive to acquire with great labour—that is to say, during these latter years, He gave me consolations and favours. I never presumed to beg Him to give me either these things or tenderness in devotion: I only asked for grace not to offend Him and for the pardon of my grievous sins. Knowing how grievous they were, I never dared consciously to desire favours or consolations. His compassion, I think, worked in me abundantly, and in truth He showed me great mercy in allowing me to be with Him and bringing me into His presence, which I knew I should not have entered had He not so disposed it.

John Calvin
(1509–1564)

It may not seem in character for Calvin to talk at much length about himself, especially about his own religious experience. Solemn and rigid in many ways, neither John Calvin nor many of his followers, as for example the Dutch and the Scots, indulged in subjective religious introspection.

But we catch a glimpse of another side to the stern Genevan reformer when he tells us in the preface to his *Commentary on the Psalms* (1557) that he once had "a sudden conversion." It is a brief, tantalizing reference, and scholars are puzzled not only about the date but about what it involved. Calvin himself provides few clues, insisting, perhaps too modestly, "I am by nature timid, mild, and cowardly."

Was Calvin's "sudden conversion" mostly an intellectual shift from the humanism of his youth to the study of the Scriptures in his maturity? Was it his "mind" (Latin *animus*) that changed, or, as in the French edition, his "heart" (French *coeur*)? Perhaps we must say it was both. In any case, Calvin's conversion marked a turning point in his reforming career. Except for faint hints elsewhere, as in his *Reply to Cardinal Sadolet* (1539), he never again referred to his conversion experience. His writings, notably his biblical commentaries and his definitive systematic theology, *The Institutes of the Christian Religion* (1559), attest to the validity and depth of his theological position, and with that legacy we must be content.

We can detect three significant features in Calvin's brief account of his conversion. (1) Since he was thinking of the book of Psalms, he likened himself to David with all his sin and weakness together with his agonizing struggle to hold on to the God who inspired his muse. (2) The conversion experience, for Calvin, is attributed to God's direct intervention and is not described in Christian terms. There is no question about the centrality of Christ in Calvin's theology, but he avoided the pious "accepting Jesus" language of so many contemporary accounts. (3) The description of his conversion as the result of God's providential grace fits exactly into Calvin's theological emphasis on election as the divine initiative in the process of redemption.

If it was uncharacteristic for Calvin to be emotional about his conversion, the depth of his inner personal gratitude at the undeserved mercy of God found poignant expression in his so-called crest or seal. Picturing a heart upon an open, outstretched hand, the motto reads, "My heart I give Thee, Lord, eagerly and earnestly."

The text for Calvin's conversion is taken from the preface to the *Commentary on the Psalms*, ed. and trans. Joseph Haroutunian and Louise Pettibone Smith, *Calvin: Commentaries*, vol. XXIII in *The Library of Christian Classics* (London: SCM Press; Philadelphia: Westminster Press, 1958). Reprinted by permission.

My father intended me as a young boy for theology. But when he saw that the science of law made those who cultivate it wealthy, he was led to change his mind by the hope of material gain for me. So it happened that I was called back from the study of philosophy to learn law. I followed my father's wish and attempted to do faithful work in this field; but God, by the secret leading of his providence, turned my course another way.

First, when I was too firmly addicted to the papal superstitions to be drawn easily out of such a deep mire, by a sudden conversion He brought my mind (already more rigid than suited my age) to submission [to him]. I was so inspired by a taste of true religion and I burned with such a desire to carry my study further, that although I did not drop other subjects, I had no zeal for them. In less than a year, all who were looking for a purer doctrine began to come to learn from me, although I was a novice and a beginner.

Then I, who was by nature a man of the country and a lover of shade and leisure, wished to find for myself a quiet hiding place—a wish which has never yet been granted me; for every retreat I found became a public lecture room. When the one thing I craved was obscurity and leisure, God fastened upon me so many cords of various kinds that he never allowed me to remain quiet, and in spite of my reluctance dragged me into the limelight.

I left my own country and departed for Germany to enjoy there, unknown, in some corner, the quiet long denied me. But lo, while I was hidden unknown at Basel, a great fire of hatred [for France] had been kindled in Germany by the exile of many godly men from France. To quench this fire, wicked and lying rumors were spread, cruelly calling the exiles Anabaptists and seditious men, men who threatened to upset, not only religion, but the whole political order with their perverse madness. I saw that this was a trick of those in [the French] court, not only to cover up with false slanders the shedding of the innocent blood of holy martyrs, but also to enable the persecutors to continue with the pitiless slaughter. Therefore I felt that I must make a strong statement against such charges; for I could not be silent without treachery. This was why I published the *Institutes*—to defend against unjust slander my brothers whose death was precious in the Lord's sight. A second reason was my desire to rouse the sympathy and concern of people outside, since the same punishment threatened many other poor people. And this volume was not a thick and laborious work like the present edition; it appeared as a brief *Enchiridion*. I had no other purpose than to bear witness to the faith of those whom I saw criminally libeled by wicked and false courtiers.

I desired no fame for myself from it; I planned to depart shortly, and no one knew that I was the writer [of the book]. For I had kept my authorship secret and intended to continue to do so. But Wilhiam Farel[1] forced me to stay in Geneva not so much by advice or urging as by command, which had the power of God's hand laid violently upon me from heaven. Since the wars had closed the direct road to Strasbourg, I had meant to pass through Geneva quickly and had determined not to be delayed there more than one night.

A short time before, by the work of the same good man [Farel], and of Peter Viret,[2] the papacy had been banished from the city; but things were still unsettled and the place was divided into evil and harmful factions. One man, who has since shamefully gone back to the papists, took immediate action to make me known. Then Farel, who was working with incredible zeal to promote the gospel, bent all his efforts to keep me in the city. And when he realized that I was determined to study in privacy in some obscure place, and saw that he gained nothing by entreaty, he descended to cursing, and said that God would surely curse my peace if I held back from giving help at a time of such great need. Terrified by his words, and conscious of my own timidity and cowardice, I gave up my journey and attempted to apply whatever gift I had in defense of my faith.

Scarcely four months had passed before we were attacked on the one side by the Anabaptists and on the other by a certain rascally apostate who, relying upon the secret aid of certain important people, was able to give us much trouble. Meanwhile, internal dissensions, coming one upon another, caused us dreadful torments.

I confess that I am by nature timid, mild, and cowardly, and yet I was forced from the very beginning to meet these violent storms. Although

[1] Guillaume Farel (1489–1565) was, like Calvin, a Frenchman. He was one of the circle of Reformers who gathered around Bishop Briconnet at Meaux near Paris. When, after much struggle in which Farel was active, the Reformed faith was established in Geneva in 1535, he was the leader of the church and induced Calvin to work with him. He was ousted with Calvin in 1538, and returned with him in 1541; but he left in 1542, and in 1544 settled in Neuchâtel. He remained Calvin's close friend, and died a year after Calvin in 1565 in Metz.

[2] Pierre Viret (1511–1571), Swiss-born Reformer, helped Farel in Geneva and stayed in the city when Farel and Calvin were expelled (1538–1541). Thereafter he worked in Lausanne, his birthplace, and also lectured on the New Testament in Bern, until he was ousted in 1559 and returned to Geneva. After a checkered career in France and much controversy with French Catholics, he died at Orthez (south of Bordeaux) in 1571. He was an extensive and respected writer as well as an effective preacher. Unfortunately he has not been studied fully or properly.

I did not yield to them, yet since I was not very brave, I was more pleased than was fitting when I was banished and forcibly expelled from the city.

Then loosed from my vocation and free [to follow my own desire], I decided to live quietly as a private individual. But that most distinguished minister of Christ, Martin Bucer,[3] dragged me back again to a new post with the same curse which Farel had used against me. Terrified by the example of Jonah which he had set before me, I continued the work of teaching. And although I always consistently avoided public notice, somehow I was dragged to the imperial assemblies.[4] There, whether I wished it or not, I had to speak before large audiences.

Afterwards the Lord had pity on the City of Geneva and quieted the deadly conflicts there. After he had by his wondrous power frustrated both the criminal conspiracies and the bloody attempts at force, I was compelled, against my own will, to take again my former position. The safety of that church was far too important in my mind for me to refuse to meet even death for its sake. But my timidity kept suggesting to me excuses of every color for refusing to put my shoulder again under so heavy a burden. However, the demand of duty and faith at length conquered, and I went back to the flock from which I had been driven away. With how much grief, with how many tears, and in how great anxiety I went, God is my best witness. Many faithful men also understood my reluctance and would have wished to see me released from this pain if they had not been constrained by the same fear which influenced me.

It would make too long a story to tell of the conflicts of all sorts in which I was active and of the trials by which I was tested. I will merely repeat briefly what I said before, so as not to offend fastidious readers with unnecessary words. Since [in the Psalms] David showed me the way with his own footsteps, I felt myself greatly comforted. The holy king was hurt more seriously by the envy and dishonesty of treacherous men at home than he was by the Philistines and other enemies who harassed him from the outside. I also have been attacked on all sides and have had scarcely a moment's relief from both external and internal conflicts. Satan has undertaken all too often in many ways to corrupt the fabric of this church. The result has been that I, who am a peaceable and timid man, was compelled to break the force of the deadly attacks by interposing my own body as a shield. . . .

---

[3] Martin Bucer (1491–1551) was the Protestant Reformer in Strasbourg, where Calvin stayed for three years (1538–1541) when he was forced out of Geneva. A man zealous for Christian unity, he had considerable influence upon Calvin, especially during this early period in the latter's activity. He commented extensively upon the Bible, and did his best-known work on the Gospels. His commentary on Romans was published in Strasbourg in 1536, shortly before Calvin began to work on his own. See Henri Strohl, *Bucer: humaniste chrétien.*

[4] At Worms in 1540 and at Regensburg in 1541, where the Catholics and the Protestants entered into futile discussions on reunion.

But this also was David's experience. He deserved well of his people, yet he was hated by many, as he laments in Ps. 69:4: *They hate me without a cause. . . . I returned what I did not rob.* When I was assailed by the undeserved hatred of those whose duty it was to help me, I received no small comfort from knowing of the glorious example [set by David].

Now these experiences were a very great help to my understanding of the Psalms, since, as I read, I was going through well-known territory. And I hope my readers will realize that when I discuss David's thoughts more intimately than those of others, I am speaking not as a remote spectator but as one who knows all about these things from his own experience.

Richard Baxter

(1615–1691)

Doubt and certainty are often seen as the two extremes of the Christian life, but in Richard Baxter one can glimpse a person who knew God through faith but confessed something less than absolute certainty. He lived among people who fought for what they believed, and their beliefs were always definite and sure. To them he preached peace and toleration of different points of view, but he was scorned by partisans on all sides. "These are my fixed resolutions and desires," he wrote in 1658, "even to be Catholick in my Estimation and respect to all, Loving all Christians of what sort soever, that may be truly called Christians ... and ... with this Catholick Charity to have the Conversation of such as the world hath long called Puritanes; and in this state I desire to die."

Baxter's Puritanism emphasized the need for a personal experience of God's forgiveness, rather than mere assent to the doctrines of the Christian faith, and Puritans constantly contrasted this "saving faith" with what they called "historical faith." And yet, as Baxter's account of his own conversion indicates, perfect proof of one's salvation was not always the result of conversion, and conversion itself could be a series of experiences, each of which brought a deeper understanding of God's love.

In 1638, Baxter was ordained in the Church of England, although he was a Non-Conformist minister, working within the Church of England but refusing to abide by some of its discipline and patterns of worship. During the English Civil War he sided with the Parliamentary cause, but then he became a vehement critic of Oliver Cromwell. When the monarchy was restored in 1660, he became a royal chaplain but also worked to keep Non-Conformists in the church. For this he was jailed in 1685 for eighteen months. During his pastorate in Kidderminster, he organized an association of all the ministers in the town, and he is often called the first leader of the ecumenical movement in England. He was an eloquent and powerful preacher, and he is renowned for The Saints Everlasting Rest (1650), a moving devotional book, and The Reformed Pastor (1656), a manual in pastoral theology.

Excerpted from The Autobiography of Richard Baxter, abridged by J. M. Lloyd Thomas and ed. N. H. Keeble (New York: E. P. Dutton; London: J. M. Dent & Sons, 1931/1973), 3-11. Reprinted by permission.

My father had only the competent estate of a freeholder, free from the temptations of poverty and riches; but having been addicted to gaming in his youth, and his father before him, it was so entangled by debts that it occasioned some excess of worldly cares before it was freed.

We lived in a country that had but little preaching at all. In the village where I was born there [were] four readers successively in six years' time, ignorant men, and two of them immoral in their lives, who were all my schoolmasters. In the village where my father lived there was a reader of about eighty years of age that never preached, and had two churches about twenty miles distant. His eyesight failing him, he said Common Prayer without book; but for the reading of the psalms and chapters he got a common thresher and day-labourer one year, and a tailor another year (for the clerk could not read well); and at last he had a kinsman of his own (the excellentest stage-player in all the country, and a good gamester and good fellow) that got Orders and supplied one of his places. After him another younger kinsman, that could write and read, got Orders. And at the same time another neighbour's son that had been a while at school turned minister, one who would needs go further than the rest, and ventured to preach (and after got a living in Staffordshire), and when he had been a preacher about twelve or sixteen years he was fain to give over, it being discovered that his Orders were forged by the first ingenious stage-player. After him another neighbour's son took Orders, when he had been a while an attorney's clerk, and a common drunkard, and tippled himself into so great poverty that he had no other way to live. It was feared that he and more of them came by their Orders the same way with the forementioned person. These were the schoolmasters of my youth (except two of them) who read Common Prayer on Sundays and Holy-Days, and taught school and tippled on the week-days, and whipped the boys, when they were drunk, so that we changed them very oft. Within a few miles about us were near a dozen more ministers that were near eighty years old apiece, and never preached; poor ignorant readers, and most of them of scandalous lives. Only three or four constant competent preachers lived near us, and those (though conformable all save one) were the common marks of the people's obloquy and reproach, and any that had but gone to hear them, when he had no preaching at home, was made the derision of the vulgar rabble under the odious name of a Puritan.

But though we had no better teachers it pleased God to instruct and change my father, by the bare reading of the Scriptures in private, without either preaching or godly company, or any other books but the Bible. And God made him the instrument of my first convictions, and approbation of a holy life, as well as of my restraint from the grosser sort of lives. When I was very young his serious speeches of God and the life to come possessed me with a fear of sinning. When I was but near ten years of age, being at school at High Ercall, we had leave to play on the day of the king's coronation; and at two of the clock in the afternoon on that day there happened an earthquake, which put all the people into a fear, and somewhat possessed them with awful thoughts of the dreadful God. (I make no commentary on the time, nor do I know certainly whether it were in other countries.)

At first my father set me to read the historical part of the Scripture, which suiting with my nature greatly delighted me; and though all that time I neither understood nor relished much the doctrinal part and mystery of redemption, yet it did me good by acquainting me with the matters of fact, drawing me on to love the Bible and to search by degrees into the rest.

But though my conscience would trouble me when I sinned, yet divers sins I was addicted to, and oft committed against my conscience; which for the warning of others I will confess here to my shame.

1. I was much addicted, when I feared correction, to lie, that I might scape.

2. I was much addicted to the excessive gluttonous eating of apples and pears; which I think laid the foundation of that imbecility and flatulency of my stomach which caused the bodily calamities of my life.

3. To this end, and to concur with naughty boys that gloried in evil, I have oft gone into other men's orchards and stolen their fruit, when I had enough at home.

4. I was somewhat excessively addicted to play, and that with covetousness, for money.

5. I was extremely bewitched with a love of romances, fables and old tales, which corrupted my affections and lost my time.

6. I was guilty of much idle foolish chat, and imitation of boys in scurrilous foolish words and actions (though I durst not swear).

7. I was too proud of my masters' commendations for learning, who all of them fed my pride, making me seven or eight years the highest in the school, and boasting of me to others, which, though it furthered my learning, yet helped not my humility.

8. I was too bold and unreverent towards my parents.

These were my sins, which, in my childhood, conscience troubled me [with] for a great while before they were overcome.

In the village where I lived the reader read the Common Prayer briefly, and the rest of the day even till dark night almost, except eating-time, was spent in dancing under a maypole and a great tree not far from my father's door, where all the town did meet together. And though one of my father's own tenants was the piper, he could not restrain him nor break the sport. So that we could not read the Scripture in our family without the great disturbance of the tabor and pipe and noise in the street. Many times my mind was inclined to be among them, and sometimes I broke loose from conscience and joined with them; and the more I did it the more I was inclined to it. But when I heard them call my father Puritan it did much to cure me and alienate me from them; for I considered that my father's exercise of reading the Scripture was better than theirs, and would surely be better thought on by all men at the last; and I considered what it was for that he and others were thus derided. . . .

About that time it pleased God of his wonderful mercy to open my eyes with a clearer insight into the concerns and case of my own soul, and to touch my heart with a livelier feeling of things spiritual than ever I had found before. And it was by the means and in the order following: stirring up my conscience more against me, by robbing an orchard or two with rude boys, than it was before; and, bringing me under some more conviction for my sin, a poor day-labourer in the town (he that I before mentioned, that was wont to read in the church for the old parson) had an old torn book which he lent my father, which was called *Bunny's Resolution* (being written by Parsons the Jesuit, and corrected by Edm. Bunny). . . . And in the reading of this book (when I was about fifteen years of age) it pleased God to awaken my soul. . . .

Yet whether sincere conversion began now, or before, or after, I was never able to this day to know; for I had before had some love to the things and people which were good, and a restraint from other sins except those forementioned; and so much from those, that I seldom committed most of them, and when I did, it was with great reluctancy. . . .

And about that time it pleased God that a poor pedlar came to the door that had ballads and some good books; and my father bought of him Dr. Sibb's *Bruised Reed*. This also I read, and found it suited to my state and seasonably sent me. . . .

When I was ready for the university my master drew me into another way which kept me thence, where were my vehement desires. He had a friend at Ludlow, Chaplain to the Council there, called Mr. Richard Wickstead; whose place having allowance from the king (who maintaineth the house) for one to attend him, he told my master that he was purposed to have a scholar fit for the university; and having but one, would be better to him than any tutor in the university could be. Whereupon my master persuaded me to accept the offer, and told me it would be better than the university to me. . . . He never read to me, nor used any savoury discourse of godliness; only he loved me, and allowed me books and time enough: so that as I had no considerable helps from him in my studies, so had I no considerable hindrance.

And though the house was great (there being four judges, the King's Attorney, the Secretary, the Clerk of the Fines, with all their servants, and all the Lord President's servants and many more), and though the town was full of temptations, through the multitude of persons (counsellors, attorneys, officers and clerks), and much given to tippling and excess, it pleased God not only to keep me from them, but also to give me one intimate companion, who was the greatest help to my seriousness in religion that ever I had before, and was a daily watchman over my soul. We walked together, we read together, we prayed together. . . . He was the first that ever I heard pray *ex tempore* (out of the pulpit), and that taught me so to pray. And his charity and liberality were equal to his zeal, so that God made him a great means of my good, who had more knowledge than he, but a colder heart.

Yet before we had been two years acquainted he fell once and a second time by the power of temptation into a degree of drunkenness, which so terrified him upon the review (especially after the second time) that he was near to despair, and went to good ministers with sad confessions. And when I had left the house and his company, he fell into it again and again so oft that at last his conscience could have no relief or ease but in changing his judgment and disowning the teachers and doctrines which had restrained him. . . . And the last I heard of him was that he was grown a fuddler and railer at strict men; but whether God recovered him, or what became of him, I cannot tell.

From Ludlow Castle, after a year and a half, I returned to my father's house, and by that time my old schoolmaster, Mr. John Owen, was sick of a consumption (which was his death); and the Lord Newport desired me to teach that school till he either recovered or died (resolving to take his brother after him if he died); which I did, about a quarter of a year or more.

After that old Mr. Francis Garbett (the faithful, learned minister at Wroxeter) for about a month read logic to me, and provoked me to a closer course of study, which yet was greatly interrupted by my bodily weakness and the troubled condition of my soul. For being in expectation of death by a violent cough, with spitting of blood, etc., of two years' continuance, supposed to be a deep degree of a consumption, I was yet more awakened to be serious and solicitous about my soul's everlasting state; and I came so short of that sense and seriousness which a matter of such infinite weight required, that I was in many years' doubt of my sincerity, and thought I had no spiritual life at all. . . .

Thus was I long kept with the calls of approaching death at one ear and the questionings of a doubtful conscience at the other; and since then I have found that this method of God's was very wise, and no other was so like to have tended to my good. . . .

It set me upon that method of my studies which since then I have found the benefit of, though at the time I was not satisfied with myself. It caused me first to seek God's Kingdom and his righteousness, and most to mind the one thing needful; and to determine first of my ultimate end; by which I was engaged to choose out and prosecute all other studies but as meant to that end. Therefore divinity was not only carried on with the rest of my studies with an equal hand, but always had the first and chiefest place. . . . And by that means all that I read did stick the better in my memory, and also less of my time was lost by lazy intermissions (but my bodily infirmities always caused me to lose or spend much of it in motion and corporal exercises, which was sometimes by walking, and sometimes at the plough and such country labours).

But one loss I had by this method which hath proved irreparable: that I missed that part of learning which stood at the greatest distance (in my thoughts) from my ultimate end (though no doubt but remotely it may be a valuable means), and I could never since find time to get it. Besides the Latin tongue and but a mediocrity in Greek (with an inconsiderable trial at the Hebrew long after), I had no great skill in languages. . . . And for the mathematics, I was an utter stranger to them, and never could find in my heart to divert any studies that way. But in order to the knowledge of divinity my inclination was most to logic and metaphysics, with that part of physics which treateth of the soul, contenting myself at first with a slighter study of the rest. And these had my labour and delight, which occasioned me (perhaps too soon) to plunge myself very early into the study of controversies, and to read all the Schoolmen I could get; for next to practical divinity, no books so suited with my disposition as Aquinas, Scotus, Durandus, Ockam and their disciples; because I thought they narrowly searched after truth and brought things out of the darkness of confusion; for I could never from my first studies endure confusion. . . . I never thought I understood any thing till I could anatomise it and see the parts distinctly, and the conjunction of the parts as they make up the whole. Distinction and method seemed to me of that necessity, that without them I could not be said to know; and the disputes which forsook them or abused them seem but as incoherent dreams.

And as for those doubts of my own salvation, which exercised me many years, the chiefest causes of them were these:

1. Because I could not distinctly trace the workings of the Spirit upon my heart in that method which Mr. Bolton, Mr. Hooker, Mr. Rogers and other divines describe; nor knew the time of my conversion, being wrought on by the forementioned degrees. But since then I understood that the soul is in too dark and passionate a plight at first to be able to keep an exact account of the order of its own operations. . . .

2. My second doubt was as aforesaid, because of the hardness of my heart or want of such lively apprehensions of things spiritual which I had about things corporal. And though I still groan under this as my sin and want, yet I now perceive that a soul in flesh doth work so much after the manner of the flesh that it much desireth sensible apprehensions; but things spiritual and distant are not so apt to work upon them, and to stir the passions, as things present and sensible are; . . . and that this is the ordinary state of a believer.

3. My next doubt was lest education and fear had done all that ever was done upon my soul, and regeneration and love were yet to seek; be-

cause I had found convictions from my childhood, and found more fear than love in all my duties and restraints.

But I afterward perceived that education is God's ordinary way for the conveyance of his grace, and ought no more to be set in opposition to the Spirit than the preaching of the Word; and that it was the great mercy of God to begin with me so soon. . . . And I understood that though fear without love be not a state of saving grace, . . . the soul of a believer groweth up by degrees from the more troublesome (but safe) operations of fear to the more high and excellent operations of complacential love. . . . And I found that my hearty love of the Word of God, and of the servants of God, and my desires to be more holy, and especially the hatred of my heart for loving God no more, and my love to love him and be pleasing to him was not without some love to himself, though it worked more sensibly on his nearer image. . . .

But I understood at last that God breaketh not all men's hearts alike. . . .

And it much increased my peace when God's providence called me to the comforting of many others that had the same complaints. While I answered their doubts I answered my own; and the charity which I was constrained to exercise for them redounded to myself and insensibly abated my fears and procured me an increase of quietness of mind.

And yet, after all, I was glad of probabilities instead of full un-doubted certainties; and to this very day, though I have no such degree of doubtfulness as is any great trouble to my soul or procureth any great disquieting fears, yet cannot I say that I have such a certainty of my own sincerity in grace as excludeth all doubts and fears of the contrary.

Blaise Pascal
(1623–1662)

The most appropriate word for describing Pascal, according to his many biographers and interpreters, is "genius." Pascal belongs to that rare circle of creative souls who cram several lifetimes into a few fleeting years. Mathematician, physicist, philosopher, theologian, and litterateur, he achieved fame in all these areas within a period of about twenty years.

A person of rigorous, scientific precision, he was also a man of deep, abiding faith. Sometimes he deliberately related the two, sharpening his geometrical mind as an instrument in the service of religious persuasion. The best-known example of this apologetic method is his so-called "wager." If god, as Pascal argued, does not exist, the skeptic loses nothing by not believing; but if God does exist, then the skeptic gains eternal life by believing. So why not make a bet!

A devout Catholic, Pascal associated himself with the controversial Jansenist movement at Port-Royal. A sort of French Catholic Puritanism, Jansenism stressed simplicity and humility of life, protesting against the moral casuistry and doctrinal remoteness of the Jesuits. Theologically, Jansenism invoked the name of Augustine and his concern to relate religious knowledge, divine grace, and human piety or spirituality. The certainties of faith, Pascal maintained, cannot be proved by reason, partly because "the heart has its reasons, which reason does not know" (*Pensées*, IV, 277).

If it may be said that Pascal's first "conversion" turned him toward Jansenism, signifying a renunciation of worldly pleasures, his second "conversion" was surrounded with a much more dramatic and enduring religious experience. He documented the exact moment when a vision (some critics say hallucination) invaded his inner being and forced itself upon him like an ecstatic revelation. Pascal wrote it all down and sewed it to the lining of his jacket, where it was found by a servant after his death nearly ten years later. Known as the *Memorial*, the full text is given here with English translations of the Latin and with biblical references supplied. "Fire" is, of course, a familiar symbol in the Bible, implying the presence of God. Whether we remember Moses and the burning bush, Isaiah's coal of fire from the altar, or the tongues of flame at Pentecost, the imagery of mysterious divine presence is inescapable — "for our God is a consuming fire" (Heb. 12:29).

In poor health most of his life, Pascal suffered through his final years in constant physical anguish. We may speculate as to whether it was meningitis, cancer of the spine, or a malignant stomach ulcer; no matter, though, for he knew he was a dying man and so he prepared a prayer, asking God to use his illness for some good purpose. The prayer, a portion of which is reprinted here, provides a fitting epilogue to his unforgettable conversion experience.

As T. S. Eliot notes in his introduction to the Everyman's Library edition of Pascal's *Pensées*: "Because of his unique combination and balance of qualities, I know of no religious writer more pertinent to our time."

The two texts for the *Memorial* and the *Prayer* are taken from *Great Shorter Works of Pascal*, trans. Emile Cailliet and John C. Blankenagel (Philadelphia: Westminster Press, 1948), 117, 220, 228. Reprinted by permission.

THE MEMORIAL

In the year of Grace, 1654,
On Monday, 23rd of November, Feast of St. Clement, Pope and Martyr, and others in the Martyrology,
Vigil of Saint Chrysogonus, Martyr, and others,
From about half past ten in the evening until about half past twelve,

FIRE

God of Abraham, God of Isaac, God of Jacob, not of the philosophers and scholars (Ex. 3:6; Matt. 22:32).
Certitude. Certitude. Feeling. Joy. Peace.
God of Jesus Christ
Deum meum et Deum vestrum ("My God and your God," John 20:17).
Forgetfulness of the world and of everything except God.
He is to be found only by the ways taught in the Gospel.
Greatness of the human soul.
"Righteous Father, the world hath not known Thee, but I have known Thee" (John 17:25).
Joy, joy, joy, tears of joy.
I have separated myself from Him
Derelinquerunt me fontem aquae vivae ("They have forsaken me, the
fountain of living waters," Jer. 2:13).
"My God, wilt Thou leave me?" (Matt. 27:46).
Let me not be separated from Him eternally.
"This is the eternal life, that they might know Thee, the only true God, and the one whom Thou has sent, Jesus Christ" (John 17:3).
Jesus Christ.
Jesus Christ.

I have separated myself from Him: I have fled from Him, denied Him, crucified Him.

Let me never be separated from Him.

We keep hold of Him only by the ways taught in the Gospel.

Renunciation, total and sweet.

Total submission to Jesus Christ and to my director.[1]

Eternally in joy for a day's training on earth.

Non obliviscar sermones tuos ("I will not forget Thy words," Psalm 118:16). *Amen.*

PRAYER ASKING GOD TO USE ILLNESS TO A GOOD END

Lord, whose spirit is so good and so gentle in all things, and who art so compassionate that not only all prosperity but even all afflictions that come to Thine elect are the results of Thy compassion: grant me grace that I may not do as the pagans do in the condition to which Thy justice has reduced me; grant that as a true Christian I may recognize Thee as my Father and as my God, in whatever estate I find myself, since the change in my condition brings no change in Thine own. For Thou art the same, though I be subject to change, and Thou art God no less when Thou dost afflict and when Thou dost punish, than when Thou dost console and when Thou dost manifest indulgence.

Thou hadst given me health that I might serve Thee, and I have profaned it; now Thou dost send me illness to correct my ways: do not permit me to use it to anger Thee by my impatience. I have misused my health, and Thou hast justly punished me for it; do not suffer me to misuse Thy punishment. And since the corruption of my nature is such that it renders Thy favors pernicious, grant, O my God, that Thine omnipotent grace may render Thy chastisements salutary to me. If my heart was filled with love for the world while it had some vigor, annihilate this vigor for my salvation, and render me incapable of enjoying the world not only through the weakness of my body, but rather through the ardor of a love which will render me capable of delight in Thee by rendering me capable of delight only in Thee.

O God, before whom I must give an exact accounting of my life unto the end of my life and unto the end of the world! O God, who dost permit the world and all things of the world to be, only that they may train Thine elect and punish sinners. O God, who dost leave hardened sinners

---

[1] Monsieur Singlin of Port-Royal.

in the delightful and criminal ways of the world and in the pleasures of the world. O God, who dost make our bodies to die, and who in the hour of death dost detach our soul from all that it loved in the world. O God, who dost wrest me in the final moment of my life from all things to which I had attached myself, and to which I had given my heart. O God, Thou who on the day of judgment must consume the earth and all creatures contained therein, to show to all men that Thou alone dost live, and hence that Thou alone art worthy of love, since nothing can endure without Thee. O God, Thou who must destroy all these vain idols and all these deadly objects of our passions, I praise Thee, my God, and I shall bless Thee all the days of my life, that Thou hast deigned to predispose this dread day in my favor, by destroying for my sake all things in the feebleness to which Thou hast reduced me. I praise Thee, my God, and I shall bless Thee all the days of my life because it has pleased Thee to lessen me so that I no longer have the capacity for enjoying the sweetness of health and the pleasures of the world. And I bless Thee for having somehow annihilated to my advantage the deceptive idols which Thou wilt indeed annihilate to confound the wicked on the day of Thy wrath. Give me, Lord, the strength to judge myself in the wake of destruction that Thou hast made with regard to me, so that Thou mayest not judge me Thyself after the complete destruction which Thou wilt make of my life and of the world. For, Lord, just as at the moment of my death I shall find myself separated from the world, devoid of all things, alone in Thy presence to answer to Thy righteousness for all the impulses of my heart, so, Lord, grant that I may consider myself in this illness as in a kind of death, separated from the world, devoid of all the objects to which I am enslaved, alone in Thy presence to implore Thy mercy for the conversion of my heart; and thus may I find unbounded consolation in Thy sending me now a kind of death to exercise Thy mercy before Thou dost in fact send me death to exercise Thy judgment. Grant then, O my God, that as Thou hast anticipated my death, so may I anticipate Thine appalling sentence, and may I examine myself before Thy judgment in order to find mercy in Thy presence.

Grant then, Lord, that I may conform to Thy will, just as I am, that, being sick as I am, I may glorify Thee in my sufferings. Without them I cannot attain to glory; without them, my Saviour, even Thou wouldst not have risen to glory. By the marks of Thy sufferings Thou wert recognized by Thy disciples, and likewise by their sufferings Thou dost recognize those who are Thy disciples. Therefore recognize me as Thy disciple by the ills that I endure, in my body and in my spirit, for the offenses which I have committed. And since nothing is pleasing to God unless it be offered by Thee, unite my will with Thine and my sufferings with those that Thou hast suffered; grant that mine may become Thine. Unite me with Thee; fill me with Thee and Thy Holy Spirit. Enter into my heart and into my soul, there to bear my sufferings and to continue in me that part of the suffering of Thy passion which yet remains to be endured, which Thou art yet completing in Thy members until the perfect consummation of Thy Body, so that it shall no longer be I who live and who suffer but that it shall be Thou who dost live and suffer in me, O my Saviour. And thus, having some small part in Thy suffering, I shall be filled wholly by Thee with the glory which it has brought to Thee, the glory in which Thou dost dwell with the Father and the Holy Spirit, forever and ever. Amen.

George Fox
(1624–1691)

George Fox was the founder of the Quakers, also known as the Society of Friends. Emerging out of the tremendous religious turmoil in England during the seventeenth century, Quakerism had its roots in English Puritanism. But Fox and his followers went beyond strict Puritanism, for they were radicals in the sense that they tried to return to what they perceived as the basic root principles of New Testament Christianity.

William Penn, one of Fox's most famous followers, called it *Primitive Christianity Revived*, and he accurately described Fox himself as "an original, being no man's copy." From Fox the Quakers emphasized the priesthood of all believers and abolished all offices of an ordained clergy. Fox proclaimed a continuing revelation by God, a revelation that centered in the Inner Light of Christ in each individual, and was not restricted simply to the Scriptures. As Fox wrote about his conversion, "Though I read the Scriptures that spoke of Christ and of God, yet I knew him not [except] by revelation, as he who hath the key did open, and as the Father of life drew me to his Son by his spirit."

Fox's doctrine of the Inner Light and his ministry to the outcasts of English society ("that which the people do trample upon") contributed to the tradition of pacifism among the Quakers and their concern for all conditions of humanity. Persecuted and even imprisoned, Fox greeted adversity and hatred with peace and charity toward others, and by the force of his personality and his witness he won others to his side.

His conversion in 1647 came after a long period of "seeking Truth," as he described it. He was born into a family of deep piety, and for a brief time was apprenticed to a shoemaker. But in 1643, feeling that he was called to reject all his ties to his family and friends, he began to travel about England in search of religious security. Fox despaired not only of his sin but also the sloth and ignorance of the priests and ministers whom he encountered. At last, Christ spoke to him directly. He began an itinerant preaching ministry, but it was not until 1652 that he attracted a significant number of converts. In 1669 he married Margaret Fell, the widow of a nobleman, and through a few such influential converts the Society of Friends developed a firm foothold in the religious landscape of England.

Fox had no intention of creating another church, but he did demonstrate a knack for organization, combining both the skills of leadership and the ability to keep the Society of Friends democratic in structure. He traveled extensively and tirelessly, making missionary journeys to Ireland, the West Indies and North America, and Holland. Although Fox dictated his famous *Journal*, his genius and spirit emerge clearly in its pages, and it has been widely read by Quakers and many others for centuries. Even those who cannot accept his theology can admire the simplicity and peaceful witness that he made. In William Penn's view, he stood alone: "Many sons have done virtuously in this day, but dear George thou excellest them all."

Excerpted from *The Journal of George Fox* (rev. ed.), ed. John L. Nickalls (Cambridge: Cambridge Univ. Press, 1952), 10-12, 14-15, 18-21. Reprinted by permission.

Now during all this time I was never joined in profession of religion with any, but gave up myself to the Lord, having forsaken all evil company, and taken leave of father and mother and all other relations, and travelled up and down as a stranger in the earth, which way the Lord inclined my heart, taking a chamber to myself in the town where I came, and tarrying sometimes a month, sometimes more, sometimes less in a place. For I durst not stay long in any place, being afraid both of professor [one who professes religion] and profane, lest, being a tender young man, I should be hurt by conversing much with either. For which reason I kept myself much as a stranger, seeking heavenly wisdom and getting knowledge from the Lord, and was brought off from outward things to rely wholly on the Lord alone. And though my exercises and troubles were very great, yet were they not so continual but that I had some intermissions, and was sometimes brought into such an heavenly joy that I thought I had been in Abraham's bosom. As I cannot declare the misery I was in, it was so great and heavy upon me, so neither can I set forth the mercies of God unto me in all my misery. Oh, the everlasting love of God to my soul when I was in great distress! When my troubles and torments were great, then was his love exceeding great. Thou, Lord, makest a fruitful field a barren wilderness, and a barren wilderness a fruitful field; thou bringest down and settest up; thou killest and makest alive; all honour and glory be to thee, O Lord of glory! The knowledge of thee in the spirit is life, but that knowledge which is fleshly works death. And while there is this knowledge in the flesh, deceit and self-will conform to anything, and will say, "Yes, yes," to that it doth not know. The knowledge which the world hath of what the prophets and apostles spake is a fleshly knowledge; and the apostates from the life in which the prophets and apostles were, have gotten their words, the Holy Scriptures, in a form, but not in their life nor spirit that gave them forth. And so all lie in confusion and are making provision for the flesh, to fulfil the lusts thereof, but not to fulfil the law and command of Christ in his power and spirit; for that, they say, they cannot do, but to fulfil the lusts of the flesh, that they can do with delight.

Now after I had received that opening from the Lord that to be bred at Oxford or Cambridge was not sufficient to fit a man to be a minister of Christ, I regarded the priests less, and looked more after the dissenting people. And among them I saw there was some tenderness, and many of them came afterwards to be convinced, for they had some openings. But as I had forsaken all the priests, so I left the separate preachers also, and those called the most experienced people; for I saw there was none among them all that could speak to my condition. And when all my hopes in them and in all men were gone, so that I had nothing outwardly to help me, nor could tell what to do, then, Oh then, I heard a voice which said, "There is one, even Christ Jesus, that can speak to thy condition," and when I heard it my heart did leap for joy. Then the Lord did let me see why there was none upon the earth that could speak to my condition, namely, that I might give him all the glory; for all are concluded under sin, and shut up in unbelief as I had been, that Jesus Christ might have the pre-eminence, who enlightens, and gives grace, and faith, and power. Thus, when God doth work who shall let [prevent] it? And this I knew experimentally [by experience].

My desires after the Lord grew stronger, and zeal in the pure knowledge of God and of Christ alone, without the help of any man, book, or writing. For though I read the Scriptures that spoke of Christ and of God, yet I knew him not but by revelation, as he who hath the key did open, and as the Father of life drew me to his Son by his spirit. And then the Lord did gently lead me along, and did let me see his love, which was endless and eternal, and surpasseth all the knowledge that men have in the natural state, or can get by history or books; and that love let me see myself as I was without him. And I was afraid of all company, for I saw them perfectly where they were, through the love of God which let me see myself. I had not fellowship with any people, priests, or professors, nor any sort of separated people, but with Christ, who hath the key, and opened the door of light and life unto me. And I was afraid of all carnal talk and talkers, for I could see nothing but corruptions, and the life lay under the burden of corruptions. And when I myself was in the deep, under all shut up, I could not believe that I should ever overcome; my troubles, my sorrows, and my temptations were so great, that I thought many times I should have despaired, I was so tempted. But when Christ opened to me how he was tempted by the same Devil, and had overcome him and bruised his head, and that through him and his power, light, grace and spirit, I should overcome also, I had confidence in him. So he it was that opened to me when I was shut up and had not hope nor faith. Christ it was who had enlightened me, that gave me his light to believe in, and gave me hope, which is himself, revealed himself in me, and gave me his spirit and gave me his grace, which I found sufficient in the deeps and in weakness. Thus, in the deepest miseries, and in greatest sorrows and temptations, that many times beset me, the Lord in his mercy did keep me. . . .

And one day when I had been walking solitarily abroad and was come home, I was taken up in the love of God, so that I could not but admire the greatness of his love. And while I was in that condition it was opened unto me by the eternal Light and power, and I therein saw clearly that all was done and to be done in and by Christ, and how he conquers and destroys this tempter, the Devil and all his works, and is atop of him, and that all these troubles were good for me, and temptations for the trial of my faith which Christ had given me. And the Lord opened me that I saw through all these troubles and temptations. My living faith was raised, that I saw all was done by Christ, the life, and my belief was in him. And when at any time my condition was veiled, my secret belief was stayed firm, and hope underneath held me, as an anchor in the bottom of the sea, and anchored my immortal soul to its Bishop, causing it to swim above the sea, the world where all the raging waves, foul weather, tempests, and temptations are. But oh, then did I see my troubles, trials, and temptations more than ever I had done! As the Light appeared, all appeared that is out of the Light, darkness, death, temptations, the unrighteous, the ungodly; all was manifest and seen in the Light.

Then after this there did a pure fire appear in me; then I saw how he sat as a refiner's fire and as the fuller's soap; and then the spiritual discerning came into me, by which I did discern my own thoughts, groans and sighs, and what it was that did veil me, and what it was that did open me. And that which could not abide in the patience nor endure the fire, in the Light I found to be the groans of the flesh (that could not give up to the will of God), which had veiled me, and that could not be patient in all trials, troubles and anguishes and perplexities, and could not give up self to die by the Cross, the power of God, that the living and quickened might follow him; and that that which would cloud and veil from the presence of Christ, that which the sword of the Spirit cuts down and which must die, might not be kept alive. And I discerned the groans of the spirit, which did open me, and made intercession to God, in which spirit is the true waiting upon God for the redemption of the body and of the whole creation. And by this true spirit, in which the true sighing is, I saw over the false sighings and groanings. And by this invisible spirit I discerned all the false hearing and the false seeing, and the false smelling which was atop, above the Spirit, quenching and grieving it; and that all they that were there were in confusion and deceit, where the false asking and praying is, in deceit, and atop in that nature and tongue that takes God's holy name in vain, and wallows in the Egyptian sea, and asketh but hath not. For they hate his light and resist the Holy Ghost, and turn the grace into wantonness, and rebel against the Spirit, and are erred from the faith they should ask in, and from the spirit they should pray by. He that knoweth these things in the true spirit, can witness them. The divine light of Christ manifesteth all things; and the spiritual fire trieth all things, and severeth all things. Several things did I then see as the Lord opened them to me, for he showed me that which can live in his holy refining fire, and that can live to God under his law. And he made me sensible how the law and the prophets were until John and how the least in the everlasting kingdom of God is greater than John. . . .

And I heard of a woman in Lancashire that had fasted two and twenty days, and I travelled to see her; but when I came to her I saw that she was under a temptation. And when I had spoken to her what I had from the Lord, I left her, her father being one high in profession. And passing on, I went among the professors at Dukinfield and Manchester, where I stayed a while and declared Truth among them. And there were some convinced, who received the Lord's teaching, by which they were confirmed and stood in the Truth. But the professors were in a rage, all pleading for sin and imperfection, and could not endure to hear talk of perfection, and of an holy and sinless life. But the Lord's power was over all; though they were chained under darkness and sin, which they pleaded for, and quenched the tender thing in them.

About this time there was a great meeting of the Baptists, at Broughton, in Leicestershire, with some that had separated from them; and people of other notions went thither, and I went also. Not many of the Baptists came, but abundance of other people were there. And the Lord opened my mouth, and his everlasting Truth was declared amongst them, and the power of the Lord was over them all. For in that day the Lord's power began to spring, and I had great openings in the Scriptures. And several were convinced in those parts, and were turned from darkness to light, and from the power of Satan unto God, and his power they did receive and by it many were raised up to praise God. And when I reasoned with professors and other people, some were convinced and did stand.

Yet I was under great temptations sometimes, and my inward sufferings were heavy; but I could find none to open my condition to but the Lord alone, unto whom I cried night and day. And I went back into Nottinghamshire, and there the Lord shewed me that the natures of those things which were hurtful without were within, in the hearts and minds of wicked men. The natures of dogs, swine, vipers, of Sodom and Egypt, Pharaoh, Cain, Ishmael, Esau, etc. The natures of these I saw within, though people had been looking without. And I cried to the Lord, saying, "Why should I be thus, seeing I was never addicted to commit those evils?" And the Lord answered that it was needful I should have a sense of all conditions, how else should I speak to all conditions; and in this I saw the infinite love of God. I saw also that there was an ocean of darkness and death, but an infinite ocean of light and love, which flowed over the ocean of darkness. And in that also I saw the infinite love of God; and I had great openings.

And as I was walking by the steeplehouse side, in the town of Mansfield, the Lord said unto me, "That which people do trample upon must be thy food." And as the Lord spoke he opened it to me how that people and professors did trample upon the life, even the life of Christ was trampled upon; and they fed upon words, and fed one another with words, but trampled upon the life, and trampled underfoot the blood of the Son of God, which blood was my life, and they lived in their airy notions, talking of him. It seemed strange to me at the first that I should feed on that which the high professors trampled upon, but the Lord opened it clearly to me by his eternal spirit and power.

In Mansfield there came a priest who was looked upon to be above others, and all that professed themselves above the priests went to hear him and cried him up. I was against their going, and spoke to them against their going, and asked them if they had not a teacher within them: the anointing to teach them, and why would they go out to man. And then when they were gone to hear him, I was in sore travail, and it came upon me that I was moved to go to the steeplehouse to tell the people and the priest, and to bid them to cease from man whose breath was in their nostrils, and to tell them where their teacher was, within them, the spirit and the light of Jesus, and how God that made the world doth not dwell in temples made with hands. And many other things concerning the Truth I spake to them. And they were pretty moderate to hear the Truth, whereby, after, many were wrought upon. Then came people from far and near to see me; and I was fearful of being drawn out by them, yet I was made to speak and open things to them.

There was one Brown, who had great prophecies and sights upon his death-bed of me. And he spoke openly of what I should be made instrumental by the Lord to bring forth. And of others he spake that they should come to nothing, which was fulfilled on some, that then were something in show. And when this man was buried, a great work of the Lord fell upon me, to the admiration of many, who thought I had been dead, and many came to see me, for about fourteen days' time. For I was very much altered in countenance and person as if my body had been new moulded or changed. And while I was in that condition, I had a sense and discerning given me by the Lord, through which I saw plainly that when many people talked of God and of Christ, etc., the Serpent spoke in them; but this was hard to be borne. Yet the work of the Lord went on in some, and my sorrows and troubles began to wear off and tears of joy dropped from me, so that I could have wept night and day with tears of joy to the Lord, in humility and brokenness of heart. And I saw into that which was without end, and things which cannot be uttered, and of the greatness and infiniteness of the love of God, which cannot be expressed by words. For I had been brought through the very ocean of darkness and death, and through the power and over the power of Satan, by the eternal glorious power of Christ. Even through that darkness was I brought, which covered-over all the world, and which chained down all, and shut up all in the death. And the same eternal power of God, which brought me through these things, was that which afterwards shook the nations, priests, professors, and people. Then could I say I had been in spiritual Babylon, Sodom, Egypt, and the grave; but by the eternal power of God I was come out of it, and was brought over it and the power of it, into the power of Christ. And I saw the harvest white, and the Seed of God lying thick in the ground, as ever did wheat that was sown outwardly, and none to gather it; and for this I mourned with tears.

And a report went abroad of me that I was a young man that had a discerning spirit; whereupon many came to me from far and near, professors, priests, and people. And the Lord's power brake forth; and I had great openings, and prophecies, and spake unto them of the things of God, and they heard with attention and silence, and went away, and spread the fame thereof. Then came the tempter, and set upon me again, charging me that I had sinned against the Holy Ghost, but I could not tell in what. And then Paul's condition came before me, how, after he had been taken up into the third heaven and seen things not lawful to be uttered, a messenger of Satan was sent to buffet him again. Thus, by the power of Christ, I got over that temptation also.

John Bunyan
(1628–1688)

John Bunyan was born into a world of violence, war, and bitter disputes about Christian doctrine. During his lifetime, the continent of Europe was engulfed in the Thirty Years' War, pitting Protestant against Catholic in what amounted to a civil war within Christianity. England saw its own civil war in the 1640s — Puritans fighting Anglicans, defenders of Parliament battling the forces of the king.

This atmosphere of war and combat is reflected in Bunyan's conversion and his vision of life. For him the world is an arena of good and evil; an individual is constantly tempted to sin; the Christian life is spiritual warfare against Satan. Because of the power of sin, a person's conversion is rarely certain or final. Conversion thus becomes a process rather than a single event.

Bunyan's understanding of God's redemption first appeared in his spiritual autobiography, *Grace Abounding to the Chief of Sinners* (1666), written while he was in prison for refusing to stop preaching without a license. A classic of the church's devotional literature, *Grace Abounding* is a powerful and dramatic tale of Bunyan's many temptations and his experiences of grace and forgiveness.

Bunyan turned this story into an allegory in *The Pilgrim's Progress* (1678), an eloquent and beautiful description of a Christian's journey through dangers and pitfalls to safety with God. *The Pilgrim's Progress* is a landmark in English literature. With the exception of the Bible, it was the most widely-read book in the English language until the twentieth century.

Bunyan says that as a youth he had "few equals . . . both for cursing, swearing, lying, and blaspheming the holy name of God." He was an impoverished tinker or general repairman who married an equally poor woman whose only dowry consisted of two devotional books: *The Practice of Piety* and *The Plain Man's Pathway to Heaven*. When he read these volumes, Bunyan began to examine his life, and one Sunday while playing tipcat, he had a sudden and deep awareness of his sin and God's anger. He searched the Scripture thoroughly, and despite occasional feelings of forgiveness, he continued to agonize over his salvation.

The selection reprinted here describes some of the heights and depths that Bunyan experienced and his final awareness of God's love. This conception of the Christian life as a journey or pilgrimage continues to be one of the most powerful and enduring ways in which Christians understand their own faith and experience, and it has been dramatically influenced by Bunyan's writings.

Bunyan's other works include *The Life and Death of Mr. Badman* (1680), *The Holy War* (1682), and seventy-four rhymes in *A Book for Boys and Girls* (1686). After being released from prison in 1672, he preached as a Baptist minister, and he died in 1688 of pneumonia after making a pastoral call.

Excerpted from *Grace Abounding to the Chief of Sinners* in *The Complete Works of John Bunyan* (Philadelphia, 1874), 54-56, 59.

Before many weeks were gone, I began to despond again, fearing, lest, notwithstanding all that I had enjoyed, that I might be deceived and destroyed at the last; for this consideration came strong into my mind, "That whatever comfort and peace I thought I might have from the word of the promise of life, yet unless there could be found in my refreshment, a concurrence and agreement in the Scriptures, let me think what I will thereof, and hold it never so fast, I should find no such thing at the end; for the Scriptures cannot be broken."

Now began my heart again to ache, and fear I might meet with a disappointment at last. Wherefore I began with all seriousness to examine my former comfort, and to consider whether one that had sinned as I had done, might with confidence trust upon the faithfulness of God, laid down in these words, by which I had been comforted, and on which I had leaned myself. But now were brought to my mind, "For it is impossible for those who were once enlightened, and have tasted the heavenly gift, and were made partakers of the Holy Ghost, and have tasted the good word of God, and the powers of the world to come, if they shall fall away, to renew them again unto repentance. For if we sin wilfully, and after we have received the knowledge of the truth, there remains no more sacrifice for sin, but certain fearful looking-for of judgment, and fiery indignation, which shall devour the adversaries; even as Esau, who for one morsel of meat, sold his birthright. For ye know how that afterwards, when he would have inherited the blessing, he was rejected; for he found no place of repentance, though he sought it carefully with tears."

Now was the word of the Gospel forced from my soul; so that no promise or encouragement was to be found in the Bible for me; and now would that saying work upon my spirit to afflict me, "Rejoice not, O Israel, for joy as other people." For I saw, indeed, there was cause of rejoicing for those that held to Jesus; but for me, I had cut myself off by my transgressions, and left myself neither foot-hold nor hand-hold, among all the stays and props in the precious word of life.

And truly, I did now feel myself to sink into a gulf, as an house whose foundation is destroyed: I did liken myself in this condition, unto the case of a child that was fallen into a mill-pit, who though it could make some shift to scrabble and sprawl in the water, yet because it could find neither hold for hand nor foot, therefore at last it must die in that condition. So soon as this fresh assault had fastened on my soul, that Scripture came into my heart, "This for many days." And indeed I found it was so; for I could not be delivered, nor brought to peace again, until well nigh two years and an half were completely finished. Wherefore these words, though in themselves they tended to no discouragement, yet to me, who feared this condition would be eternal, they were at sometimes as an help and refreshment to me.

For, thought I, many days are not for ever, many days will have an end; therefore seeing I was to be afflicted not a few, but many days, yet I was glad it was but for many days. Thus, I say, I could recall myself sometimes and give myself an help, for as soon as even the word came into my mind, at first I knew my trouble would be long, yet this would be but sometimes; for I could not always think on this, nor ever be helped by it, though I did.

Now while the Scriptures lay before me, and laid sin anew at my door, that saying in Luke xviii. 1, with others, did encourage me to prayer; then the tempter again laid at me very sore, suggesting, "That neither the mercy of God, nor yet the blood of Christ, did at all concern me, nor could they help me for my sin; therefore it was but in vain to pray." Yet, thought I, "I will pray." "But, said the tempter, your sin is unpardonable." "Well, said I, I will pray." "It is to no boot, said he." "Yet, said I, I will pray." So I went to prayer with God; and while I was at prayer, I uttered words to this effect: "Lord, Satan tells me, that neither thy mercy, nor Christ's blood is sufficient to save my soul; Lord, shall I honour thee most, by believing thou wilt, and canst? or him, by believing that thou neither wilt, nor canst? Lord, I would fain honour thee, by believing that thou wilt, and canst."

And as I was thus before the Lord, that Scripture fastened on my heart, "O man, great is thy faith:" even as if one had clapped me on the back, as I was on my knees before God: yet I was not able to believe this, that this was a prayer of faith, till almost six months after; for I could not think that I had faith, or that there should be a word for me to act faith on; therefore I should still be, as sticking in the jaws of desperation, and went mourning up and down in a sad condition.

There was nothing now that I longed for more than to be put out of doubt, as to this thing in question, and as I was vehemently desiring to know, if there was indeed hope for me, these words came rolling into my mind, "Will the Lord cast off for ever? and will he be favourable no more? Is his mercy clean gone for ever? Doth his promise fail for evermore? Hath God forgotten to be gracious? Hath he in anger shut up his tender mercies?" And all the while they run in my mind, methought I had still this as the answer: " 'Tis a question whether he hath or no; it may be he hath not."

Yea, the interrogatory seemed to me to carry in it a sure affirmation that
indeed he had not, nor would so cast off, but would be favourable; that his
promise doth not fail, and that he hath not forgotten to be gracious, nor
would in anger shut up his tender mercy. Something also there was upon
my heart at the same time, which I now cannot call to mind, which with
this text did sweeten my heart, and make me conclude, that this mercy
might not be quite gone, not gone for ever.

At another time I remembered, I was again much under this question, "Whether the blood of Christ was sufficient to save my soul?" in
which doubt I continued from morning, till about seven or eight at night;
and at last, when I was, as it were, quite worn out with fear, lest it should
not lay hold on me, these words did sound suddenly within my heart, "He
is able." But methought this word *able*, was spoke so loud to me, it showed
a great word, it seemed to be writ in great letters, and gave such a jostle
to my fear and doubt, (I mean for the time it tarried with me, which was
about a day,) as I never had from that, all my life, either before or after.
(Heb. vii. 25.)

But one morning as I was again at prayer and trembling under the
fear of this, that no word of God could help me, that piece of a sentence
darted in upon me, "My grace is sufficient." At this methought I felt some
stay, as if there might be hopes; but oh! how good a thing it is for God to
send his word! for about a fortnight before, I was looking on this very
place, and then I thought it could not come near my soul with comfort,
therefore I threw down my book in a pet; then I thought it was not large
enough for me; no, not large enough, but now it was as if it had arms of
grace so wide, that it could not only enclose me, but many more beside.

By these words I was sustained, yet not without exceeding conflicts,
for the space of seven or eight weeks; for my peace would be in it, and
out, sometimes twenty times a day, comfort now, and trouble presently;
peace now, and before I could go a furlong, as full of fear and guilt as ever
heart could hold; and this was not only now and then, but my whole seven
weeks' experience. For this about the sufficiency of grace, and that of Esau's
parting with his birthright, would be like a pair of scales within my mind,
sometimes one end would be uppermost and sometimes again the other;
according to which would be my peace or troubles.

Therefore I did still pray to God, that he would come in with his
Scripture more fully on my heart; to wit, that he would help me to apply
the whole sentence, for as yet I could not; what he gave, that I gathered;
but further I could not go, for as yet it only helped me to hope there might
be mercy for me, "My grace is sufficient:" and though it came no farther,
it answered my former question; to wit, that there was hope; yet because
"for thee" was left out, I was not contented, but prayed to God for that
also. Wherefore, one day, when I was in a meeting of God's people, full
of sadness and terror, for my fears again were strong upon me, and as I

was now thinking my soul was never the better, but my case most sad and fearful, these words did with great power suddenly break in upon me, "My power is sufficient for thee, My grace is sufficient for thee, My grace is sufficient for thee," three times together: and oh! methought that every word was a mighty word unto me; as "my," and "grace," and "sufficient," and "for thee;" they were then, and sometimes are still, far bigger than others be.

At which time my understanding was so enlightened, that I was as though I had seen the Lord Jesus look down from heaven, through the tiles upon me, and direct these words unto me. This sent me mourning home; it broke my heart, and filled me full of joy, and laid me low as the dust; only it stayed not long with me, I mean in this glory and refreshing comfort; yet it continued with me for several weeks, and did encourage me to hope; but as soon as that powerful operation of it was taken from my heart, that other, about Esau, returned upon me as before; so my soul did hang as in a pair of scales again, sometimes up, and sometimes down; now in peace, and anon again in terror.

Thus I went on for many weeks, sometimes comforted, and sometimes tormented; and especially at some times my torment would be very sore. . . .

But one day, as I was passing into the field, and that too with some dashes on my conscience, fearing lest yet all was not right, suddenly this sentence fell upon my soul, "Thy righteousness is in heaven;" and methought withal, I saw with the eyes of my soul, Jesus Christ at God's right hand; there, I say, as my righteousness; so that wherever I was, or whatever I was doing, God could not say to me, "He wants my righteousness," for that was just before him. I also saw moreover, that it was not my good frame of heart that made my righteousness better, nor yet my bad frame that made my righteousness worse; for my righteousness was Jesus Christ himself, "the same yesterday, to-day and for ever."

Now did my chains fall off my legs indeed; I was loosed from my afflictions and irons; my temptations also fled away; so that from that time those dreadful Scriptures of God left off to trouble me: now went I also home rejoicing, for the grace and love of God; so when I came home, I looked to see if I could find that sentence, "Thy righteousness is in heaven," but could not find such a saying; wherefore my heart began to sink again, only that was brought to my remembrance, "He is made unto us of God, wisdom, righteousness, sanctification, and redemption." By this word I saw the other sentence true.

For by this Scripture I saw that the man Christ Jesus, as he is distinct from us, as touching his bodily presence, so he is our righteousness and sanctification before God. Here therefore I lived, for some time, very sweetly at peace with God through Christ. Oh! methought, Christ! Christ! there was nothing but Christ that was before my eyes: I was now only for looking upon this and the other benefits of Christ apart, as of his blood, burial, or his resurrection, but considering him as a whole Christ! as he in whom all these, and all other virtues, relations, offices, and operations met together, and that he sat on the right hand of God in heaven.

'Twas glorious to me to see his exaltation, and the worth and prevalency of all his benefits, and that because now I could look from myself to him, and would reckon, that all those graces of God that now were green on me, were yet but like those cracked groats and four-pence-half-pennies that rich men carry in their purses, when their gold is in their trunks at home: Oh! I saw my gold was in my trunk at home! In Christ my Lord and Saviour. Now Christ was all; all my righteousness, all my sanctification, and all my redemption.

Further, the Lord did also lead me into the mystery of the union with the Son of God, that I was joined to him, and that I was flesh of his flesh, and bone of his bone, and now was that a sweet word unto me, in Ephes. v. 30. By this also was my faith in him, as my righteousness, the more confirmed in me; for if he and I were one, then his righteousness was mine, his merits mine, his victory also mine. Now I could see myself in heaven and earth at once, in heaven by my Christ, by my head, by my righteousness and life, though on earth by body or person.

Now I saw Christ Jesus was looked upon of God; and should also be looked upon by us, as that common or public person, in whom the whole body of his elect are always to be considered and reckoned; that we fulfilled the law by him, died by him, rose from the dead by him, got the victory over sin, death, and hell, by him; when he died, we died; and so of his resurrection. "Thy dead men shall live together, with my dead body shall they arise," saith he. And again, "After two days he will revive us, and the third day we shall live in his sight." Which is now fulfilled by the sitting down of the Son of man on the right hand of the Majesty in the heavens, according to that of the Ephesians, "He hath raised us up together, and made us sit together in heavenly places in Christ Jesus."

Ah! these blessed considerations and Scriptures, with many others of like nature, were in those days made to spangle in mine eye, so that I have cause to say, "Praise ye the Lord God in his sanctuary; praise him in the firmament of his power: praise him for his mighty acts; praise him according to his excellent greatness."

John Wesley
(1703-1791)

John Wesley's conversion on May 24, 1738 has been widely recognized as an epoch-making date. It marks the beginning of Methodism, a denomination which has exerted a profound influence in Great Britain, the United States, and throughout the world. Signaling the rise of evangelicalism in Christianity, Wesley's conversion is a model of the datable, instantaneous, certain experience of grace that has become so characteristic of some forms of the evangelical movement.

Although Wesley emphasized the sinfulness of his life prior to this date, he was born into what would be called a Christian home. His father, Samuel, was a scholarly but somewhat prickly rector in the Church of England. His mother, Susanna, was an extraordinary woman of beauty, learning, efficiency, and piety. She gave birth to nineteen children, only nine of whom lived to adulthood. Among them were John and his brother Charles, the author of innumerable hymns, and together they transformed the history of Christianity. Their mother left a permanent imprint on their lives, perhaps greater in the case of John who had difficulty relating to women throughout his life. She educated all the children not simply in the three R's but also in Latin, Greek, history, literature, and of course religion. She set aside one evening a week for each of her children to converse about the child's educational and spiritual development. When John left for Oxford University, he continued the rigorous pattern that his mother had taught him at home. He joined a group of students who trained themselves in Christian spirituality, and because of their disciplined life, the members of this "Holy Club" were derisively called "Methodists."

As a child, John Wesley nearly died in a fire that devastated the parsonage, and when he was saved by two men of the town, his mother praised God and exclaimed, "Is this not a brand plucked out of the burning?" The phrase stayed with Wesley throughout his life. He left Oxford for a disastrous missionary tour in Georgia, suffered through a disappointing love affair, and, in frail health, he returned to England on a ship buffeted by terrible gales. The images of these experiences — fire, storms, illness — characterize much of his preaching and piety, as well as the ethos of this kind of evangelicalism.

It was in Georgia that Wesley first encountered the Moravians, who impressed him because of the serenity and certainty of their faith. When he arrived back in London, he met the Moravian Peter Böhler, to whom he confessed that despite his knowledge of Christianity, he still felt he lacked saving faith and wondered if he should stop preaching. "By no means," Böhler said. "But what shall I preach?" Wesley asked, and Böhler replied, "Preach faith till you have it; and then, because you have it, you will preach faith." Shortly after that, Wesley visited the house on Aldersgate where a group of Moravians were meeting, and as someone read from Luther's preface to his commentary on Romans, Wesley's heart was "strangely warmed."

The influence of Luther on Wesley is appropriate, for Wesley's conversion was a renewed sense that assurance of salvation came by grace through faith, not by works. But, as Wesley's own account reveals, he was afflicted by doubt immediately after the experience and resolved, "Well may fears be within me; but I must go on, and tread them under my feet." He almost literally did just that, beginning an itinerant ministry that lasted for fifty years — into his eighties — traveling 250,000 miles, and preaching 40,000 to 50,000 sermons. Early on he wrote his brother Samuel, "Leisure and I have taken leave of each other," and they never met again. He considered all the world his parish, and to a considerable degree, later Methodists and evangelicals have fulfilled his charge.

The text of Wesley's account is taken from *The Journal of John Wesley, A.M.*, ed. Nehemiah Curnock (New York: Eaton & Mains, 1909), I: 465-78, with the annotation omitted.

W hat occurred on *Wednesday* the 24th, I think best to relate at large, after premising what may make it the better understood. Let him that cannot receive it ask of the Father of lights that He would give more light to him and me.

1. I believe, till I was about ten years old I had not sinned away that "washing of the Holy Ghost" which was given me in baptism, having been strictly educated and carefully taught that I could only be saved "by universal obedience, by keeping all the commandments of God"; in the meaning of which I was diligently instructed. And those instructions, so far as they respected outward duties and sins, I gladly received and often thought of. But all that was said to me of inward obedience or holiness I neither understood nor remembered. So that I was indeed as ignorant of the true meaning of the law as I was of the gospel of Christ.

2. The next six or seven years were spent at school; where, outward restraints being removed, I was much more negligent than before, even of outward duties, and almost continually guilty of outward sins, which I knew to be such, though they were not scandalous in the eye of the world. However, I still read the Scriptures, and said my prayers morning and evening. And what I now hoped to be saved by, was, (1) not being so bad as other people; (2) having still a kindness for religion; and (3) reading the Bible, going to church, and saying my prayers.

3. Being removed to the University for five years, I still said my prayers both in public and in private, and read, with the Scriptures, several other books of religion, especially comments on the New Testament. Yet I had not all this while so much as a notion of inward holiness; nay, went on habitually, and for the most part very contentedly, in some or other known sin: indeed, with some intermission and short struggles, especially before and after the Holy Communion, which I was obliged to receive thrice a year. I cannot well tell what I hoped to be saved by now, when I was continually sinning against that little light I had; unless by those transient fits of what many divines taught me to call repentance.

4. When I was about twenty-two, my father pressed me to enter into holy orders. At the same time, the providence of God directing me to Kempis's *Christian Pattern,* I began to see, that true religion was seated in the heart, and that God's law extended to all our thoughts as well as words and actions. I was, however, very angry at Kempis for being too strict; though I read him only in Dean Stanhope's translation. Yet I had frequently much sensible comfort in reading him, such as I was an utter stranger to before; and meeting likewise with a religious friend, which I never had till now, I began to alter the whole form of my conversation, and to set in earnest upon a new life. I set apart an hour or two a day for religious retirement. I communicated every week. I watched against all sin, whether in word or deed. I began to aim at, and pray for, inward holiness. So that now, "doing so much, and living so good a life," I doubted not but I was a good Christian.

5. Removing soon after to another College, I executed a resolution which I was before convinced was of the utmost importance,—shaking off at once all my trifling acquaintance—I began to see more and more the value of time. I applied myself closer to study. I watched more carefully against actual sins; I advised others to be religious, according to that scheme of religion by which I modelled my own life. But meeting now with Mr. Law's *Christian Perfection* and *Serious Call,* although I was much offended at many parts of both, yet they convinced me more than ever of the exceeding height and breadth and depth of the law of God. The light flowed in so mightily upon my soul, that everything appeared in a new view. I cried to God for help, and resolved not to prolong the time of obeying Him as I had never done before. And by my continued endeavour to keep His whole law, inward and outward, to the utmost of my power, I was persuaded that I should be accepted of Him, and that I was even then in a state of salvation.

6. In 1730 I began visiting the prisons; assisting the poor and sick in town; and doing what other good I could, by my presence or my little fortune, to the bodies and souls of all men. To this end I abridged myself of all superfluities, and many that are called necessaries of life. I soon became a by-word for so doing, and I rejoiced that my name was cast out as evil. The next spring I began observing the Wednesday and Friday Fasts,

commonly observed in the ancient Church; tasting no food till three in the afternoon. And now I knew not how to go any further. I diligently strove against all sin. I omitted no sort of self-denial which I thought lawful; I carefully used, both in public and in private, all the means of grace at all opportunities. I omitted no occasion of doing good; I for that reason suffered evil. And all this I knew to be nothing, unless as it was directed toward inward holiness. Accordingly this, the image of God, was what I aimed at in all, by doing His will, not my own. Yet when, after continuing some years in this course, I apprehended myself to be near death, I could not find that all this gave me any comfort or any assurance of acceptance with God. At this I was then not a little surprised; not imagining I had been all this time building on the sand, nor considering that "other foundation can no man lay than that which is laid" by God, "even Christ Jesus."

7. Soon after, a contemplative man "convinced me still more than I was convinced before, that outward works are nothing, being alone; and in several conversations instructed me how to pursue inward holiness, or a union of the soul with God. But even of his instructions (though I then received them as the words of God) I cannot but now observe (1) that he spoke so incautiously against trusting in outward works, that he discouraged me from doing them at all; (2) that he recommended (as it were, to supply what was wanting in them) *mental prayer,* and the like exercises, as the most effectual means of purifying the soul and uniting it with God. Now these were, in truth, as much my own works as visiting the sick or clothing the naked; and the union with God thus pursued was as really my own righteousness as any I had before pursued under another name.

8. In this refined way of trusting to my own works and my own righteousness (so zealously inculcated by the Mystic writers), I dragged on heavily, finding no comfort or help therein till the time of my leaving England. On shipboard, however, I was again active in outward works; where it pleased God of His free mercy to give me twenty-six of the Moravian brethren for companions, who endeavoured to show me "a more excellent way." But I understood it not at first. I was too learned and too wise. So that it seemed foolishness unto me. And I continued preaching, and following after, and trusting in, that righteousness whereby no flesh can be justified.

9. All the time I was at Savannah I was thus beating the air. Being ignorant of the righteousness of Christ, which, by a living faith in Him, bringeth salvation "to every one that believeth," I sought to establish my own righteousness; and so labored in the fire all my days. I was now properly "under the law"; I knew that "the law" of God was "spiritual; I consented to it that it was good." Yea, "I delighted in it, after the inner man." Yet was I "carnal, sold under sin." Every day was I constrained to cry out, "What I do, I allow not: for what I would, I do not; but what I hate, that I do. To will is" indeed "present with me: but how to perform that which

is good, I find not. For the good which I would, I do not; but the evil which I would not, that I do. I find a law, that when I would do good, evil is present with me": even "the law in my members, warring against the law of my mind," and still "bringing me into captivity to the law of sin."

10. In this vile, abject state of bondage to sin, I was indeed fighting continually, but not conquering. Before, I had willingly served sin: now it was unwillingly; but still I served it. I fell, and rose, and fell again. Sometimes I was overcome, and in heaviness: sometimes I overcame, and was in joy. For as in the former state I had some foretastes of the terrors of the law; so had I in this, of the comforts of the gospel. During this whole struggle between nature and grace, which had now continued above ten years, I had many remarkable returns to prayer, especially when I was in trouble; I had many sensible comforts, which are indeed no other than short anticipations of the life of faith. But I was still "under the law," not "under grace" (the state most who are called Christians are content to live and die in); for I was only striving with, not freed from, sin. Neither had I the witness of the Spirit with my spirit, and indeed could not; for I "sought it not by faith, but as it were by the works of the law."

11. In my return to England, January 1738, being in imminent danger of death, and very uneasy on that account, I was strongly convinced that the cause of that uneasiness was unbelief; and that the gaining a true, living faith was the "one thing needful" for me. But still I fixed not this faith on its right object: I meant only faith in God, not faith in or through Christ. Again, I knew not that I was wholly void of this faith; but only thought I had not enough of it. So that when Peter Böhler, whom God prepared for me as soon as I came to London, affirmed of true faith in Christ (which is but one) that it had those two fruits inseparably attending it, "dominion over sin and constant peace from a sense of forgiveness," I was quite amazed, and looked upon it as a new gospel. If this was so, it was clear I had not faith. But I was not willing to be convinced of this. Therefore I disputed with all my might, and laboured to prove that faith might be where these were not: for all the scriptures relating to this I had been long since taught to construe away; and to call all Presbyterians who spoke otherwise. Besides, I well saw no one could, in the nature of things, have such a sense of forgiveness, and not *feel* it. But I felt it not. If, then, there was no faith without this, all my pretensions to faith dropped at once.

12. When I met Peter Böhler again, he consented to put the dispute upon the issue which I desired, namely, Scripture and experience. I first consulted the Scripture. But when I set aside the glosses of men, and simply considered the words of God, comparing them together, endeavouring to illustrate the obscure by the plainer passages, I found they all made against me, and was forced to retreat to my last hold, "that experience would never agree with the *literal interpretation* of those scriptures. Nor could I therefore allow it to be true, till I found some living witnesses of it." He replied, he

could show me such at any time; if I desired it, the next day. And accordingly the next day he came again with three others, all of whom testified, of their own personal experience, that a true living faith in Christ is inseparable from a sense of pardon for all past and freedom from all present sins. They added with one mouth that this faith was the gift, the free gift of God; and that He would surely bestow it upon every soul who earnestly and perseveringly sought it. I was now thoroughly convinced; and, by the grace of God, I resolved to seek it unto the end, (1) By absolutely renouncing all dependence, in whole or in part, upon *my own* works or righteousness; on which I had really grounded my hope of salvation, though I knew it not, from my youth up; (2) by adding to the constant use of all the other means of grace, continual prayer for this very thing, justifying, saving faith, a full reliance on the blood of Christ shed for *me*; a trust in Him, as *my* Christ, as *my* sole justification, sanctification, and redemption.

13. I continued thus to seek it (though with strange indifference, dullness, and coldness, and unusually frequent relapses into sin) till *Wednesday*, May 24. I think it was about five this morning, that I opened my Testament on those words, Τὰ μέγιστα ἡμῖν καὶ τίμια ἐπαγγέλματα δεδώρηται, ἵνα γένησθε θείας κοινωνοὶ φύσεως. "There are given unto us exceeding great and precious promises, even that ye should be partakers of the divine nature" (2 Pet. i. 4). Just as I went out, I opened it again on those words, "Thou art not far from the kingdom of God." In the afternoon I was asked to go to St. Paul's. The anthem was, "Out of the deep have I called unto Thee, O Lord: Lord, hear my voice. O let Thine ears consider well the voice of my complaint. If Thou, Lord, wilt be extreme to mark what is done amiss, O Lord, who may abide it? For there is mercy with Thee; therefore shalt Thou be feared. O Israel, trust in the Lord: for with the Lord there is mercy, and with Him is plenteous redemption. And He shall redeem Israel from all his sins."

14. In the evening I went very unwillingly to a society in Aldersgate Street, where one was reading Luther's preface to the *Epistle to the Romans*. About a quarter before nine, while he was describing the change which God works in the heart through faith in Christ, I felt my heart strangely warmed. I felt I did trust in Christ, Christ alone for salvation; and an assurance was given me that He had taken away *my* sins, even *mine,* and saved *me* from the law of sin and death.

15. I began to pray with all my might for those who had in a more especial manner despitefully used me and persecuted me. I then testified openly to all there what I now first felt in my heart. But it was not long before the enemy suggested, "This cannot be faith; for where is thy joy?" Then was I taught that peace and victory over sin are essential to faith in the Captain of our salvation; but that, as to the transports of joy that usually attend the beginning of it, especially in those who have mourned deeply,

God sometimes giveth, sometimes withholdeth them, according to the counsels of His own will.

16. After my return home, I was much buffeted with temptations; but cried out, and they fled away. They returned again and again. I as often lifted up my eyes, and He "sent me help from His holy place." And herein I found the difference between this and my former state chiefly consisted. I was striving, yea, fighting with all my might under the law, as well as under grace. But then I was sometimes, if not often, conquered; now, I was always conqueror.

17. *Thur. 25.*—The moment I awaked, "Jesus, Master," was in my heart and in my mouth; and I found all my strength lay in keeping my eye fixed upon Him, and my soul waiting on Him continually. Being again at St. Paul's in the afternoon, "My song shall be always of the loving-kindness of the Lord: with my mouth will I ever be showing forth Thy truth from one generation to another." Yet the enemy injected a fear, "If thou dost believe, why is there not a more sensible change?" I answered (yet not I), "That I know not. But this I know, I have 'now peace with God.' And I sin not to-day, and Jesus my Master has forbid me to take thought for the morrow."

18. "But is not any sort of fear," continued the tempter, "a proof that thou dost not believe?" I desired my Master to answer for me, and opened His Book upon those words of St. Paul, "Without were fightings, within were fears." Then, inferred I, well may fears be within me; but I must go on, and tread them under my feet.

George Whitefield
(1714–1770)

George Whitefield (pronounced "Witfield") was without doubt one of the greatest preachers in the history of Christianity. In his youth he loved plays, and while reading one to his sister, he declared boldly, "God intends something for me which we know not of." That turned out to be a ministry of preaching, and Whitefield's stage became the pulpit, the platform, and even the open field. He later called theaters "nurseries of debauchery," but he never lost his love for drama nor his histrionic flair. The great Shakespearean actor David Garrick went to hear the same sermon by Whitefield forty times. He believed that Whitefield could sway an audience just in the way he said "Mesopotamia," and he vowed that he would give a hundred guineas to be able to pronounce "O!" the way the preacher did.

Whitefield was a combination of arrogance and zeal, and once confessed, "I can truly say I was froward from my mother's womb. I was so brutish as to hate instruction, and used purposely to shun all opportunities of receiving it." Converted to Methodism by the Wesleys at Oxford in 1735, Whitefield prayed for humility, but his escalating fame often prevented him from displaying that Christian virtue. His associations with dissenters and Methodists caused him to be banned from many churches, and so he took to the fields, often preaching to crowds of over 20,000 — and without any amplification for his voice.

His fame and infamy were intimately connected with the outbreak of revivals in North America which has come to be known as the First Great Awakening. Whitefield traveled to the colonies first in 1738 and again in 1739 for a three-year journey up and down the Atlantic coast, making converts wherever he preached. He was supported and encouraged by such Awakening leaders as Jonathan Edwards and Gilbert Tennent, but to others, like the members of the Harvard faculty, he was "an Enthusiast, a censorious uncharitable Person, and a Deluder of the People."

He separated from the Wesleys for a brief time because he believed that they placed too much stress on the role a person could play in achieving his or her salvation, a doctrine that was labeled "Arminianism." He emphasized rather a more Calvinistic understanding of the plight of people before God and their inability to save themselves, but his theology was for the masses and his message one of repentance. As one of

61

his biographers notes, "He professed Calvinism, lived by the Arminian faith, and preached them both."

Whitefield worked hard to support an orphanage known as Bethesda near Savannah, and he collected funds to maintain it. He also purchased a plantation in Georgia, using slave labor to raise crops, with the proceeds going to the orphanage. His slaveholding and his poor financial accounting of the contributions undermined the reputation of the orphanage and his own as well.

Always controversial in his day, he yet stands out as a major figure in the birth of evangelicalism and the history of preaching. As the great pulpiteer of the nineteenth century, Charles H. Spurgeon, declared, "There is no end to the interest which attaches to such a man as George Whitefield. Often as I have read his life, I am conscious of distinct quickening whenever I turn to it. He Lived. Other men seem to be only half-alive; but Whitefield was all life, fire, wind, force."

As he gazed out over rapt congregations between squinty eyes scarred by measles, Whitefield described the terrors of sin and the majesty of forgiveness, and his preaching mirrored his own experience of conversion.

Excerpted from A Short Account of God's Dealings with George Whitefield From His Infancy to His Ordination, 1714 – 1736 in George Whitefield's Journals (Banner of Truth Trust, 1960), 50-58. Reprinted by permission of the Banner of Truth Trust, Carlisle, Pa., and Edinburgh, Scotland.

At my first setting out, in compassion to my weakness, I grew in favour both with God and man, and used to be much lifted up with sensible devotion, especially at the blessed Sacrament. But when religion began to take root in my heart, and I was fully convinced my soul must totally be renewed ere it could see God, I was visited with outward and inward trials.

The first thing I was called to give up for God was what the world calls my fair reputation. I had no sooner received the sacrament publicly on a week-day at St. Mary's, but I was set up as a mark for all the polite students that knew me to shoot at. By this they knew that I was commenced Methodist; for though there is a sacrament at the beginning of every term, at which all, especially the seniors, are by statute, obliged to be present, yet so dreadfully has that once faithful city played the harlot, that very few Masters, and no undergraduates but the Methodists, attended upon it.

Mr. Charles Wesley, whom I must always mention with the greatest deference and respect, walked with me, in order to confirm me, from the church even to the college. I confess, to my shame, I would gladly have excused him; and the next day, going to his room, one of our Fellows passing by, I was ashamed to be seen to knock at his door. But, blessed be God! this fear of man gradually wore off. As I had imitated Nicodemus in his cowardice, so, by the Divine assistance, I followed him in his courage. I confessed the Methodists more and more publicly every day. I walked openly with them, and chose rather to bear contempt with those people of God, than to enjoy the applause of almost-Christians for a season.

Soon after this, I incurred the displeasure of the Master of the College, who frequently chid, and once threatened to expel me, if I ever visited the poor again. Being surprised at this treatment, and overawed by his authority, I spake unadvisedly with my lips, and said, if it displeased him, I would not. My conscience soon pricked me for this sinful compliance. I immediately repented, and visited the poor the first opportunity, and told my companions, if ever I was called to a stake for Christ's sake, I would serve my tongue as Archbishop Cranmer served his hand, *viz.,* make that burn first.

My tutor, being a moderate man, did not oppose me much, but thought, I believe, that I went a little too far. He lent me books, gave me money, visited me, and furnished me with a physician when sick. In short, he behaved in all respects like a father; and I trust God will remember him for good, in answer to the many prayers I have put up in his behalf.

My relations were quickly alarmed at the alteration of my behaviour, conceived strong prejudices against me, and, for some time, counted my life madness. I daily underwent some contempt at college. Some have thrown dirt at me; others, by degrees, took away their pay from me; and two friends, that were dear unto me, grew shy of and forsook me, when they saw me resolved to deny myself, take up my cross daily, and follow Jesus Christ. But our Lord, by His Spirit, soon convinced me that I must know no one after the flesh; and I soon found that promise literally fulfilled, "That no one hath left father or mother, brethren or sisters, houses or lands, for Christ's sake and the Gospel's, but he shall receive a hundredfold in this life, with persecutions, as well as eternal life in the world to come."

These, though little, were useful trials. They inured me to contempt, lessened self-love, and taught me to die daily. My inward sufferings were of a more uncommon nature. Satan seemed to have desired me in particular to sift me as wheat. God permitted him, for wise reasons I have seen already, *viz.,* that His future blessings might not prove my ruin.

From my first awakenings to the Divine life, I felt a particular hungering and thirsting after the humility of Jesus Christ. Night and day I prayed to be a partaker of that grace, imagining that the habit of humility would be instantaneously infused into my soul. But as Gideon taught the men of Succoth with thorns, so God, if I am yet in any measure blessed with true proverty of spirit, taught it me by the exercise of strong temptations.

I observed before how I used to be favoured with sensible devotion; those comforts were soon withdrawn, and a horrible fearfulness and dread permitted to overwhelm my soul. One morning in particular, rising from my bed, I felt an unusual impression and weight upon my breast, attended with inward darkness. I applied to my friend, Mr. Charles Wesley. He advised me to keep upon my watch, and referred me to a chapter in Kempis.

In a short time I perceived this load gradually increase, till it almost weighed me down, and fully convinced me that Satan had as real possession

of, and power given over, my body, as he had once over Job's. All power
of meditating, or even thinking, was taken from me. My memory quite
failed me. My whole soul was barren and dry, and I could fancy myself to
be like nothing so much as a man locked up in iron armour.

Whenever I kneeled down, I felt great heavings in my body, and
have often prayed under the weight of them till the sweat came through
me. At this time, Satan used to terrify me much, and threatened to punish
me if I discovered his wiles. It being my duty, as servitor, in my turn to
knock at the gentlemen's rooms by ten at night, to see who were in their
rooms, I thought the Devil would appear to me every stair I went up. And
he so troubled me when I lay down to rest, that for some weeks I scarce
slept above three hours at a time.

God only knows how many nights I have lain upon my bed groaning
under the weight I felt, and bidding Satan depart from me in the Name of
Jesus. Whole days and weeks have I spent in lying prostrate on the ground,
and begging for freedom from those proud hellish thoughts that used to
crowd in upon and distract my soul. But God made Satan drive out Satan;
for these thoughts and suggestions created such a self-abhorrence within
me, that I never ceased wrestling with God, till He blessed me with a
victory over them. Self-love, self-will, pride and envy, so buffeted me in
their turns, that I was resolved either to die or conquer. I wanted to see
sin as it was, but feared, at the same time, lest the sight of it should terrify
me to death.

Whilst my inward man was thus exercised, my outward man was not
unemployed. I soon found what a slave I had been to my sensual appetite,
and now resolved to get the mastery over it by the help of Jesus Christ.
Accordingly, by degrees, I began to leave off eating fruits and such like,
and gave the money I usually spent in that way to the poor. Afterward, I
always chose the worst sort of food, though my place furnished me with
variety. I fasted twice a week. My apparel was mean. I thought it unbe-
coming a penitent to have his hair powdered. I wore woollen gloves, a
patched gown and dirty shoes; and though I was then convinced that the
Kingdom of God did not consist in meats and drinks, yet I resolutely
persisted in these voluntary acts of self-denial, because I found them great
promoters of the spiritual life.

For many months, I went on in this state, faint, yet pursuing, and
travelling along in the dark, in hope that the Star I had before once seen,
would hereafter appear again. . . .

As I daily got strength, by continued, though almost silent, prayer,
in my study, my temptations grew stronger also, particularly for two or
three days before deliverance came.

Near five or six weeks I had now spent in my study, except when
I was obliged to go out. During this time I was fighting with my corruptions,
and did little else besides kneeling down by my bedside, feeling, as it were,

a heavy pressure upon my body, as well as an unspeakable oppression of mind, yet offering up my soul to God, to do with me as it pleased Him. It was now suggested to me, that Jesus Christ was amongst the wild beasts when He was tempted, and that I ought to follow His example; and being willing, as I thought, to imitate Jesus Christ, after supper I went into Christ Church Walk, near our College, and continued in silent prayer under one of the trees for near two hours, sometimes lying flat on my face, sometimes kneeling upon my knees, all the while filled with fear and concern lest some of my brethren should be overwhelmed with pride. The night being stormy, it gave me awful thoughts of the Day of Judgment. I continued, I think till the great bell rung for retirement to the college, not without finding some reluctance in the natural man against staying so long in the cold.

The next night I repeated the same exercise at the same place. But the hour of extremity being now come, God was pleased to make an open show of those diabolical devices by which I had been deceived.

By this time, I had left off keeping my diary, using my forms, or scarce my voice in prayer, visiting the prisoners, etc. Nothing remained for me to leave, unless I forsook public worship, but my religious friends. Now it was suggested that I must leave them also for Christ's sake. This was a sore trial; but rather than not be, as I fancied, Christ's disciple, I resolved to renounce them, though as dear to me as my own soul. Accordingly, the next day being Wednesday, whereon we kept one of our weekly fasts, instead of meeting with my brethren as usual, I went out into the fields, and prayed silently by myself. Our evening meeting I neglected also, and went not to breakfast, according to appointment, with Mr. Charles Wesley the day following. This, with many other concurring circumstances, made my honoured friend, Mr. Charles Wesley, suspect something more than ordinary was the matter. He came to my room, soon found out my case, apprised me of my danger if I would not take advice, and recommended me to his brother John, Fellow of Lincoln College, as more experienced in the spiritual life. God gave me—blessed be His Holy Name—a teachable temper, I waited upon his brother, with whom from that time I had the honour of growing intimate. He advised me to resume all my externals, though not to depend on them in the least. From time to time he gave me directions as my various and pitiable state required; and, at length, by his excellent advice and management of me, under God, I was delivered from those wiles of Satan. Praise the Lord, O my soul, and all that is within me praise His Holy Name! . . .

Soon after this, the holy season of Lent came on, which our friends kept very strictly, eating no flesh during the six weeks, except on Saturdays also, and ate nothing on the other days, except on Sunday, but sage-tea without sugar, and coarse bread. I constantly walked out in the cold mornings till part of one of my hands was quite black. This, with my continued abstinence, and inward conflicts, at length so emaciated my body, that, at Passion-week, finding I could scarce creep upstairs, I was obliged to inform my kind tutor of my condition, who immediately sent for a physician to me.

This caused no small triumph amongst the collegians, who began to cry out, "What is his fasting come to now?" But I rejoiced in this reproach, knowing that, though I had been imprudent, and lost much of my flesh, yet, I had nevertheless increased in the Spirit.

This fit of sickness continued upon me for seven weeks, and a glorious visitation it was. The blessed Spirit was all this time purifying my soul. All my former gross and notorious, and even my heart sins also, were now set home upon me, of which I wrote down some remembrance immediately, and confessed them before God morning and evening. Though weak, I often spent two hours in my evening retirements, and prayed over my Greek Testament and Bishop Hall's most excellent *Contemplations*, every hour that my health would permit. About the end of the seven weeks, and after I had been groaning under an unspeakable pressure both of body and mind for above a twelve-month, God was pleased to set me free in the following manner. One day, perceiving an uncommon drought and a disagreeable clamminess in my mouth and using things to allay my thirst, but in vain, it was suggested to me, that when Jesus Christ cried out, "I thirst," His sufferings were near at an end. Upon which I cast myself down on the bed, crying out, "I thirst! I thirst!" Soon after this, I found and felt in myself that I was delivered from the burden that had so heavily oppressed me. The spirit of mourning was taken from me, and I knew what it was truly to rejoice in God my Saviour; and, for some time, could not avoid singing psalms wherever I was; but my joy gradually became more settled, and, blessed be God, has abode and increased in my soul, saving a few casual intermissions, ever since.

Thus were the days of my mourning ended. After a long night of desertion and temptation, the Star, which I had seen at a distance before, began to appear again, and the Day Star arose in my heart. Now did the Spirit of God take possession of my soul, and, as I humbly hope, seal me unto the day of redemption.

Jonathan Edwards
(1703–1758)

Like John Wesley, Jonathan Edwards brought one age to a close as a very new and different era made ready to appear. Reared in the Calvinistic tradition of New England, Edwards was the last of the Puritans as he carried forward their vigorous intellectual life.

Regarded by many as the greatest American theologian, Edwards personified what has been called "the New England mind." Philosophically reflective and literately articulate, it was a perspective that viewed the whole created panorama under the premise of the sovereignty of God.

Educated at Yale, Edwards served in Northampton for nearly twenty-five years. During this time, the revivalistic movement known as the Great Awakening swept through the churches and created not only religious enthusiasm but divisive controversy among the clergy. Edwards sided with the new movement and wrote at length about it, praising the place of the emotions in religious experience. "Our people," he said, "do not so much need to have their heads stored, as to have their hearts touched."

Three significant documents, written by Edwards, were an outgrowth of this Great Awakening period: A *Faithful Narrative of the Surprising Work of God in the Conversion of Many Hundred Souls in Northampton and the Neighboring Towns and Villages* (1737); *Sinners in the Hands of an Angry God* (1741); and A *Treatise concerning Religious Affections* (1746). The first report circulated widely in England; the second was a hell-fire sermon, though not typical of Edwards' preaching; the third was a rational argument in favor of religious emotions.

After a dispute with his congregation over requirements for church membership, Edwards was forced to leave Northampton. He moved to Stockbridge in the unlikely role of missionary and teacher to a community of Housatunnock Indians. It was during this period that he wrote his most significant and thoughtful books. The volume on the *Freedom of the Will* (1754) was Edwards' most philosophical work. *The Nature of True Virtue* (1755) was his lucid essay on Christian ethics. Also written at this time but not published until 1758 was his greatest theological work, *Original Sin*. The same year he became president of the College of New Jersey (now Princeton University), but within five weeks he died of the newly developed inoculation for smallpox.

The relation between the emotional upheaval of the Great Awakening and his erudite theological works corresponds to two important sides of Edwards' life and personality. He could be rigid and demanding in thought, brilliant in debate, and verbally persuasive, and yet at the same time he often seemed inwardly self-conscious, quietly contemplative, and personally introspective.

Many of his sermons and letters reflect this inner side of the thinker, and his own more private writings reveal this clearly. In this latter category belong such items as his early nature essays on insects, colors, and the rainbow, as well as jottings in his diary and a carefully kept list of "resolutions" (which he reminded himself to read over "once a week"). Edwards also wrote (in 1739) an account of his own conversion experience. Known as the *Personal Narrative* or the *Narrative of His Conversion*, the document illustrates Edwards' facility in combining the personal and the theological.

The text comes from *The Works of President Edwards*, vol. 1 (New York: S. Converse, 1829), 60-61; 65-66; 132; 133-34; 135.

The first instance, that I remember, of that sort of inward, sweet delight in God and divine things, that I have lived much in since, was on reading those words, 1 Tim. i. 17. *Now unto the King eternal, immortal, invisible, the only wise God, be honour and glory for ever and ever, Amen.* As I read the words, there came into my soul, and was as it were diffused through it, a sense of the glory of the Divine Being; a new sense, quite different from any thing I ever experienced before. Never any words of Scripture seemed to me as these words did. I thought with myself, how excellent a Being that was, and how happy I should be, if I might enjoy that God, and be rapt up to him in heaven, and be as it were swallowed up in him for ever! I kept saying, and as it were singing, over these words of scripture to myself; and went to pray to God that I might enjoy him, and prayed in a manner quite different from what I used to do; with a new sort of affection. But it never came into my thought, that there was any thing spiritual, or of a saving nature in this.

From about that time, I began to have a new kind of apprehensions and ideas of Christ, and the work of redemption, and the glorious way of salvation by him. An inward, sweet sense of these things, at times, came into my heart; and my soul was led away in pleasant views and contemplations of them. And my mind was greatly engaged to spend my time in reading and meditating on Christ, on the beauty and excellency of his person, and the lovely way of salvation by free grace in him. . . .

On *January* 12, 1723, I made a solemn dedication of myself to God, and wrote it down; giving up myself, and all that I had to God; to be for the future, in no respect, my own; to act as one that had no right to himself, in any respect. And solemnly vowed, to take God for my whole portion and felicity; looking on nothing else, as any part of my happiness, nor acting as if it were; and his law for the constant rule of my obedience: engaging to fight, with all my might, against the world, the flesh, and the devil, to the end of my life. But I have reason to be infinitely humbled, when I consider, how much I have failed, of answering my obligation. . . .

I have loved the doctrines of the gospel; they have been to my soul like green pastures. The gospel has seemed to me the richest treasure; the treasure that I have most desired, and longed that it might dwell richly in me. The way of salvation by Christ, has appeared, in a general way, glorious and excellent, most pleasant and most beautiful. It has often seemed to me, that it would, in a great measure, spoil heaven, to receive it in any other way. That text has often been affecting and delightful to me, Isa. xxxii. 2, *A man shall be an hiding place from the wind, and a covert from the tempest, &c.*

It has often appeared to me delightful, to be united to Christ; to have him for my head, and to be a member of his body; also to have Christ for my teacher and prophet. I very often think with sweetness, and long-ings, and pantings of soul, of being a little child, taking hold of Christ, to be led by him through the wilderness of this world. That text, Matt. xviii. 3, has often been sweet to me, *Except ye be converted, and become as little children, &c.* I love to think of coming to Christ, to receive salvation of him, poor in spirit, and quite empty of self, humbly exalting him alone; cut off entirely from my own root, in order to grow into, and out of Christ: to have God in Christ to be all in all; and to live by faith on the Son of God, a life of humble, unfeigned confidence in him. . . .

Once, as I rode out into the woods for my health, in 1737, having alighted from my horse in a retired place, as my manner commonly has been, to walk for divine contemplation and prayer, I had a view, that for me was extraordinary, of the glory of the Son of God, as Mediator between God and man, and his wonderful, great, full, pure and sweet grace and love, and meek and gentle condescension. This grace that appeared so calm and sweet, appeared also great above the heavens. The person of Christ appeared ineffably excellent, with an excellency great enough to swallow up all thought and conception—which continued, as near as I can judge, about an hour; which kept me the greater part of the time, in a flood of tears, and weeping aloud. I felt an ardency of soul to be, what I know not otherwise how to express, emptied and annihilated; to lie in the dust, and to be full of Christ alone; to love him with a holy and pure love; to trust in him; to live upon him; to serve and follow him; and to be perfectly sanctified and made pure, with a divine and heavenly purity. I have, several other times, had views very much of the same nature, and which have had the same effects.

I have, many times, had a sense of the glory of the Third Person in the Trinity, in his office of Sanctifier; in his holy operations, communicating divine light and life to the soul. God in the communications of his holy spirit, has appeared as an infinite fountain of divine glory and sweetness;

being full and sufficient to fill and satisfy the soul; pouring forth itself in sweet communications, like the sun in its glory, sweetly and pleasantly diffusing light and life. And I have sometimes had an affecting sense of the excellency of the word of God as a word of life; as the light of life; a sweet, excellent, life-giving word; accompanied with a thirsting after that word, that it might dwell richly in my heart. . . .

Though it seems to me, that in some respects, I was a far better christian, for two or three years after my first conversion, than I am now; and lived in a more constant delight and pleasure; yet of late years, I have had a more full and constant sense of the absolute sovereignty of God, and a delight in that sovereignty; and have had more of a sense of the glory of Christ, as a Mediator revealed in the gospel. On one Saturday night, in particular, I had such a discovery of the excellency of the gospel above all other doctrines, that I could not but say to myself, "This is my chosen light, my chosen doctrine," and of Christ, "This is my chosen Prophet." It appeared sweet, beyond all expression, to follow Christ, and to be taught, and enlightened, and instructed by him; to learn of him, and live to him.

David Brainerd
(1718–1747)

David Brainerd was a candle that burned brilliantly but briefly. He died before his thirtieth birthday, but through his diary he influenced thousands and achieved more fame in death than in life. In that diary he recorded his deep spiritual turmoil, his desire to sacrifice himself for God, and his relentless and persistent quest for holiness and purity. To another age, Brainerd's piety seems extreme, but he was a mystic for whom both the awesome power of God and his own unworthiness were real.

Brainerd was born in Haddam, Connecticut; his father died when he was seven, and by the age of fourteen he was an orphan. By his own admission Brainerd was a melancholy, introspective lad, and his fears about his salvation plagued him until his conversion in 1739. This occurred during his first year at Yale, and Brainerd was gradually swept up in the enthusiasm of the Great Awakening. His ardent defense of George White-field and Jonathan Edwards prompted him to describe his Yale tutor, Mr. Whittelsey, as having "no more grace than this chair." The remark was reported to the Yale authorities, and in 1742 Brainerd was summarily dismissed from the college, much to the dismay and anger of ministers in the area. In 1743 he offered to make a complete apology in order to receive his degree, but his offer was rejected.

The incident scarred an already fragile personality, and in 1742 Brainerd began his missionary work among the Indians — first in western Massachusetts and New York, then at the Forks of the Delaware River, and finally in central New Jersey. Hampered by continuing bouts of illness, Brainerd resolved to stay with the Indian tribes, sacrificing his health for his missionary purpose.

He became engaged to the daughter of Jonathan Edwards, and finally as tuberculosis began to erode his strength, he left his missionary post to his brother, traveled to Edwards' home in Northampton, and died.

Edwards was deeply impressed with Brainerd's pious journal, and in 1749 he published An Account of the Life of the late Reverend Mr. David Brainerd. Edwards declared that Brainerd's conversion "was not the end of his work, or of the course of his diligence and strivings in religion; so neither was it the end of the work of the Spirit of God on his heart."

Edwards hoped that the journal might show "the right way to success in the work of the ministry" and "afford instruction to missionaries in particular."

Edwards' expectation was fully realized, for Brainerd's diary became a best-seller. More than thirty different editions appeared before the end of the nineteenth century, making this the most popular of all of Edwards' works. Brainerd became a model for Protestant missionaries, and his journal became an inspiration to some of the greatest names in missions — the English Baptist William Carey; Methodist Thomas Coke; Robert Morrison, Bible translator in China; Henry Martyn, Anglican missionary and Bible translator; Samuel Marsden, missionary in New Zealand; Samuel Mills, American missionary leader; and Thomas Chalmers, missionary statesman of the Church of Scotland. Because of his diary, others picked up the cause of missions to which Brainerd devoted himself and to which he gave his life.

Excerpted from *Memoirs of the Rev. David Brainerd, Missionary to the Indians ... Chiefly Taken from his own Diary by Rev. Jonathan Edward...*, ed. Sereno Edwards Dwight (New Haven, 1822), 38-47. This was the first complete edition of the diary.

Sometime in the beginning of winter, 1738, it pleased God, one Sabbath morning, as I was walking out for prayer, to give me on a sudden such a sense of my *danger,* and the wrath of God, that I stood amazed, and my former good frames presently vanished. From the view which I had of my sin and vileness, I was much distressed all that day, fearing that the vengeance of God would soon overtake me. I was much dejected; kept much alone; and sometimes envied the birds and beasts their happiness, because they were not exposed to eternal misery, as I evidently saw that I was. Thus I lived from day to day, being frequently in great distress: sometimes there appeared mountains before me to obstruct my hopes of mercy; and the work of conversion appeared so great, that I thought I should never be the subject of it. I used, however, to pray and cry to God, and perform other duties with great earnestness; and thus hoped by some means to make the case better.

Hundreds of times, I renounced all pretences of any *worth* in my duties, as I thought, even while performing them, and often confessed to God that I deserved nothing, for the very best of them, but eternal condemnation; yet still I had a secret hope of *recommending* myself to God by my religious duties. When I prayed affectionately, and my heart seemed in some measure to melt, I hoped that God would be thereby moved to pity me. My prayers then looked with some appearance of *goodness* in them, and I seemed to *mourn* for sin. Then I could in some measure venture on the mercy of God in Christ, as I thought; though the *preponderating* thought, the *foundation* of my hope was some imagination of *goodness* in my meltings of heart, the warmth of my affections, and my extraordinary enlargements in prayer. Though at times the gate appeared so very strait, that it looked next to impossible to enter; yet, at other times, I flattered myself that it was not so very difficult, and hoped I should by diligence and watchfulness soon gain the point. Sometimes after enlargement in duty and considerable affection, I hoped I had made a *good step* towards heaven; and imagined that God was affected as I was, and would hear such *sincere cries,* as I called them. And so sometimes, when I withdrew for secret prayer in great distress, I returned comfortable; and thus healed myself with my *duties.*

In February 1739, I set apart a day for secret fasting and prayer, and spent the day in almost incessant cries to God for mercy, that he would open my eyes to see the evil of sin, and the way of life by Jesus Christ. God was pleased that day to make considerable discoveries of my heart to me. Still I *trusted* in all the duties I performed, though there was no manner of *goodness* in them; there being in them no respect to the glory of God, nor any such principle in my heart. Yet God was pleased to make my endeavours, that day, a means to shew me my *helplessness* in some measure.

Sometimes I was greatly *encouraged,* and imagined that God loved me, and was pleased with me,—and thought I should soon be fully reconciled to God. But the whole was founded on mere *presumption,* arising from enlargement in duty, or warmth of affections, or some good resolutions, or the like. And when, at times, great distress began to arise, on a sight of my vileness, and inability to deliver myself from a sovereign God, I used to put off the discovery, as what I could not bear. Once, I remember, a terrible pang of distress seized me; and the thought of renouncing myself, and standing naked before God, stripped of all goodness, was so dreadful to me, that I was ready to say to it, as Felix to Paul, "Go thy way for this time." Thus, though I daily longed for greater conviction of sin; supposing that I must see more of my dreadful state in order to a remedy; yet, when the discoveries of my vile, wicked heart, were made to me, the sight was so dreadful, and shewed me so plainly my exposedness to damnation, that I could not endure it. I constantly strove after whatever *qualifications* I imagined others obtained before the reception of Christ, in order to *recommend* me to his favour. Sometimes I felt the power of a *hard heart,* and supposed it must be *softened* before Christ would accept of me; and when I felt any meltings of heart, I hoped now the work was almost done. Hence, when my distress still remained, I was wont to murmur at God's dealings with me; and thought, when others felt their hearts softened, God shewed them mercy; but my distress remained still.

At times I grew *remiss* and *sluggish,* without any great convictions of sin, for a considerable time together; but after such a season, convictions seized me more violently. One night I remember in particular, when I was walking solitarily abroad, I had opened to me such a view of my sin, that I feared the ground would cleave asunder under my feet, and become my grave; and would send my soul quick into hell, before I could get home.

Though I was forced to go to bed, lest my distress should be discovered by others, which I much feared; yet I scarcely durst sleep at all, for I thought it would be a great wonder if I should be out of hell in the morning. And though my distress was sometimes thus great, yet I greatly dreaded the loss of *convictions,* and returning back to a state of carnal security, and to my former insensibility of impending wrath; which made me exceedingly exact in my behaviour, lest I should stifle the motions of God's Holy Spirit. When at any time I took a view of my convictions, and thought the degree of them to be considerable, I was wont to trust in them; but this confidence, and the hopes of soon making some notable advances towards deliverance, would ease my mind, and I soon became more senseless and remiss.— Again, when I discerned my convictions to grow languid, and thought them about to leave me; this immediately alarmed and distressed me.—Sometimes I expected to take a large step, and get very far towards conversion, by some particular opportunity or means I had in view.

The many disappointments, great distresses and perplexity which I experienced, put me into a most *horrible frame* of *contesting* with the Almighty; with an inward vehemence and virulence finding fault with his ways of dealing with mankind. I found great fault with the imputation of Adam's sin to his posterity: and my wicked heart often wished for some other way of salvation, than by Jesus Christ. Being like the troubled sea, my thoughts confused, I used to contrive to *escape* the wrath of God by some *other* means. I had strange projects, full of Atheism, contriving to *disappoint* God's designs and decrees concerning me, or to escape his *notice,* and hide myself from him. But when, upon reflection, I saw these projects were vain, and would not serve me, and that I could contrive nothing for my own relief; this would throw my mind into the most horrid frame, to wish there was no God, or to wish there were some *other* God that could control him. These thoughts and desires were the secret inclinations of my heart, frequently acting before I was aware; but, alas! they were *mine,* although I was frightened when I came to reflect on them. When I considered, it distressed me to think, that my heart was so full of enmity against God; and it made me tremble, lest his vengeance should suddenly fall upon me. I used before to imagine, that my heart was not so bad as the scriptures and some other books represented it. Sometimes I used to take much pains to work it up into the good frame, a humble submissive disposition; and hoped there was *then* some goodness in me. But, on a sudden, the thoughts of the strictness of the law, or the sovereignty of God, would so irritate the corruption of my heart, that I had so watched over, and hoped I had brought to a good frame, that it would break over all bounds, and burst forth on all sides, like floods of waters when they break down their dam.

Being sensible of the necessity of deep humiliation in order to a saving interest in Christ, I used to set myself to produce in my own heart the *convictions* requisite in such a humiliation; as, a conviction that God would be just, if he cast me off for ever; that if ever God should bestow mercy on me, it would be mere grace, though I should be in distress many years first, and be never so much engaged in duty; and that God was not in the least obliged to pity me the more for all past duties, cries, and tears. I strove to my utmost to bring myself to a firm belief of these things and a hearty assent to them; and hoped that now I was brought off from *myself,* truly humbled, and that I bowed to the divine sovereignty. I was wont to tell God in my prayers, that now I had those very dispositions of soul which he required, and on which he shewed mercy to others, and thereupon to beg and plead for mercy to me. But when I found no relief, and was still oppressed with guilt, and fears of wrath, my soul was in a tumult, and my heart rose against God, as dealing hardly with me. Yet *then* my conscience flew in my face, putting me in mind of my late confession to God of his *justice* in my condemnation. This, giving me a sight of the badness of my heart, threw me again into distress; and I wished that I had watched my heart more narrowly, to keep it from breaking out against God's dealings with me. I even wished that I had not pleaded for mercy on account of my humiliation; because thereby I had lost all my seeming goodness.—Thus, scores of times, I vainly imagined myself humbled and prepared for saving mercy. While I was in this distressed, bewildered, and tumultuous state of mind, the *corruption* of my heart was especially *irritated* with the following things.

1. The *strictness* of the divine *Law.* For I found it was impossible for me, after my utmost pains, to answer its demands. I often made new resolutions, and as often broke them. I imputed the whole to carelessness, and the want of being more watchful, and used to call myself a fool for my negligence. But when, upon a stronger resolution, and greater endeavours, and close application to fasting and prayer, I found all attempts fail; then I quarrelled with the law of God, as unreasonably rigid. I thought, if it extended only to my *outward* actions and behaviours, that I could *bear* with it; but I found that it condemned me for my evil thoughts, and sins of my *heart,* which I could not possibly prevent. I was extremely loth to own my utter helplessness in this matter: but after repeated disappointments, thought that, rather than perish, I could do a *little* more still; especially if such and such circumstances might but attend my endeavours and strivings. I *hoped,* that I should strive more earnestly than ever, if the matter came to extremity, though I never could find the time to do my utmost, in the manner I intended. This hope of future more favourable circumstances, and of doing something great hereafter, kept me from utter despair in myself, and from seeing myself fallen into the hands of a sovereign God, and dependent on nothing but free and boundless grace.

2. That *faith alone* was the *condition of salvation*; that God would not come down to lower terms; and that he would not promise life and salvation upon my sincere and hearty prayers and endeavours. That word, Mark xvi.

16, "He that believeth not, shall be damned," cut off all hope there.—I found that faith was the sovereign gift of God; that I could not get it as of myself; and could not oblige God to bestow it upon me, by any of my performances. (Eph. ii. 1.8.) *This,* I was ready to say, *is a hard saying, who can hear it?* I could not bear, that all I had done should stand for mere nothing; as I had been very conscientious in duty, had been exceeding religious a great while, and had, as I thought, done much more than many others who had obtained mercy. I *confessed* indeed the vileness of my duties; but then, what made them at that time seem vile, was my *wandering* thoughts in them; not because I was all over defiled like a devil, and the *principle* corrupt from whence they flowed, so that I could not possibly do any thing that was good. Hence I called what I did by the name of *honest faithful endeavours*; and could not bear it, that God had made no promises of salvation to them.

3. That I could not find out *what* faith was; or *what* it was to believe and come to Christ. I read the *calls* of Christ to the *weary* and *heavy laden*; but could find no *way* that he directed them to come in. I thought I would gladly come, if I knew *how*; though the path of duty were never so difficult. I read Stoddard's *Guide to Christ,* (which I trust was, in the hand of God, the happy means of my conversion), and my *heart rose* against the author; for though he told me my very heart all along under convictions, and seemed to be very beneficial to me in his directions; yet here he failed; he did not tell me any thing I could *do* that would bring me to Christ, but left me as it were with a great gulph between, without any direction to get through. For I was not yet effectually and experimentally taught, that there *could* be no way prescribed, whereby a *natural* man could, of his own strength, obtain that which is *supernatural,* and which the highest angel cannot give.

4. The *sovereignty* of God. I could not bear, that it should be wholly at God's pleasure, to save or damn me, just as he would. That passage, Rom. ix. 11–23. was a constant vexation to me, especially verse 21. Reading or meditating on this, always destroyed my seeming good frames; for when I thought I was almost humbled, and almost resigned, this passage would make my enmity against the sovereignty of God appear. When I came to reflect on the inward enmity and blasphemy, which arose on this occasion, I was the more afraid of God, and driven further from any hopes of reconciliation with him. It gave me a dreadful view of myself; I dreaded more than ever to see myself in God's hands, at his sovereign disposal; and it made me more opposite than ever to submit to his sovereignty; for I thought God designed my damnation.

All this time the Spirit of God was powerfully at work with me; and I was inwardly pressed to relinquish all *self-confidence,* all hopes of ever helping myself by any means whatsoever. The conviction of my *lost* estate was sometimes so clear and manifest before my eyes, that it was as if it had been declared to me in so many words, "It is done, it is done, it is for ever impossible to deliver yourself." For about three or four days my soul was thus greatly distressed. At some turns, for a few moments, I seemed to myself *lost* and *undone*; but then would shrink back immediately from the sight, because I dared not venture myself into the hands of God, as wholly helpless, and at the disposal of his sovereign pleasure. I dared not see that important truth concerning myself, that I was *dead in trespasses and sins.* But when I had, as it were, thrust away these views of myself at any time, I felt distressed to have the same discoveries of myself again; for I greatly feared being given over of God to final stupidity. When I thought of putting it off to a *more convenient season,* the conviction was so close and powerful, with regard to the *present* time, that it was the best, and probably the *only* time, that I dared not put it off.

It was the sight of *truth* concerning myself, *truth* respecting my state, as a creature fallen and alienated from God, and that consequently could make no demands on God for mercy, but must subscribe to the absolute sovereignty of the divine Being; the sight of the *truth,* I say, my soul shrank away from, and trembled to think of beholding. Thus, *he that doth evil,* as all unregenerate men continually do, *hates the light of truth* neither cares to *come to it,* because it will *reprove his deeds,* and shew him his just deserts, John iii. 20. Sometime before, I had taken much pains, as I thought, to submit to the sovereignty of God; yet I mistook the thing,— and did not once imagine, that seeing and being made experimentally sensible of this truth, which my soul now so much dreaded and trembled at, was the frame of soul which I had so earnestly desired. I had ever hoped, that when I had attained to that *humiliation,* which I supposed necessary to precede faith, then it would not be fair for God to *cast me off;* but now I saw it was so far from any goodness in me, to own myself spiritually dead, and destitute of all goodness, that, on the contrary, *my mouth* would be for ever *stopped* by it; and it looked as *dreadful* to me, to see myself, and the relation I stood in to God—I a sinner and criminal, and he a great judge and Sovereign—as it would be to a poor trembling creature, to venture off some high precipice. Hence I put it off for a minute or two, and tried for better circumstances to do it in; either I must read a passage or two, or pray first, or something of the like nature; or else put off my submission to God's sovereignty with an objection, that I did not know how to submit. But the truth was, I could see no safety in owning myself in the hands of a sovereign God, and could lay no claim to any thing better than damnation. . . .

After a considerable time spent in similar exercises and distresses, one morning, while I was walking in a solitary place, as usual, I at once saw that all my contrivances and projects to effect or procure deliverance and salvation for myself, were utterly *in vain*; I was brought quite to a stand, as finding myself totally *lost.* I had thought many times before, that the difficulties in my way were very great; but now I saw, in another and very different light, that it was for ever impossible for me to do any thing towards helping or delivering myself. I then thought of blaming myself, that I had not done more, and been more engaged, while I had opportunity—for it seemed now as if the season of doing was for ever over and gone—but I instantly saw, that, let me have done what I would, it would no more have tended to my helping myself, than what I had done; that I had made all the pleas I ever could have made to all eternity; and that all my pleas were vain. The *tumult* that had been before in my mind, was now *quieted*; and I was somewhat eased of that distress which I felt while struggling against a sight of myself, and of the divine sovereignty. I had the greatest certainty, that my state was forever miserable, for all that I *could* do; and wondered that I had never been sensible of it before.

While I remained in this state, my *notions* respecting my *duties* were quite different from what I had ever entertained in times past. Before this, the more I did in duty, the more hard I thought it would be for God to cast me off; though at the same time I confessed, and thought I saw, that there was no goodness or merit in my duties; but now, the more I did in prayer or any other duty, the more I saw that I was indebted to God for *allowing* me to ask for mercy; for I saw that self-interest had led me to pray, and that I had never once prayed from any respect to the glory of God. Now I saw that there was no necessary connection between my prayers and the bestowment of divine mercy; that they laid not the least *obligation* upon God to bestow his grace upon me; and that there was no more virtue or goodness in them, than there would be in my *paddling with my hand in the water*, (which was the comparison I had then in my mind;) and this because they were not performed from any love or regard to God. I saw that I had been heaping up my devotions before God, fasting, praying, &c. pretending, and indeed really thinking sometimes, that I was aiming at the glory of God; whereas I never once *truly* intended it, but only my own happiness. I saw that as I had never done any thing *for* God, I had no claim on any thing *from* him, but perdition, on account of my hypocrisy and mockery. Oh, how different did my duties now appear from what they used to do! I used to charge them with sin and imperfection; but this was only on account of the wanderings and vain thoughts attending them, and not because I had no regard to God in them; for this I thought I had. But when I saw evidently that I had regard to nothing but self-interest; then they appeared a vile mockery of God, self-worship, and a continual course of lies.—I saw that something worse had attended my duties than barely a few wanderings; for the whole was nothing but *self-worship*, and an horrid abuse of God.

I continued, as I remember, in this state of mind, from Friday morning till the Sabbath evening following, (July 12, 1739,) when I was walking again in the same solitary place, where I was brought to see myself lost and helpless, as before mentioned. Here, in a mournful melancholy state, I was attempting to pray; but found no heart to engage in that or any other duty; my former concern, exercise, and religious affections were now gone. I thought that the Spirit of God had *quite* left me; but still was not distressed; yet disconsolate, as if there was nothing in heaven or earth could make me happy. Having been thus endeavouring to pray—though, as I thought, very stupid and senseless—for near half an hour; then, as I was walking in a dark thick grove, *unspeakable glory* seemed to open to the view and apprehension of my soul. I do not mean any *external* brightness, for I saw no such thing; nor do I intend any imagination of a body of light, some where in the third heavens, or any thing of that nature; but it was a new inward apprehension or view that I had of *God,* such as I never had before, nor any thing which had the least resemblance of it. I stood still; wondered; and admired! I knew that I never had seen before any thing comparable to it for excellency and beauty; it was widely different from all the conceptions that ever I had of God, or things divine. I had no particular apprehension of any one person in the Trinity, either the Father, the Son, or the Holy Ghost; but it appeared to be *Divine glory.* My soul *rejoiced with joy unspeakable,* to see such a God, such a glorious divine Being; and I was inwardly pleased and satisfied, that he should be *God over all* for ever and ever. My soul was so captivated and delighted with the excellency, loveliness, greatness, and other perfections of God, that I was even swallowed up in him; at least to that degree, that I had no thought (as I remember) at *first,* about my own salvation, and scarce reflected that there was such a creature as myself.

Thus God, I trust, brought me to a hearty disposition to *exalt him,* and set him on the throne, and principally and ultimately to aim at his honour and glory, as King of the universe. I continued in this state of inward joy, peace, and astonishment, till near dark, without any sensible abatement; and then began to think and examine what I had seen; and felt sweetly *composed* in my mind all the evening following. I felt myself in a new world, and every thing about me appeared with a different aspect from what it was wont to do. At this time, the *way of salvation* opened to me with such infinite wisdom, suitableness, and excellency, that I wondered I should ever think of any other way of salvation; was amazed that I had not dropped my own contrivances, and complied with this lovely, blessed, and excellent way before. If I could have been saved by my own duties, or any other way that I had formerly contrived, my whole soul would now have refused it. I wondered that all the world did not see and comply with this way of salvation, entirely by the *righteousness of Christ.*

The sweet relish of what I then felt, continued with me for several days, almost constantly, in a greater or less degree.—I could not but sweetly rejoice in God, lying down and rising up. The next Lord's day I felt something of the same kind, though not so powerful as before. But not long after I was again involved in *thick darkness,* and under great distress; yet not of the same kind with my distress under convictions. I was guilty, afraid, and ashamed to come before God; was exceedingly pressed with a sense of guilt: but it was not long before I felt, I trust, true repentance and joy in God.—About the latter end of August, I again fell under great darkness; it seemed as if the presence of God was *clean gone for ever*; though I was not so much distressed about my spiritual *state,* as I was at my being shut out from God's *presence,* as I then sensibly was. But it pleased the Lord to return graciously to me not long after.

John Woolman
(1720–1772)

If Quakers had saints, John Woolman would certainly be one. In his own lifetime, he proclaimed the equality of all people and became the most important Quaker voice in opposition to slavery. Austere in his life-style, he urged people not to accumulate more possessions than they needed. War and violence were abhorrent to his conscience, and he sought justice for the poor and good working conditions for laborers. These attitudes were rooted in a vibrant, mystical piety and in Woolman's understanding of the Bible. For him, the results of conversion were works of charity and love for all God's creatures.

Born into a relatively well-to-do Quaker family in New Jersey, Woolman was nurtured in Quaker faith and practice. He entered the bakery business, but feeling guilty about his increasing affluence, he turned to part-time tailoring and serving as a scribe or secretary for others. Here he had his first encounter with slavery (described below), and he always later regretted this early compromise.

A regular attender at "meetings," as the Friends called their religious services, Woolman was commissioned a Quaker "minister" at the age of twenty-three. For thirty years he traveled as a Quaker missionary to England and throughout the American colonies.

On his travels, Woolman adopted the tactic of confronting slaveholding Quakers, and he managed to do so without incurring the bitterness and wrath of those he criticized. If he stayed in a Quaker home where slaves were held, he insisted on paying for his lodging.

Woolman had a strong sense of God's activity in human history, and he felt certain that God's judgment would fall on those who held "fellow men in property." A century before the Civil War he declared, "The seeds of great calamity and desolation are sown and growing fast on this continent." Under Woolman's influence, the Quaker Yearly Meeting resolved in 1758 that all Quakers should free their slaves, and in 1776, four years after Woolman's death, the Quakers became the first American denomination to prohibit slaveholding by its members.

Woolman might have been a footnote in history were it not for his Journal, a classic in American literature and a devotional manual of enduring power. Begun when he was thirty-six and maintained sporadically throughout his life, it was published in 1774, two years after his death. William

Ellery Channing called it "the sweetest and purest autobiography in the language," and Samuel Taylor Coleridge declared, "I should almost despair of that man who could peruse the life of John Woolman without an amelioration of heart." Woolman's other influential writings, *Some Considerations on the Keeping of Negroes* and *A Plea for the Poor*, had wide circulation as well, but the religious depth and moral vision of his *Journal* continue to speak across the centuries to the problems of religious people living in a sinful world.

Excerpted from *The Journal of John Woolman* (Boston, 1871), 51-65. This was a famous edition because the introduction was written by John Greenleaf Whittier. A critical edition of Woolman's writings was edited by Phillips P. Moulton, *The Journal and Major Essays of John Woolman* (New York: Oxford Univ. Press, 1971).

I have often felt a motion of love to leave some hints in writing of my experience of the goodness of God, and now, in the thirty-sixth year of my age, I begin this work.

I was born in Northampton, in Burlington County, West Jersey, in the year 1720. Before I was seven years old I began to be acquainted with the operations of Divine love. Through the care of my parents, I was taught to read nearly as soon as I was capable of it; and as I went from school one day, I remember that while my companions were playing by the way, I went forward out of sight, and, sitting down, I read the twenty-second chapter of Revelation: "He showed me a pure river of water of life, clear as crystal, proceeding out of the throne of God and of the Lamb, &c." In reading it, my mind was drawn to seek after that pure habitation which I then believed God had prepared for his servants. The place where I sat, and the sweetness that attended my mind, remain fresh in my memory. This, and the like gracious visitations, had such an effect upon me that when boys used ill language it troubled me; and, through the continued mercies of God, I was preserved from that evil. . . .

Advancing in age, the number of my acquaintance increased, and thereby my way grew more difficult. Though I had found comfort in reading the Holy Scriptures and thinking on heavenly things, I was not estranged therefrom. I knew I was going from the flock of Christ and had no resolution to return, hence serious reflections were uneasy to me, and youthful vanities and diversions were my greatest pleasure. In this road I found many like myself, and we associated in that which is adverse to true friendship.

In this swift race it pleased God to visit me with sickness, so that I doubted of recovery; then did darkness, horror, and amazement with full force seize me, even when my pain and distress of body were very great. I thought it would have been better for me never to have had being, than to see the day which I now saw. I was filled with confusion, and in great affliction, both of mind and body, I lay and bewailed myself. I had not confidence to lift up my cries to God, whom I had thus offended; but in a deep sense of my great folly I was humbled before him. At length that word which is as a fire and a hammer broke and dissolved my rebellious heart; my cries were put up in contrition; and in the multitude of his mercies I found inward relief, and a close engagement that if he was pleased to restore my health I might walk humbly before him.

After my recovery this exercise remained with me a considerable time, but by degrees giving way to youthful vanities, and associating with wanton young people, I lost ground. The Lord had been very gracious, and spoke peace to me in the time of my distress, and I now most ungratefully turned again to folly; at times I felt sharp reproof, but I did not get low enough to cry for help. I was not so hardy as to commit things scandalous, but to exceed in vanity and to promote mirth was my chief study. Still I retained a love and esteem for pious people, and their company brought an awe upon me. My dear parents several times admonished me in the fear of the Lord, and their admonition entered into my heart and had a good effect for a season; but not getting deep enough to pray rightly, the tempter, when he came, found entrance. Once having spent a part of the day in wantonness, when I went to bed at night there lay in a window near my bed a Bible, which I opened, and first cast my eye on the text, "We lie down in our shame, and our confusion covereth us." This I knew to be my case, and meeting with so unexpected a reproof I was somewhat affected with it, and went to bed under remorse of conscience, which I soon cast off again. . . .

All this time I lived with my parents, and wrought on the plantation; and having had schooling pretty well for a planter, I used to improve myself in winter evenings, and other leisure times. Being now in the twenty-first year of my age, with my father's consent I engaged with a man, in much business as a shop-keeper and baker, to tend shop and keep books. At home I had lived retired; and now having a prospect of being much in the way of company, I felt frequent and fervent cries in my heart to God, the Father of Mercies, that he would preserve me from all taint and corruption; that, in this more public employment, I might serve him, my gracious Redeemer, in that humility and self-denial which I had in a small degree exercised in a more private life.

The man who employed me furnished a shop in Mount Holly, about five miles from my father's house, and six from his own, and there I lived alone and tended his shop. Shortly after my settlement here I was visited by several young people, my former acquaintance, who supposed that vanities would be as agreeable to me now as ever. At these times I cried to the Lord in secret for wisdom and strength; for I felt myself encompassed with difficulties, and had fresh occasion to bewail the follies of times past, in contracting a familiarity with libertine people; and as I had now left my father's house outwardly, I found my Heavenly Father to be merciful to me beyond what I can express.

By day I was much amongst people, and had many trials to go through; but in the evenings I was mostly alone, and I may with thankfulness acknowledge, that in those times the spirit of supplication was often poured upon me; under which I was frequently exercised, and felt my strength renewed.

After a while, my former acquaintance gave over expecting me as one of their company, and I began to be known to some whose conversation was helpful to me. And now, as I had experienced the love of God, through Jesus Christ, to redeem me from many pollutions, and to be a succor to me through a sea of conflicts, with which no person was fully acquainted, and as my heart was often enlarged in this heavenly principle, I felt a tender compassion for the youth who remained entangled in snares like those which had entangled me. This love and tenderness increased, and my mind was strongly engaged for the good of my fellow-creatures. I went to meetings in an awful frame of mind, and endeavored to be inwardly acquainted with the language of the true Shepherd. One day, being under a strong exercise of spirit, I stood up and said some words in a meeting; but not keeping close to the Divine opening, I said more than was required of me. Being soon sensible of my error, I was afflicted in mind some weeks, without any light or comfort, even to that degree that I could not take satisfaction in anything. I remembered God, and was troubled, and in the depth of my distress he had pity upon me, and sent the Comforter. I then felt forgiveness for my offence; my mind became calm and quiet, and I was truly thankful to my gracious Redeemer for his mercies. About six weeks after this, feeling the spring of Divine love opened, and a concern to speak, I said a few words in a meeting, in which I found peace. Being thus humbled and disciplined under the cross, my understanding became more strengthened to distinguish the pure spirit which inwardly moves upon the heart, and which taught me to wait in silence sometimes many weeks together, until I felt that rise which prepares the creature to stand like a trumpet, through which the Lord speaks to his flock.

From an inward purifying, and steadfast abiding under it springs a lively operative desire for the good of others. All the faithful are not called to the public ministry; but whoever are, are called to minister of that which they have tasted and handled spiritually. The outward modes of worship are various; but whenever any are true ministers of Jesus Christ, it is from the operation of his Spirit upon their hearts, first purifying them, and thus giving them a just sense of the conditions of others. This truth was early fixed in my mind, and I was taught to watch the pure opening, and to take heed lest, while I was standing to speak, my own will should get uppermost, and cause me to utter words from worldly wisdom, and depart from the channel of the true gospel ministry. . . .

About the twenty-third year of my age, I had many fresh and heavenly openings, in respect to the care and providence of the Almighty over his creatures in general, and over man as the most noble amongst those which are visible. And being clearly convinced in my judgment that to place my whole trust in God was best for me, I felt renewed engagements that in all things I might act on an inward principle of virtue, and pursue worldly business no further than as truth opened my way.

About the time called Christmas I observed many people, both in town and from the country, resorting to public-houses, and spending their time in drinking and vain sports, tending to corrupt one another; on which account I was much troubled. At one house in particular there was much disorder; and I believed it was a duty incumbent on me to speak to the master of that house. I considered I was young, and that several elderly friends in town had opportunity to see these things; but though I would gladly have been excused, yet I could not feel my mind clear.

The exercise was heavy; and as I was reading what the Almighty said to Ezekiel, respecting his duty as a watchman, the matter was set home more clearly. With prayers and tears I besought the Lord for his assistance, and He, in loving-kindness, gave me a resigned heart. At a suitable opportunity I went to the public-house; and seeing the man amongst much company, I called him aside, and in the fear and dread of the Almighty expressed to him what rested on my mind. He took it kindly, and afterwards showed more regard to me than before. In a few years afterwards he died, middle-aged; and I often thought that had I neglected my duty in that case it would have given me great trouble; and I was humbly thankful to my gracious Father, who had supported me herein.

My employer, having a Negro woman, sold her, and desired me to write a bill of sale, the man being waiting who bought her. The thing was sudden; and though I felt uneasy at the thoughts of writing an instrument of slavery for one of my fellow-creatures, yet I remembered that I was hired by the year, that it was my master who directed me to do it, and that it was an elderly man, a member of our Society, who bought her; so through weakness I gave way, and wrote it; but at the executing of it I was so afflicted in my mind, that I said before my master and the Friend that I believed slave-keeping to be a practice inconsistent with the Christian religion. This, in some degree, abated my uneasiness; yet as often as I reflected seriously upon it I thought I should have been clearer if I had desired to be excused from it, as a thing against my conscience; for such it was. Some time after this a young man of our Society spoke to me to write a conveyance of a slave to him, he having lately taken a Negro into his house. I told him I was not easy to write it; for, though many of our meeting and in other places kept slaves, I still believed the practice was not right, and desired to be excused from the writing. I spoke to him in good-will; and he told me that keeping slaves was not altogether agreeable to his mind; but that the slave being a gift made to his wife he had accepted her.

John Newton
(1725–1807)

It would be difficult to exaggerate the sheer drama of John Newton's life story. Son of an English sea captain, he himself went to sea at eleven years of age. Under sail on many voyages through the Mediterranean and to the West Indies, Newton became a slave-ship captain during the most dreadful years of that traffic in black humanity. Then he was converted, sought ordination, and served as a minister with distinction. During these years he wrote poems and hymns, and died at age eighty-three, full of grace and highly respected everywhere.

During his long and lonely sea voyages, Newton educated himself by mastering Euclid, learning Latin to read Virgil and Erasmus, studying the Bible (in Hebrew and Greek), and conducting Sunday worship for his crews. A friend of Whitefield and Wesley, he applied, after retiring from the sea, for ordination in the Church of England but was refused. In 1764, with the help of Lord Dartmouth, he was appointed to the more evangelical curacy of the church at Olney.

Newton soon became known as a preacher, and his little church added a gallery to accommodate the crowds who came to hear him. The poet William Cowper (1731 – 1800) moved to Olney and collaborated with Newton in the publishing of the "Olney Hymns." Newton contributed nearly three hundred hymns, including "How Sweet the Name of Jesus Sounds," "Glorious Things of Thee Are Spoken," and "Amazing Grace," which in our own time has become phenomenally popular with people from diverse religious backgrounds.

The anguish of his former slave-trade experience could not be forgotten, and, in later years, Newton became the motivating influence upon William Wilberforce (1759 – 1833) and the ultimate abolition of the slave trade in Great Britain. The emancipation of the slaves in America would not come until 1863, but in 1792 the College of New Jersey (now Princeton University) conferred an honorary degree upon John Newton. Two other recipients of honorary degrees at the same time were Alexander Hamilton and Thomas Jefferson.

The first verse of "Amazing Grace" (originally titled "Faith's Review and Expectation") sums up John Newton's religious experience.

> Amazing grace! (how sweet the sound!)
>   That saved a wretch like me;
> I once was lost, but now am found;
>   Was blind, but now I see.

Before he died, he prepared his own epitaph which read, in part:

John Newton, once an infidel and libertine, a servant of slaves in Africa, was, by the rich mercy of our Lord and Saviour, Jesus Christ, preserved, restored, pardoned, and appointed to preach the faith he had long laboured to destroy....

The excerpts are taken from *The Works of the Rev. John Newton*, ed. Richard Cecil (New York: Robert Carter Co., 1844), I: 95-110.

I went to bed that night in my usual security and indifference, but was awakened from a sound sleep by the force of a violent sea, which broke on board us; so much of it came down below as filled the cabin I lay in with water. This alarm was followed by a cry from the deck, that the ship was going down or sinking. As soon as I could recover myself, I essayed to go upon deck: but was met upon the ladder by the captain, who desired me to bring a knife with me. While I returned for the knife, another person went up in my room, who was instantly washed overboard. We had no leisure to lament him, nor did we expect to survive him long; for we soon found the ship was filling with water very fast. The sea had torn away the upper timbers on one side, and made a mere wreck in a few minutes. I shall not affect to describe this disaster in marine dialect, which would be understood by few; and therefore I can give you but a very inadequate idea of it. Taking in all circumstances, it was astonishing, and almost miraculous, that any of us survived to relate the story. We had immediate recourse to the pumps; but the water increased against our efforts. Some of us were set to baling in another part of the vessel; that is, to lade it out with buckets and pails. We had but eleven or twelve people to sustain this service; and, notwithstanding all we could do, she was full, or very near it: and then, with a common cargo, she must have sunk of course; but we had a great quantity of bees' wax and wood on board, which were specifically lighter than the water; and as it pleased God that we received this shock in the very crisis of the gale, towards morning we were enabled to employ some means for our safety, which succeeded beyond hope. In about an hour's time, the day began to break, and the wind abated. We expended most of our clothes and bedding to stop the leaks (though the weather was exceedingly cold, especially to us, who had so lately left a hot climate;) over these we nailed pieces of boards, and at last perceived the water abate. At the beginning of this hurry, I was little affected. I pumped hard, and endeavoured to animate myself and companions: I told one of them, that in a few days, this distress would serve us to talk of over a glass of wine; but he being a less hardened sinner than myself, replied, with tears, "No; it is too late now." About nine o'clock, being almost spent with cold and labour, I went to speak with the captain, who was busied elsewhere, and just as I was returning from him, I said almost without any meaning, "If this will not do the Lord have mercy upon us." This (though spoken with little reflection) was the first desire I had breathed for mercy for the space of many years. I was instantly struck with my own words; and, as Jehu said once, "what hast thou to do with peace!" so it directly occurred, "What mercy can there be for me!" I was obliged to return to the pump, and there I continued till noon, almost every passing wave breaking over my head; but we made ourselves fast with ropes, that we might not be washed away. Indeed, I expected that every time the vessel descended in the sea, she would rise no more; and though I dreaded death now, and my heart foreboded the worst, if the scriptures, which I had long since opposed, were indeed true; yet still I was but half convinced, and remained for a space of time in a sullen frame, a mixture of despair and impatience. I thought, if the Christian religion was true, I could not be forgiven; and was, therefore, expecting, and almost, at times, wishing, to know the worst of it. . . .

. . . For about the space of six years, the Lord was pleased to lead me in a secret way. I had learned something of the evil of my heart; I had read the Bible over and over, with several good books, and had a general view of gospel truths. But my conceptions were, in many respects, confused; not having, in all this time, met with one acquaintance who could assist my inquiries. But upon my arrival at St. Christopher's, this voyage, I found a captain of a ship from London, whose conversation was greatly helpful to me. He was, and is a member of Mr. B——r's church, a man of experience in the things of God, and of a lively, communicative turn. We discovered each other by some casual expressions in mixed company, and soon became (so far as business would permit) inseparable. For near a month, we spent every evening together, on board each other's ship alternately, and often prolonged our visits till towards day-break. I was all ears; and what was better, he not only informed my understanding, but his discourse inflamed my heart. He encouraged me to open my mouth in social prayer; he taught me the advantage of christian converse; he put me upon an attempt to make my profession more public, and to venture to speak for God. From him, or rather from the Lord, by his means, I received an increase of knowledge; my conceptions became clearer and more evangelical, and I was delivered from a fear which had long troubled me, the fear of relapsing into my former apostasy. But now I began to understand the security of the covenant of grace, and to expect to be preserved, not by my own power and holiness, but by the mighty power and promise of God, through faith in an unchangeable Saviour. He likewise gave me a general view of the state of religion, with the errors and controversies of the times (things to which I had been entirely a stranger,) and finally directed me where to apply in London for further instruction. With these newly acquired advantages, I left him, and my passage homewards gave me leisure to digest what I had received. I had much comfort and freedom during those seven weeks, and my sun was seldom clouded. I arrived safe in [Liverpool], August, 1754.

My stay at home was intended to be but short, and by the beginning of November, I was again ready for the sea: but the Lord saw fit to over-rule my design. During the time I was engaged in the slave trade, I never had the least scruple as to its lawfulness. I was, upon the whole, satisfied with it, as the appointment Providence had marked out for me; yet it was, in many respects, far from eligible. It is, indeed, accounted a genteel employment, and is usually very profitable, though to me it did not prove so, the Lord seeing that a large increase of wealth could not be good for me. However, I considered myself as a sort of gaoler or turnkey; and I was sometimes shocked with an employment that was perpetually conversant with chains, bolts, and shackles. In this view I had often petitioned, in my prayers, that the Lord, in his own time, would be pleased to fix me in a more humane calling, and, if it might be, place me where I might have more frequent converse with his people and ordinances, and be freed from those long separations from home, which very often were hard to bear. My prayers were now answered, though in a way I little expected. I now ex-perienced another sudden, unforeseen change of life. I was within two days of sailing, and, to all appearance, in good health as usual; but in the after-noon, as I was sitting with Mrs. [Newton], by ourselves, drinking tea, and talking over past events, I was in a moment seized with a fit which deprived me of sense and motion, and left me no other sign of life than that of breathing. I suppose it was of the apoplectic kind. It lasted about an hour, and when I recovered, it left a pain and dizziness in my head, which con-tinued with such symptoms as induced the physicians to judge it would not be safe or prudent for me to proceed on the voyage. Accordingly, by the advice of my friend, to whom the ship belonged, I resigned the command the day before she sailed; and thus I was unexpectedly called from that service, and freed from a share of the future consequences of that voyage, which proved extremely calamitous. The person who went in my room, most of the officers, and many of the crew, died, and the vessel was brought home with great difficulty.

As I was now disengaged from business. I left [Liverpool], and spent most of the following year at London, and in Kent. But I entered upon a new trial. You will easily conceive that Mrs. [Newton] was not an uncon-cerned spectator, when I lay extended, and, as she thought, expiring upon the ground. In effect, the blow that struck me reached her in the same instant: she did not, indeed, immediately feel it, till her apprehensions on my account began to subside; but as I grew better, she became worse: her surprise threw her into a disorder, which no physicians could define, or medicines remove. Without any of the ordinary symptoms of a consumption, she decayed almost visibly, till she became so weak that she could hardly bear any one to walk across the room she was in. I was placed for about eleven months in what Dr. Young calls the

"—dreadful post of observation,
Darker every hour"

It was not till after my settlement in my present station, that the Lord was pleased to restore her by his own hand, when all hopes from ordinary means were at an end. But before this took place, I have some other particulars to mention. . . .

All this while I had two trials, more or less, upon my mind; the first and principal was Mrs. [Newton's] illness; she still grew worse, and I had daily more reason to fear that the hour of separation was at hand. When faith was in exercise, I was in some measure resigned to the Lord's will; but too often my heart rebelled, and I found it hard either to trust or to submit. I had likewise some care about my future settlement; the African trade was overdone that year, and my friends did not care to fit out another ship till mine returned. I was sometime in suspense. . . .

One word concerning my view to the ministry, and I have done. I have told you, that this was my dear mother's hope concerning me; but her death, and the scenes of life in which I afterwards engaged, seemed to cut off the probability. The first desires of this sort of my own mind, arose many years ago, from a reflection on Gal. i. 23, 24. I could not but wish for such a public opportunity to testify the riches of divine grace. I thought I was, above most living, a fit person to proclaim that faithful saying, "That Jesus Christ came into the world to save the chief of sinners," and as my life had been full of remarkable turns, and I seemed selected to show what the Lord could do, I was in some hopes that, perhaps, sooner or later, he might call me into his service.

Barton Stone

(1772–1844)

The experiences of the American frontier are the stuff of which legends are made, but the history of westward expansion in the United States includes the stories of real men and women who were caught up in the religious enthusiasm of the camp meeting and the frontier church. After the American Revolution, settlers streamed west, and with them went the preachers. One of them was Barton Stone, a Presbyterian who moved from Pennsylvania to eastern Kentucky to preach, evangelize, and farm the land.

Stone had been converted at the age of nineteen by another Presbyterian revivalist, James McGready. Ten years later, in Cane Ridge, Kentucky, a series of revivals broke out under Stone's preaching. News spread rapidly, inspiring other mass conversions and extending the practice of the camp meeting. But most importantly, the fact and the symbol of Cane Ridge captured the imagination of thousands.

Presbyterians looked askance at some of the activities at Cane Ridge, and although Stone admitted there were excesses, he defended what had happened as the work of the Holy Spirit. Under fire of criticism, he finally left the Presbyterian Church to form what eventually became the Disciples of Christ. The new denomination was a creation of the frontier and its ethos: each congregation was autonomous and self-governing; its members simply called themselves Christians; there were no creeds except for the Bible; salvation was for all who accepted Christ; and only adults could be baptized.

Preeminently a preacher, and despite some physical paralysis that restricted him during the last decade of his life, Barton Stone was a dedicated, life-long preacher. As he lived, so he died – in the pulpit, on a preaching mission at the age of seventy-two.

The following account is taken from Stone's autobiography, and though written decades after the Cane Ridge revivals, it reveals his own awe and astonishment at the power of the revival meeting and the excitement it generated. Excerpted from *The Biography of Eld. Barton Warren Stone, Written by Himself* (Cincinnati, 1847), 39–42.

The bodily agitations or exercises, attending the excitement in the beginning of this century, were various, and called by various names;—as, the falling exercise—the jerks—the dancing exercise—the barking exercise—the laughing and singing exercise, &c.—the falling exercise was very common among all classes, the saints and sinners of every age and of every grade, from the philosopher to the clown. The subject of this exercise would, generally, with a piercing scream, fall like a log on the floor, earth, or mud, and appear as dead. Of thousands of similar cases, I will mention one. At a meeting, two gay young ladies, sisters, were standing together attending to the exercises and preaching at the time. Instantly they both fell, with a shriek of distress, and lay for more than an hour apparently in a lifeless state. Their mother, a pious Baptist, was in great distress, fearing they would not revive. At length they began to exhibit symptoms of life, by crying fervently for mercy, and then relapsed into the same death-like state, with an awful gloom on their countenances. After awhile, the gloom on the face of one was succeeded by a heavenly smile, and she cried out, precious Jesus, and rose up and spoke of the love of God—the preciousness of Jesus, and of the glory of the gospel, to the surrounding crowd, in language almost superhuman, and pathetically exhorted all to repentance. In a little while after, the other sister was similarly exercised. From that time they became remarkably pious members of the church.

I have seen very many pious persons fall in the same way, from a sense of the danger of their unconverted children, brothers, or sisters— from a sense of the danger of their neighbors, and of the sinful world. I have heard them agonizing in tears and strong crying for mercy to be shown to sinners, and speaking like angels to all around.

The jerks cannot be so easily described. Sometimes the subject of the jerks would be affected in some one member of the body, and sometimes in the whole system. When the head alone was affected, it would be jerked backward and forward, or from side to side, so quickly that the features of the face could not be distinguished. When the whole system was affected, I have seen the person stand in one place, and jerk backward and forward in quick succession, their head nearly touching the floor behind and before. All classes, saints and sinners, the strong as well as the weak, were thus affected. I have inquired of those thus affected. They could not account for it; but some have told me that those were among the happiest seasons of their lives. I have seen some wicked persons thus affected, and all the time cursing the jerks, while they were thrown to the earth with violence. Though so awful to behold, I do not remember that any one of the thousands I have seen ever sustained an injury in body. This was as strange as the exercise itself.

The dancing exercise. This generally began with the jerks, and was peculiar to professors of religion. The subject, after jerking awhile, began to dance, and then the jerks would cease. Such dancing was indeed heavenly to the spectators; there was nothing in it like levity, nor calculated to excite levity in the beholders. The smile of heaven shone on the countenance of the subject, and assimilated to angels appeared the whole person. Sometimes the motion was quick and sometimes slow. Thus they continued to move forward and backward in the same track or alley till nature seemed exhausted, and they would fall prostrate on the floor or earth, unless caught by those standing by. While thus exercised, I have heard their solemn praises and prayers ascending to God.

The barking exercise (as opposers contemptuously called it) was nothing but the jerks. A person affected with the jerks, especially in his head, would often make a grunt, or bark, if you please, from the suddenness of the jerk. This name of barking seems to have had its origin from an old Presbyterian preacher of East Tennessee. He had gone into the woods for private devotion, and was seized with the jerks. Standing near a sapling, he caught hold of it, to prevent his falling, and as his head jerked back, he uttered a grunt or kind of noise similar to a bark, his face being turned upwards. Some wag discovered him in this position, and reported that he found him barking up a tree.

The laughing exercise was frequent, confined solely with the religious. It was a loud, hearty laughter, but one *sui generis*; it excited laughter in none else. The subject appeared rapturously solemn, and his laughter excited solemnity in saints and sinners. It is truly indescribable.

The running exercise was nothing more than, that persons feeling something of these bodily agitations, through fear, attempted to run away, and thus escape from them; but it commonly happened that they ran not far, before they fell, or became so greatly agitated that they could proceed no farther. I knew a young physician of a celebrated family, who came some distance to a big meeting to see the strange things he had heard of. He and a young lady had sportively agreed to watch over, and take care of each other, if either should fall. At length the physician felt something very uncommon, and started from the congregation to run into the woods; he was discovered running as for life, but did not proceed far till he fell down, and there lay till he submitted to the Lord, and afterwards became a zealous member of the church. Such cases were common.

I shall close this chapter with the singing exercise. This is more unaccountable than any thing else I ever saw. The subject in a very happy state of mind would sing most melodiously, not from the mouth or nose, but entirely in the breast, the sounds issuing thence. Such music silenced every thing, and attracted the attention of all. It was most heavenly. None could ever be tired of hearing it. Doctor J. P. Campbell and myself were together at a meeting, and were attending to a pious lady thus exercised, and concluded it to be something surpassing any thing we had known in nature.

Thus have I given a brief account of the wonderful things that appeared in the great excitement in the beginning of this century. That there were many eccentricities, and much fanaticism in this excitement, was acknowledged by its warmest advocates; indeed it would have been a wonder, if such things had not appeared, in the circumstances of that time. Yet the good effects were seen and acknowledged in every neighborhood, and among the different sects it silenced contention, and promoted unity for awhile; and these blessed effects would have continued, had not men put forth their unhallowed hands to hold up their tottering ark, mistaking it for the ark of God.

Peter Cartwright
(1785–1872)

Peter Cartwright's life captures the story of religion on the American frontier. Born in Virginia, he grew up in Logan County, Kentucky, known as
Rogue's Harbor because of the wild life of its residents. His father "was
quite a poor man and not so much a bad as a good-for-nothing kind of
man." His mother, who influenced Peter greatly, was a devout and pious
Methodist, but one brother was hanged for murder and a sister led a life
of debauchery. Peter himself enjoyed the drinking, gambling, horse-racing,
and dancing of the frontier, but then he was converted in 1801 by the
Presbyterian revivalist, James McGready.

In 1803 "the Kentucky boy" began his life-long ministry as an itinerant Methodist preacher, traveling through Kentucky, Tennessee, Ohio,
Indiana, and Illinois. Some settlers on the frontier battled the elements
for survival, but Cartwright waged war against sin, Satan, and sects. He
ridiculed the Presbyterians and wrote a famous letter to the devil de-
nouncing Calvinism; he condemned the Shakers; and he wrestled rival
religionists if he had to — and always won. His theology was simple, if not
simplistic: repent and believe. His preaching was emotional and powerful,
but some of the excesses of revivalism violated his own common sense.
Theological education was useless for ministers, as far as Cartwright was
concerned, and late in life he looked back wistfully and wished that "camp-
meetings, class-meetings, prayer-meetings, and love-feasts" would continue "eternally."

Although he devoted his life to building the Methodist Church, he
also entered politics. A vehement opponent of slavery, he was elected to
the Illinois legislature in 1824, defeated Abraham Lincoln in 1832, but then
lost to Lincoln in the 1846 Congressional race. When Methodists split over
slavery in 1844, he sided with the antislavery party in the church.

His account of his conversion and his report on the famous Cane
Ridge revival of 1801 vividly portray the revivalism of the frontier and the
life of early Methodist preachers who established the denomination in the
American heartland. Through Cartwright's account also comes his strength
and vigor.

Excerpted from *Autobiography of Peter Cartwright* (Cincinnati, 1856),
36-47.

In 1801, when I was in my sixteenth year, my father, my eldest half brother, and myself, attended a wedding about five miles from home, where there was a great deal of drinking and dancing, which was very common at marriages in those days. I drank little or nothing; my delight was in dancing. After a late hour in the night, we mounted our horses and started for home. I was riding my race-horse.

A few minutes after we had put up the horses, and were sitting by the fire, I began to reflect on the manner in which I had spent the day and evening. I felt guilty and condemned. I rose and walked the floor. My mother was in bed. It seemed to me, all of a sudden, my blood rushed to my head, my heart palpitated, in a few minutes I turned blind; an awful impression rested on my mind that death had come and I was unprepared to die. I fell on my knees and began to ask God to have mercy on me.

My mother sprang from her bed, and was soon on her knees by my side, praying for me, and exhorting me to look to Christ for mercy, and then and there I promised the Lord that if he would spare me, I would seek and serve him; and I never fully broke that promise. My mother prayed for me a long time. At length we lay down, but there was little sleep for me. Next morning I rose, feeling wretched beyond expression. I tried to read in the Testament, and retired many times to secret prayer through the day, but found no relief. I gave up my race-horse to my father, and requested him to sell him. I went and brought my pack of cards, and gave them to mother, who threw them into the fire, and they were consumed. I fasted, watched, and prayed, and engaged in regular reading of the Testament. I was so distressed and miserable, that I was incapable of any regular business.

My father was greatly distressed on my account, thinking I must die, and he would lose his only son. He bade me retire altogether from business, and take care of myself.

Soon it was noised abroad that I was distracted, and many of my associates in wickedness came to see me, to try and divert my mind from those gloomy thoughts of my wretchedness; but all in vain. I exhorted them to desist from the course of wickedness which we had been guilty of together. The class-leader and local preacher were sent for. They tried to point me to the bleeding Lamb, they prayed for me most fervently. Still I found no comfort, and although I had never believed in the doctrine of unconditional election and reprobation, I was sorely tempted to believe I was a reprobate, and doomed, and lost eternally, without any chance of salvation.

At length one day I retired to the horse-lot, and was walking and wringing my hands in great anguish, trying to pray, on the borders of utter despair. It appeared to me that I heard a voice from heaven, saying, "Peter, look at me." A feeling of relief flashed over me as quick as an electric shock. It gave me hopeful feelings, and some encouragement to seek mercy, but still my load of guilt remained. I repaired to the house, and told my mother what had happened to me in the horse-lot. Instantly she seemed to understand it, and told me the Lord had done this to encourage me to hope for mercy, and exhorted me to take encouragement, and seek on, and God would bless me with the pardon of my sins at another time.

Some days after this, I retired to a cave on my father's farm to pray in secret. My soul was in an agony; I wept, I prayed, and said, "Now, Lord, if there is mercy for me, let me find it," and it really seemed to me that I could almost lay hold of the Saviour, and realize a reconciled God. All of a sudden, such a fear of the devil fell upon me that it really appeared to me that he was surely personally there, to seize and drag me down to hell, soul and body, and such a horror fell on me that I sprang to my feet and ran to my mother at the house. My mother told me this was a device of Satan to prevent me from finding the blessing then. Three months rolled away, and still I did not find the blessing of the pardon of my sins. . . .

In the spring of this year, Mr. M'Grady, a minister of the Presbyterian Church, who had a congregation and meeting-house, as we then called them, about three miles north of my father's house, appointed a sacramental meeting in this congregation, and invited the Methodist preachers to attend with them, and especially John Page, who was a powerful Gospel minister, and was very popular among the Presbyterians. Accordingly he came, and preached with great power and success.

There were no camp-meetings in regular form at this time, but as there was a great waking up among the Churches, from the revival that had broken out at Cane Ridge . . . many flocked to those sacramental meetings. The church would not hold the tenth part of the congregation. Accordingly, the officers of the Church erected a stand in a contiguous shady grove, and prepared seats for a large congregation.

The people crowded to this meeting from far and near. They came in their large wagons, with victuals mostly prepared. The women slept in the wagons, and the men under them. Many stayed on the ground night and day for a number of nights and days together. Others were provided for among the neighbors around. The power of God was wonderfully displayed; scores of sinners fell under the preaching, like men slain in mighty battle; Christians shouted aloud for joy.

To this meeting I repaired, a guilty, wretched sinner. On the Saturday evening of said meeting, I went, with weeping multitudes, and bowed before the stand, and earnestly prayed for mercy. In the midst of a solemn struggle of soul, an impression was made on my mind, as though a voice said to me, "Thy sins are all forgiven thee." Divine light flashed all round me, unspeakable joy sprung up in my soul. I rose to my feet, opened my eyes, and it really seemed as if I was in heaven; the trees, the leaves on them, and everything seemed, and I really thought were, praising God. My mother raised the shout, my Christian friends crowded around me and joined me in praising God; and though I have been since then, in many instances, unfaithful, yet I have never, for one moment, doubted that the Lord did, then and there, forgive my sins and give me religion. . . .

Elizabeth Bayley Seton
(1774–1821)

The first American-born canonized saint of the Roman Catholic Church, Elizabeth Bayley Seton began to question her Episcopal background during a visit to Leghorn, Italy. Her father was a distinguished physician and professor of medicine at King's College, New York (now Columbia), and her mother's father was rector of St. Andrew's Episcopal Church, Staten Island.

When she was twenty years old, she married William M. Seton, a wealthy merchant who promptly lost his fortune and his health. With their five children, the Setons visited Italy in search of rest and physical restoration. William died, and Elizabeth was befriended by the Filicchi family in Leghorn where she came into direct contact with the Catholic faith.

Returning to New York, Mrs. Seton struggled with her religious commitment, and, mostly for reasons of historical priority, she joined the Catholic Church. It was, she wrote later, "where true faith first began." Deserted and ostracized by friends and family, she retreated to Canada until she was invited to Baltimore to found a new religious community.

It was a time of bitter animosity between Protestants and Catholics. The former were polemical and unfair in their criticism, and the latter became overly sensitive and defensive. For both Christian traditions, it marked an ebb tide for theology, biblical scholarship, and simple human tolerance.

In Baltimore, Mrs. Seton and a few like-minded associates established what came to be known as the Sisters of Charity. Dedicated to social work among the poor, the order also began new programs of education for Catholic children, a local effort credited with establishing the widespread and sometimes controversial Catholic parochial school system.

Against the formidable intolerance of the times, Mother Seton made her way without bluster or attack and in time received the respect not only of Protestants but of civic leaders. Many years later, Pope John XXIII became involved in the process that led to her canonization by Pope Paul VI in 1975.

The account of Mrs. Seton's decision to join the Roman Catholic Church comes from *Memoir, Letters and Journal of Elizabeth Seton, Convert to the Catholic Faith and Sister of Charity,* ed. Robert Seton, Prothonotary Apostolic (New York: P. O'Shea, Publisher, 1869), I: 203-13.

The Catholic religion so fully satisfied my heart and soul in Italy, that had not my duty towards my children deterred me, I would have retired into a convent after my husband's death. In losing him, my father, and my sister Rebecca, all seems ended here on earth; for although my children are indeed a treasure, I dare not rest a hope of happiness on such frail young beings whose lives are so uncertain. When I arrived here from Leghorn, the clergy had much to say to me on the score of religion, and spoke of Antichrist, idolatry, and urged any number of objections, all of which, without altering the opinions I had formed, were quite enough to frighten me into irresolution as to what step I should take; and here now I am in God's hands, praying day and night for His heavenly direction, which alone can guide me straight. I instruct my children in the religion of Catholics as well as I can, without, however, taking any decided course, although my greatest comfort is found in imagining myself a member of their church. . . .

In desperation of heart I went last Sunday to St. George's [Episcopal] Church; the wants and necessities of my soul were so pressing, that I looked straight up to God, and I told Him since I can not see the way to please You, whom alone I wish to please, every thing is indifferent to me, and until You do show me the way You mean me to go, I will walk on in the path You suffered me to be placed on at my birth, and even go to the very sacrament where I once used to find you. So away I went, but if I left the house a Protestant, I returned to it a Catholic I think, since I determined to go no more to the Protestants, being much more troubled than ever I thought I could be. But so it was that at the bowing of my head before the bishop to receive his absolution, which is given publicly and universally to all in the church, I had not the least faith in his prayer, and looked for an apostolic loosing from my sins. . . .

Then, trembling, I went to communion, half dead with the inward struggles, when they said: "The body and blood of Christ". . . I became half crazy, and for the first time could not bear the sweet caresses of my darlings or bless their little dinner. O my God! that day. But it finished calmly at last, abandoning all to God with a renewed confidence in the Blessed Virgin, whose mild and peaceful look reproached my bold excesses, and reminded me to fix my heart above with better hopes.

Now, my friends tell me to take care, that I am a mother, and must answer for my children at the judgment-seat, whatever faith I lead them to. That being so, I will go peaceably and firmly to the Catholic Church. For if faith is so important to our salvation, I will seek it where true faith first began, will seek it among those who received it from God Himself. The controversies on it I am quite incapable of deciding, and as the strictest Protestant allows salvation to a good Catholic, to the Catholics will I go, and try to be a good one. May God accept my good intention and pity me. As to supposing the word of our Lord has failed, and that He suffered His first foundation to be built on by Antichrist, I can not stop on that without stopping on every other word of our Lord, and being tempted to be no Christian at all. For if the chief church became Antichrist's, and the second holds her rights from it, then I should be afraid both might be antichristian, and I be lost by following either.

Charles G. Finney
(1792–1875)

American Protestantism has produced many revivalist preachers, but few can compare with Charles Grandison Finney. In a long and productive life, he transformed American evangelicalism and gave it most of its distinctive theological emphases and many of its evangelistic methods. In a democratic age, he made grace available to common people and reinterpreted theology for the understanding of ordinary individuals.

Finney's conversion, according to one biographer, "is one of the classics of American religious folklore." Nominally religious in his youth, he became a lawyer, and his work brought him to the study of the Mosaic law. This exposed him to more of the Bible, and eventually he decided, as he characteristically put it, "that I would settle the question of my soul's salvation at once." For Finney, the burden of salvation lay with the sinful individual, not in God's mysterious election of the saved, and his own powerful conversion experience served as the basis of his theology.

He became a lawyer in the pulpit, for as he told one of his clients immediately after his conversion, "I have a retainer from the Lord Jesus Christ to plead his cause, and I cannot plead yours." He convicted people of their sins, and then offered them the choice: plead innocent, and die in sin, or plead guilty, accept Jesus Christ, and be saved. Although his theology collided with the strict Calvinism of the Presbyterian Church, Finney sought ordination as a Presbyterian minister. His presbytery wanted him to go to Princeton Theological Seminary, but he coolly refused, saying he did not like the way Princeton influenced its graduates. He called the Westminster Confession "this wonderful theological fiction" and its doctrines "cannotism." Nevertheless, his presbytery ordained him, and he soon won fame as a revivalist in New York, leading a series of important evangelistic services throughout the state from 1821 to 1832.

His theology, he said, was based on his own reason and the Bible, and his methods were pragmatic. Revivals were not simply the work of God, he argued, but the right application of the right methods. He later published a "how-to-do-it" manual for preachers, *Lectures on Revivals of Religion* (1835), insisting that revivals were like planting grain: sow the seed and then reap the harvest. Finney also developed what were known as "new measures": the anxious bench (where potential converts were directly addressed by the preacher); protracted meetings which built up the intensity of the appeals to repent; allowing women to pray in public worship in the presence of men; and direct appeals by name to individuals in the congregation. Such practices were controversial, but for Finney they worked. His followers made them a staple of American revivalism.

Finney also believed that it was impossible for a person to be both holy and sinful at the same time, and this belief encouraged a tendency toward perfectionism. He was opposed to slavery but focused most of his attention on converting sinners. His influence was widespread, not only through his preaching but also his association with Oberlin College, Ohio, where he served on the faculty from 1835 to 1875 and as president from 1851 to 1866.

Finney's conversion changed his life and dramatically influenced American Protestantism. He embodied the spirit of nineteenth-century America in its self-reliance and independence, and by choosing salvation, Finney also opened the door for others.

Excerpted from *Memoirs of Rev. Charles G. Finney* (New York, 1876), 12-23.

On a Sabbath evening in the autumn of 1821, I made up my mind that I would settle the question of my soul's salvation at once, that if it were possible I would make my peace with God. But as I was very busy in the affairs of the office, I knew that without great firmness of purpose, I should never effectually attend to the subject. I therefore, then and there resolved, as far as possible, to avoid all business, and everything that would divert my attention, and to give myself wholly to the work of securing the salvation of my soul. I carried this resolution into execution as sternly and thoroughly as I could. I was, however, obliged to be a good deal in the office. But as the providence of God would have it, I was not much occupied either on Monday or Tuesday; and had opportunity to read my Bible and engage in prayer most of the time.

But I was very proud without knowing it. I had supposed that I had not much regard for the opinions of others, whether they thought this or that in regard to myself; and I had in fact been quite singular in attending prayer meetings, and in the degree of attention that I had paid to religion, while in Adams. In this respect I had been so singular as to lead the church at times to think that I must be an anxious inquirer. But I found, when I came to face the question, that I was very unwilling to have any one know that I was seeking the salvation of my soul. When I prayed I would only whisper my prayer, after having stopped the key-hole to the door, lest some one should discover that I was engaged in prayer. Before that time I had my Bible lying on the table with the law-books; and it never had occurred to me to be ashamed of being found reading it, any more than I should be ashamed of being found reading any of my other books.

But after I had addressed myself in earnest to the subject of my own salvation, I kept my Bible, as much as I could, out of sight. If I was reading it when anybody came in, I would throw my law-books upon it, to create the impression that I had not had it in my hand. Instead of being outspoken and willing to talk with anybody and everybody on the subject as before, I found myself unwilling to converse with anybody. I did not want to see my minister, because I did not want to let him know how I felt, and I had no confidence that he would understand my case, and give me the direction that I needed. For the same reasons I avoided conversation with the elders of the church, or with any of the Christian people. I was ashamed to let them know how I felt, on the one hand; and on the other, I was afraid they would misdirect me. I felt myself shut up to the Bible.

During Monday and Tuesday my convictions increased; but still it seemed as if my heart grew harder. I could not shed a tear; I could not pray. I had no opportunity to pray above my breath; and frequently I felt, that if I could be alone where I could use my voice and let myself out, I should find relief in prayer. I was shy, and avoided, as much as I could, speaking to anybody on any subject. I endeavored, however, to do this in a way that would excite no suspicion, in any mind, that I was seeking the salvation of my soul.

Tuesday night I had become very nervous; and in the night a strange feeling came over me as if I was about to die. I knew that if I did I should sink down to hell; but I quieted myself as best I could until morning.

At an early hour I started for the office. But just before I arrived at the office, something seemed to confront me with questions like these: indeed, it seemed as if the inquiry was within myself, as if an inward voice said to me, "What are you waiting for? Did you not promise to give your heart to God? And what are you trying to do? Are you endeavoring to work out a righteousness of your own?"

Just at this point the whole question of Gospel salvation opened to my mind in a manner most marvellous to me at the time. I think I then saw, as clearly as I ever have in my life, the reality and fulness of the atonement of Christ. I saw that his work was a finished work; and that instead of having, or needing, any righteousness of my own to recommend me to God, I had to submit myself to the righteousness of God through Christ. Gospel salvation seemed to me to be an offer of something to be accepted; and that it was full and complete; and that all that was necessary on my part, was to get my own consent to give up my sins, and accept Christ. Salvation, it seemed to me, instead of being a thing to be wrought out, by my own works, was a thing to be found entirely in the Lord Jesus Christ, who presented himself before me as my God and my Saviour.

Without being distinctly aware of it, I had stopped in the street right where the inward voice seemed to arrest me. How long I remained in that position I cannot say. But after this distinct revelation had stood for some little time before my mind, the question seemed to be put, "Will you accept it now, to-day?" I replied, "Yes; I will accept it to-day, or I will die in the attempt."

North of the village, and over a hill, lay a piece of woods, in which I was in the almost daily habit of walking, more or less, when it was pleasant weather. It was now October, and the time was past for my frequent walks there. Nevertheless, instead of going to the office, I turned and bent my course toward the woods, feeling that I must be alone, and away from all human eyes and ears, so that I could pour out my prayer to God.

But still my pride must show itself. As I went over the hill, it occurred to me that some one might see me and suppose that I was going away to pray. Yet probably there was not a person on earth that would have suspected such a thing, had he seen me going. But so great was my pride, and so much was I possessed with the fear of man, that I recollect that I skulked along under the fence, till I got so far out of sight that no one from the village could see me. I then penetrated into the woods, I should think, a quarter of a mile, went over on the other side of the hill, and found a place where some large trees had fallen across each other, leaving an open place between. There I saw I could make a kind of closet. I crept into this place and knelt down for prayer. As I turned to go up into the woods, I recollect to have said, "I will give my heart to God, or I never will come down from there." I recollect repeating this as I went up—"I will give my heart to God before I ever come down again."

But when I attempted to pray I found that my heart would not pray. I had supposed that if I could only be where I could speak aloud, without being overheard, I could pray freely. But lo! when I came to try, I was dumb; that is, I had nothing to say to God; or at least I could say but a few words, and those without heart. In attempting to pray I would hear a rustling in the leaves, as I thought, and would stop and look up to see if somebody were not coming. This I did several times.

Finally I found myself verging fast to despair. I said to myself, "I cannot pray. My heart is dead to God, and will not pray." I then reproached myself for having promised to give my heart to God before I left the woods. When I came to try, I found I could not give my heart to God. My inward soul hung back, and there was no going out of my heart to God. I began to feel deeply that it was too late; that it must be that I was given up of God and was past hope.

The thought was pressing me of the rashness of my promise, that I would give my heart to God that day or die in the attempt. It seemed to me as if that was binding upon my soul; and yet I was going to break my vow. A great sinking and discouragement came over me, and I felt almost too weak to stand upon my knees.

Just at this moment I again thought I heard some one approach me, and I opened my eyes to see whether it were so. But right there the revelation of my pride of heart, as the great difficulty that stood in the way, was distinctly shown to me. An overwhelming sense of my wickedness in being ashamed to have a human being see me on my knees before God, took such powerful possession of me, that I cried at the top of my voice, and exclaimed that I would not leave that place if all the men on earth and all the devils in hell surrounded me. "What!" I said, "such a degraded sinner as I am, on my knees confessing my sins to the great and holy God; and ashamed to have any human being, and a sinner like myself, find me on my knees endeavoring to make my peace with my offended God!" The sin appeared awful, infinite. It broke me down before the Lord.

Just at that point this passage of Scripture seemed to drop into my mind with a flood of light: "Then shall ye go and pray unto me, and I will hearken unto you. Then shall ye seek me and find me, when he shall search for me with all your heart." I instantly seized hold of this with my heart. I had intellectually believed the Bible before; but never had the truth been in my mind that faith was a voluntary trust instead of an intellectual state. I was as conscious as I was of my existence, of trusting at that moment in God's veracity. Somehow I knew that that was a passage of Scripture, though I do not think I had ever read it. I knew that it was God's word, and God's voice, as it were, that spoke to me. I cried to Him, "Lord, I take thee at thy word. Now thou knowest that I do search for thee with all my heart, and that I have come here to pray to thee; and thou hast promised to hear me."

That seemed to settle the question that I could then, that day, perform my vow. The Spirit seemed to lay stress upon that idea in the text, "When you search for me with all your heart." The question of when, that is of the present time, seemed to fall heavily into my heart. I told the Lord that I should take him at his word; that he could not lie; and that therefore I was sure that he heard my prayer, and that he would be found of me.

He then gave me many other promises, both from the Old and the New Testament, especially some most precious promises respecting our Lord Jesus Christ. I never can, in words, make any human being understand how precious and true those promises appeared to me. I took them one after the other as infallible truth, the assertions of God who could not lie. They did not seem so much to fall into my intellect as into my heart, to be put within the grasp of the voluntary powers of my mind; and I seized hold of them, appropriated them, and fastened upon them with the grasp of a drowning man.

I continued thus to pray, and to receive and appropriate promises for a long time, I know not how long. I prayed till my mind became so full that, before I was aware of it, I was on my feet and tripping up the ascent toward the road. The question of my being converted had not so much as arisen to my thought; but as I went up, brushing through the leaves and bushes, I recollect saying with great emphasis, "If I am ever converted, I will preach the Gospel."

I soon reached the road that led to the village, and began to reflect upon what had passed; and I found that my mind had become most wonderfully quiet and peaceful. I said to myself. "What is this? I must have grieved the Holy Ghost entirely away. I have lost all my conviction. I have not a particle of concern about my soul; and it must be that the Spirit has left me." "Why!" thought I, "I never was so far from being concerned about my own salvation in my life."

Then I remembered what I had said to God while I was on my knees—that I had said I would take him at his word; and indeed I recollected a good many things that I had said, and concluded that it was no wonder that the Spirit had left me; that for such a sinner as I was to take hold of God's word in that way, was presumption if not blasphemy. I concluded that in my excitement I had grieved the Holy Spirit, and perhaps committed the unpardonable sin.

I walked quietly toward the village; and so perfectly quiet was my mind that it seemed as if all nature listened. It was on the 10th of October, and a very pleasant day. I had gone into the woods immediately after an early breakfast; and when I returned to the village I found it was dinner time. Yet I had been wholly unconscious of the time that had passed; it appeared to me that I had been gone from the village but a short time.

But how was I to account for the quiet of my mind? I tried to recall my convictions, to get back again the load of sin under which I had been laboring. But all sense of sin, all consciousness of present sin or guilt, had departed from me. I said to myself, "What is this, that I cannot arouse any sense of guilt in my soul, as great a sinner as I am?" I tried in vain to make myself anxious about my present state. I was so quiet and peaceful that I tried to feel concerned about that, lest it should be a result of my having grieved the Spirit away. But take any view of it I would, I could not be anxious at all about my soul, and about my spiritual state. The repose of my mind was unspeakably great. I never can describe it in words. The thought of God was sweet to my mind, and the most profound spiritual tranquillity had taken full possession of me. This was a great mystery; but it did not distress or perplex me.

I went to my dinner, and found I had no appetite to eat. I then went to the office, and found that Squire W—— had gone to dinner. I took down my bass-viol, and, as I was accustomed to do, began to play and sing some pieces of sacred music. But as soon as I began to sing those sacred words, I began to weep. It seemed as if my heart was all liquid; and my feelings were in such a state that I could not hear my own voice in singing without causing my sensibility to overflow. I wondered at this, and tried to suppress my tears, but could not. After trying in vain to suppress my tears, I put up my instrument and stopped singing.

After dinner we were engaged in removing our books and furniture to another office. We were very busy in this, and had but little conversation all the afternoon. My mind, however, remained in that profoundly tranquil state. There was a great sweetness and tenderness in my thoughts and feelings. Everything appeared to be going right, and nothing seemed to ruffle or disturb me in the least.

Just before evening the thought took possession of my mind, that as soon as I was left alone in the new office, I would try to pray again— that I was not going to abandon the subject of religion and give it up, at any rate; and therefore, although I no longer had any concern about my soul, still I would continue to pray.

By evening we got the books and furniture adjusted; and I made up, in an open fire-place, a good fire, hoping to spend the evening alone. Just at dark Squire W——, seeing that everything was adjusted, bade me good-night and went to his home. I had accompanied him to the door; and as I closed the door and turned around, my heart seemed to be liquid within me. All my feelings seemed to rise and flow out; and the utterance of my heart was, "I want to pour my whole soul out to God." The rising of my soul was so great that I rushed into the room back of the front office, to pray.

There was no fire, and no light, in the room; nevertheless it appeared to me as if it were perfectly light. As I went in and shut the door after me, it seemed as if I met the Lord Jesus Christ face to face. It did not occur to me then, nor did it for some time afterward, that it was wholly a mental state. On the contrary it seemed to me that I saw him as I would see any other man. He said nothing, but looked at me in such a manner as to break me right down at his feet. I have always since regarded this as a most remarkable state of mind; for it seemed to me a reality, that he stood before me, and I fell down at his feet and poured out my soul to him. I wept aloud like a child, and made such confessions as I could with my choked utterance. It seemed to me that I bathed his feet with my tears; and yet I had no distinct impression that I touched him, that I recollect.

I must have continued in this state for a good while; but my mind was too much absorbed with the interview to recollect anything that I said. But I know, as soon as my mind became calm enough to break off from the interview, I returned to the front office, and found that the fire that I had made of large wood was nearly burned out. But as I turned and was about to take a seat by the fire, I received a mighty baptism of the Holy Ghost. Without any expectation of it, without ever having the thought in my mind that there was any such thing for me, without any recollection that I had ever heard the thing mentioned by any person in the world, the Holy Spirit descended upon me in a manner that seemed to go through me, body and soul. I could feel the impression, like a wave of electricity, going through and through me. Indeed it seemed to come in waves and waves of liquid love; for I could not express it in any other way. It seemed like the very breath of God. I can recollect distinctly that it seemed to fan me, like immense wings.

No words can express the wonderful love that was shed abroad in my heart. I wept aloud with joy and love; and I do not know but I should say, I literally bellowed out the unutterable gushings of my heart. These waves came over me, and over me, and over me, one after the other, until I recollect I cried out, "I shall die if these waves continue to pass over me." I said, "Lord, I cannot bear any more;" yet I had no fear of death.

How long I continued in this state, with this baptism continuing to roll over me and go through me, I do not know. But I know it was late in the evening when a member of my choir—for I was the leader of the choir—came into the office to see me. He was a member of the church. He found me in this state of loud weeping, and said to me, "Mr. Finney, what ails you?" I could make him no answer for some time. He then said, "Are you in pain?" I gathered myself up as best I could, and replied, "No, but so happy that I cannot live."

He turned and left the office, and in a few minutes returned with one of the elders of the church, whose shop was nearly across the way from our office. This elder was a very serious man; and in my presence had been very watchful, and I had scarcely ever seen him laugh. When he came in, I was very much in the state in which I was when the young man went out to call him. He asked me how I felt, and I began to tell him. Instead of saying anything, he fell into a most spasmodic laughter. It seemed as if it was impossible for him to keep from laughing from the very bottom of his heart.

There was a young man in the neighborhood who was preparing for college, with whom I had been very intimate. Our minister, as I afterward learned, had repeatedly talked with him on the subject of religion, and warned him against being misled by me. He informed him that I was a very careless young man about religion; and he thought that if he associated much with me his mind would be diverted, and he would not be converted.

After I was converted, and this young man was converted, he told me that he had said to Mr. Gale several times, when he had admonished him about associating so much with me, that my conversations had often affected him more, religiously, than his preaching. I had, indeed, let out my feelings a good deal to this young man.

But just at the time when I was giving an account of my feelings to this elder of the church, and to the other member who was with him, this young man came into the office. I was sitting with my back toward the door, and barely observed that he came in. He listened with astonishment to what I was saying, and the first I knew he partly fell upon the floor, and cried out in the greatest agony of mind, "Do pray for me!" The elder of the church and the other member knelt down and began to pray for him;

and when they had prayed, I prayed for him myself. Soon after this they all retired and left me alone.

The question then arose in my mind, "Why did Elder B—— laugh so? Did he not think that I was under a delusion, or crazy?" This suggestion brought a kind of darkness over my mind; and I began to query with myself whether it was proper for me—such a sinner as I had been—to pray for that young man. A cloud seemed to shut in over me; I had no hold upon anything in which I could rest; and after a little while I retired to bed, not distressed in mind, but still at a loss to know what to make of my present state. Notwithstanding the baptism I had received, this temptation so obscured my view that I went to bed without feeling sure that my peace was made with God.

I soon fell asleep, but almost as soon awoke again on account of the great flow of the love of God that was in my heart. I was so filled with love that I could not sleep. Soon I fell asleep again, and awoke in the same manner. When I awoke, this temptation would return upon me, and the love that seemed to be in my heart would abate; but as soon as I was asleep, it was so warm within me that I would immediately awake. Thus I continued till, late at night, I obtained some sound repose.

When I awoke in the morning the sun had risen, and was pouring a clear light into my room. Words cannot express the impression that this sunlight made upon me. Instantly the baptism that I had received the night before, returned upon me in the same manner. I arose upon my knees in the bed and wept aloud with joy, and remained for some time too much overwhelmed with the baptism of the Spirit to do anything but pour out my soul to God. It seemed as if this morning's baptism was accompanied with a gentle reproof, and the Spirit seemed to say to me, "Will you doubt?" "Will you doubt?" I cried, "No! I will not doubt; I cannot doubt." He then cleared the subject up so much to my mind that it was in fact impossible for me to doubt that the Spirit of God had taken possession of my soul.

In this state I was taught the doctrine of justification by faith, as a present experience. That doctrine had never taken any such possession of my mind, that I had ever viewed it distinctly as a fundamental doctrine of the Gospel. Indeed, I did not know at all what it meant in the proper sense. But I could now see and understand what was meant by the passage, "Being justified by faith, we have peace with God through our Lord Jesus Christ." I could see that the moment I believed, while up in the woods all sense of condemnation had entirely dropped out of my mind; and that from that moment I could not feel a sense of guilt or condemnation by any effort that I could make. My sense of guilt was gone; my sins were gone; and I do not think I felt any more sense of guilt than if I never had sinned.

This was just the revelation that I needed. I felt myself justified by faith; and, so far as I could see, I was in a state in which I did not sin. Instead of feeling that I was sinning all the time, my heart was so full of love that it overflowed. My cup ran over with blessing and with love; and I could not feel that I was sinning against God. Nor could I recover the least sense of guilt for my past sins. Of this experience I said nothing that I recollect, at the time, to anybody; that is, of this experience of justification.

Sojourner Truth
(1797?–1883)

"Isabella" was born a slave in New York, the property of a wealthy Dutch landowner, and for the rest of her life she spoke with a heavy Dutch accent. She served several masters and gave birth to five children; in 1827 she was emancipated by Isaac Van Wagener, one year before New York state outlawed slavery. She moved to New York City in 1829 where she became involved with a religious visionary, Elijah Pierson, but the Pierson sect dissolved in 1835 in a scandal over its sexual mores.

After her initial conversion, she had religious visions and mystical experiences, and in 1843, following one divine encounter, she changed her name to Sojourner Truth. Taking to the pulpit and the lecture platform, she traveled throughout New England, describing her religious experience and attracting huge crowds. After 1843, however, she was not content to confine herself to religious subjects, and she became a powerful voice opposing slavery. Like other abolitionists, she also moved to the point of likening black slavery to discrimination against women, and she spoke out forcefully for women's suffrage and women's rights.

During the Civil War she helped outfit volunteer black regiments, successfully campaigned to desegregate streetcars in Washington, D.C., and was received at the White House by Abraham Lincoln. After the war, she worked for the National Freedmen's Relief Association in Virginia, assisting in resettlement, health, and education programs.

In her faith and in her life, she held forth the promise of the freedom proclaimed by Paul in Galatians 3: "There is neither Jew nor Greek, there is neither slave nor free, there is neither male nor female; for you are all one in Christ Jesus." She asked Americans to make that freedom a reality for all.

During her lifetime she was known as "The Libyan Sibyl," and fellow abolitionist leader Parker Pillsbury said of her, "The wondrous experiences of that most remarkable woman would make a library, if not indeed a literature, could they all be gathered and spread before the world."

Sojourner Truth, like many former slaves, dictated her autobiography to a white person, a friend named Olive Gilbert. "Isabella" is referred to, in the account, in the third person. Such slave narratives were extremely important in shaping antislavery sentiment in the North, and in 1850 Sojourner Truth distributed her own account at rallies and meetings.

The following excerpt is taken from the last revision of the autobiography, *Narrative of Sojourner Truth; A Bondswoman of Olden Time ... Drawn from Her "Book of Life"* (Battle Creek, Mich., 1878), 64-71.

When Isabella had been at Mr. Van Wagener's a few months, she saw in prospect one of the festivals approaching. She knows it by none but the Dutch name, Pingster, as she calls it—but I think it must have been Whitsuntide, in English. She says she "looked back into Egypt," and everything looked "so pleasant there," as she saw retrospectively all her former companions enjoying their freedom for at least a little space, as well as their wonted convivialities, and in her heart she longed to be with them. With this picture before her mind's eye, she contrasted the quiet, peaceful life she was living with the excellent people of Wahkendall, and it seemed so dull and void of incident, that the very contrast served but to heighten her desire to return, that, at least, she might enjoy with them, once more, the coming festivities. These feelings had occupied a secret corner of her breast for some time, when, one morning, she told Mrs. Van Wagener that her old master Dumont would come that day, and that she should go home with him on his return. They expressed some surprise, and asked her where she obtained her information. She replied, that no one had told her, but she felt that he would come.

It seemed to have been one of those "events that cast their shadows before"; for, before night, Mr. Dumont made his appearance. She informed him of her intention to accompany him home. He answered, with a smile, "I shall not take you back again; you ran away from me." Thinking his manner contradicted his words, she did not feel repulsed, but made herself and child ready; and when her former master had seated himself in the open dearborn, she walked towards it, intending to place herself and child in the rear, and go with him. But, ere she reached the vehicle, she says that God revealed himself to her, with all the suddenness of a flash of lightning, showing her, "in the twinkling of an eye, that he was *all over"*— that he pervaded the universe—"and that there was no place where God was not." She became instantly conscious of her great sin in forgetting her almighty Friend and "ever-present help in time of trouble." All her unfulfilled promises arose before her, like a vexed sea whose waves run mountains high; and her soul, which seemed but one mass of lies, shrunk back aghast from the "awful look" of Him whom she had formerly talked to, as if he had been a being like herself; and she would now fain have hid herself in the bowels of the earth, to have escaped his dread presence. But she plainly saw there was no place, not even in hell, where he was not: and where could she flee? Another such "a look," as she expressed it, and she felt that she must be extinguished forever, even as one, with the breath of his mouth, "blows out a lamp," so that no spark remains.

A dire dread of annihilation now seized her, and she waited to see if, by "another look," she was to be stricken from existence,—swallowed up, even as the fire licketh up the oil with which it comes in contact.

When at last the second look came not, and her attention was once more called to outward things, she observed her master had left, and exclaiming aloud, "Oh, God, I did not know you were so big," walked into the house, and made an effort to resume her work. But the workings of the inward man were too absorbing to admit of much attention to her avocations. She desired to talk to God, but her vileness utterly forbade it, and she was not able to prefer a petition. "What!" said she, "shall I lie again to God? I have told him nothing but lies; and shall I speak again, and tell another lie to God?" She could not; and now she began to wish for some one to speak to God for her. Then a space seemed opening between her and God, and she felt that if some one, who was worthy in the sight of heaven, would but plead *for* her in their own name, and not let God know it came from *her,* who was so unworthy, God might grant it. At length a friend appeared to stand between herself and an insulted Deity; and she felt as sensibly refreshed as when, on a hot day, an umbrella had been interposed between her scorching head and a burning sun. But who was this friend? became the next inquiry. Was it Deencia, who had so often befriended her? She looked at her with her new power of sight—and, lo! she, too, seemed all "bruises and putrifying sores," like herself. No, it was some one very different from Deencia.

"Who *are* you?" she exclaimed, as the vision brightened into a form distinct, beaming with the beauty of holiness, and radiant with love. She then said, audibly addressing the mysterious visitant—"I *know* you, and I *don't* know you." Meaning, "You seem perfectly familiar; I feel that you not only love me, but that you always *have* loved me—yet I know you not— I cannot call you by name." When she said, "I know you," the subject of the vision remained distinct and quiet. When she said, "I don't know you," it moved restlessly about, like agitated waters. So while she repeated, without intermission, "I know you, I know you," that the vision might remain— "Who are you?" was the cry of her heart, and her whole soul was in one deep prayer that this heavenly personage might be revealed to her, and remain with her. At length, after bending both soul and body with the intensity of this desire, till breath and strengh seemed failing, and she could maintain her position no longer, an answer came to her, saying distinctly, "It is Jesus." "Yes," she responded, "it is *Jesus.*"

Previous to these exercises of mind, she heard Jesus mentioned in reading or speaking, but had received from what she heard no impression that he was any other than an eminent man, like a Washington or a Lafayette. Now he appeared to her delighted mental vision as so mild, so good, and so every way lovely, and he loved her so much! And, how strange that he had always loved her, and she had never known it! And how great a blessing he conferred, in that he should stand between her and God! And God was no longer a terror and a dread to her.

She stopped not to argue the point, even in her own mind, whether he had reconciled her to God, or God to herself, (though she thinks the former now,) being but too happy that God was no longer to her as a consuming fire, and Jesus was "altogether lovely." Her heart was now full of joy and gladness, as it had been of terror, and at one time of despair. In the light of her great happiness, the world was clad in new beauty, the very air sparkled as with diamonds, and was redolent of heaven. She contemplated the unapproachable barriers that existed between herself and the great of this world, as the world calls greatness, and made surprising comparisons between them, and the union existing between herself and Jesus,— Jesus, the transcendently lovely as well as great and powerful; for so he appeared to her, though he seemed but human; and she watched for his bodily appearance, feeling that she should know him, if she saw him; and when he came, she should go and dwell with him, as with a dear friend.

It was not given her to see that he loved any other; and she thought if others came to know and love him, as she did, she should be thrust aside and forgotten, being herself but a poor ignorant slave, with little to recommend her to his notice. And when she heard him spoken of, she said mentally—"What! others know Jesus! I thought no one knew Jesus but me!" and she felt a sort of jealousy, lest she should be robbed of her newly found treasure.

She conceived, one day, as she listened to reading, that she heard an intimation that Jesus was married, and hastily inquired if Jesus had a wife. "What!" said the reader, "*God* have a wife?" "Is Jesus *God*?" inquired Isabella. "Yes, to be sure he is," was the answer returned. From this time, her conceptions of Jesus became more elevated and spiritual; and she sometimes spoke of him as God, in accordance with the teaching she had received.

But when she was simply told, that the Christian world was much divided on the subject of Christ's nature—some believing him to be co-equal with the Father—to be God in and of himself, "very God, of very God;"—some, that he is the "well-beloved," "only begotten Son of God;"— and others, that he is, or was, rather, but a mere man—she said, "Of that I only know as I saw. I did not see him to be God; else, how could he stand between me and God? I saw him as a friend, standing between me and God, through whom, love flowed as from a fountain." Now, so far from expressing her views of Christ's character and office in accordance with any system of theology extant, she says she believes Jesus is the same spirit that was in our first parents, Adam and Eve, in the beginning, when they came from the hand of their Creator. When they sinned through disobedience, this pure spirit forsook them, and fled to heaven; that there it remained, until it returned again in the person of Jesus; and that, previous to a personal union with him, man is but a brute, possessing only the spirit of an animal.

She avers that, in her darkest hours, she had no fear of any worse hell than the one she then carried in her bosom; though it had ever been pictured to her in its deepest colors, and threatened her as a reward for all her misdemeanors. Her vileness and God's holiness and all-pervading presence, which filled immensity, and threatened her with instant annihilation, composed the burden of her vision of terror. Her faith in prayer is equal to her faith in the love of Jesus. Her language is, "Let others say what they will of the efficacy of prayer, *I* believe in it, and *I* shall pray. Thank God! Yes, *I shall always pray,*" she exclaims, putting her hands together with the greatest enthusiasm.

For some time subsequent to the happy change we have spoken of, Isabella's prayers partook largely of their former character; and while, in deep affliction, she labored for the recovery of her son, she prayed with constancy and fervor; and the following may be taken as a specimen:— "Oh, God, you know how much I am distressed, for I have told you again and again. Now, God, help me get my son. If you were in trouble, as I am, and I could help you, as you can me, think I wouldn't do it? Yes, God, you *know* I would do it." "Oh, God, you know I have no money, but you can make the people do for me, and you must make the people do for me. I will never give you peace till you do, God." "Oh, God, make the people hear me—don't let them turn me off, without hearing and helping me." And she has not a particle of doubt, that God heard her, and especially disposed the hearts of thoughtless clerks, eminent lawyers, and grave judges and others—between whom and herself there seemed to her almost an infinite remove—to listen to her suit with patient and respectful attention, backing it up with all needed aid. The sense of her nothingness, in the eyes of those with whom she contended for her rights, sometimes fell on her like a heavy weight, which nothing but her unwavering confidence in an arm which she believed to be stronger than all others combined could have raised from her sinking spirit. "Oh! how little I did feel," she repeated, with a powerful emphasis. "Neither would you wonder, if you could have seen me, in my ignorance and destitution, trotting about the streets, meanly clad, bare-headed, and bare-footed! Oh, God only could have made such people hear me; and he did it in answer to my prayers." And this perfect trust, based on the rock of Deity, was a soul-protecting fortress, which, raising her above the battlements of fear, and shielding her from the machinations of the enemy, impelled her onward in the struggle, till the foe was vanquished, and the victory gained.

David Livingstone
(1813–1873)

Perhaps no figure has had a greater influence on Western attitudes toward Africa than David Livingstone, the missionary explorer. Through a combination of incredible physical endurance and evangelical zeal, he "opened" the continent of Africa, literally and figuratively, traveling widely through southern and central Africa, coast to coast. An imperialist as well as a forerunner of African nationalism and self-determination, Livingstone believed that the combination of Christianity and commerce would be the salvation of Africa, and yet he also urged that native-born Africans should carry out the task of evangelization. He was passionately committed to the abolition of African slavery, and his writings and speeches were influential in awakening Great Britain and the West to the horrors of the slave trade. But he was also an example of Victorian paternalism in his relationships with black people.

Born near Glasgow into a poor Scottish family, Livingstone was raised in the ethos of Scots Calvinism with its emphases on piety, self-discipline, hard work, education, and duty. At the age of ten he entered the cotton mill to help his family — and worked with a book before him, reading a sentence or two as the machine spun. In 1834 he responded to an appeal for medical missionaries in China, working part-time in the mill while he studied Greek, theology, and medicine for two years at the University of Glasgow. In 1838, he was accepted by the London Missionary Society, but his determination to go to China was frustrated by the Opium War. Then in London he met the South African missionary Robert Moffat, who convinced him to come to Africa.

In 1840, he was ordained as a missionary by the London Missionary Society, and took the first of his African journeys. He arrived in South Africa in 1841, and within a year had pushed farther north than any other white person. He married Moffat's daughter in 1845, and she and their children accompanied him on his journeys; however, one child died in infancy and his wife became gravely ill. For the sake of their health, security, and education, he sent them back to Britain in 1852 and confessed later that one of his chief regrets was that he had not taken an hour a day to play with his children.

Africa and destiny beckoned, and in 1853 he declared, "I shall open up a path into the interior, or perish." From 1853 to 1856, with a small band of Africans, he pushed deeper into the continent of Africa, finally discovering the mammoth waterfalls on the Zambezi River and naming them, with a burst of British patriotism, Victoria Falls. In 1857 he published his *Missionary Travels and Researches in South Africa*, which became a best-seller and captured the imagination of the English-speaking world. Quietly severing his relationship with the London Missionary Society, Livingstone left for his Zambezi expedition (1858 – 1864) as a British consul, and in 1866 he departed again on his famous search for the origin of the Nile. It was on this journey that the explorer H. M. Stanley was commissioned by the *New York Herald* to discover whether Livingstone was alive or dead. Upon reaching him, Stanley greeted him with typical British propriety, "Dr. Livingstone, I presume." Stanley tried to persuade Livingstone to return with him, but he refused, and on May 1, 1873, Livingstone was found dead, kneeling at his bedside, apparently in prayer.

A complex man of strong ego but also selfless determination to explore Africa, Livingstone possessed a fervent but understated faith. The following account of his conversion is tantalizingly brief and restrained, but one can glimpse his piety and his passion for discovery in a portion of his diary, written on his birthday and shortly before his death:

> 19 March 1872 – Birthday. My Jesus, my King, my life, my All; I again dedicate my whole self to Thee. Accept me and grant, O gracious Father, that ere this year is gone I may finish my task. In Jesus' name I ask it. Amen, so let it be. David Livingstone.

When he died, his African companions buried his heart and entrails in Africa and shipped his body back to England, where he was buried in Westminster Abbey.

Excerpted from *Missionary Travels and Researches in South Africa* (New York, 1958), 4-5.

Great pains had been taken by my parents to instill the doctrines of Christianity into my mind, and I had no difficulty in understanding the theory of our free salvation by the atonement of our Savior, but it was only about this time that I really began to feel the necessity and value of a personal application of the provisions of that atonement to my own case. The change was like what may be supposed would take place were it possible to cure a case of "color blindness." The perfect freeness with which the pardon of all our guilt is offered in God's book drew forth feelings of affectionate love to Him who bought us with his blood, and a sense of deep obligation to Him for his mercy has influenced, in some small measure, my conduct ever since. But I shall not again refer to the inner spiritual life which I believe then began, nor do I intend to specify with any prominence the evangelistic labors to which the love of Christ has since impelled me. This book will speak, not so much of what has been done, as of what still remains to be performed, before the Gospel can be said to be preached to all nations.

In the glow of love which Christianity inspires, I soon resolved to devote my life to the alleviation of human misery. Turning this idea over in my mind, I felt that to be a pioneer of Christianity in China might lead to the material benefit of some portions of that immense empire; and therefore set myself to obtain a medical education, in order to be qualified for that enterprise.

John Henry Newman
(1801–1890)

Meek and mild in many ways, scholarly and remote in others, Newman was probably more surprised than many to become the focus of the most controversial church dispute in England since Henry VIII. Oxford vicar, teacher, writer, authority on the early church Patristic period, John Henry Newman belonged to the high church tradition of the Church of England. Many who later sang his well-loved hymn, "Lead, Kindly Light," might not guess that the lines were autobiographical.

About the same time as he wrote the hymn, in 1833, the so-called Oxford or Tractarian Movement began to distribute a series of pamphlets or tracts critical of the present state of Anglicanism. Newman soon became the recognized leader of the Tractarians, urging his fellow clergy to reconsider the distinctive marks of their own heritage.

It was not a time of vigorous theological ideas, and religious life in the Church of England had become bland and lackluster. Newman drew definite lines of distinction between Protestants (Lutherans and Calvinists), Roman Catholics, and Anglicans. He regarded the Reformation, as did Catholics, as a historical offshoot and hence a heretical departure from apostolic continuity. But at this time he also regarded Catholics as non-apostolic because of later Roman developments such as papal infallibility. Within his own Anglican tradition, he detected the debasing influences of what he called "liberalism," the incursion of science and rationalism into the domain of Christian culture.

Striving to authenticate the apostolic validity of his own tradition, Newman and his Tractarian colleagues disrupted the church. The famous "Tract 90" sought to interpret "The Thirty-Nine Articles" of the Church of England as compatible with the doctrines of the Catholic Council of Trent. This drew down upon Newman such persistent criticism from his fellow clerics and especially from the bishops that he began, on the one hand, to doubt the validity of the Anglican claim, and, on the other, to look more favorably on the Catholic Church as the true custodian of apostolic orthodoxy.

Newman resigned his Oxford ecclesiastical position in 1843, and after an agonizing time of isolation and reflection, he was quietly received into the Roman Catholic Church on October 9, 1845. When his sincerity was questioned, he responded, painfully and at considerable length, in what came to be known as *Apologia Pro Vita Sua* (1864).

He thoroughly vindicated himself in the eyes of the world, and at the same time produced one of the great spiritual classics of all time. In 1879, Pope Leo XIII made him a cardinal and henceforth he was known as John Henry Cardinal Newman. Perhaps he did not know it at the time, but his famous hymn was a perfect expression of his inner spiritual struggle:

> Lead, kindly Light, amid th' encircling gloom,
>   Lead Thou me on;
> The night is dark, and I am far from home;
>   Lead Thou me on;
> Keep Thou my feet; I do not ask to see
> The distant scene — one step enough for me.

Whatever may be thought of his decision, and he was applauded and vilified on all sides, subsequent generations have agreed that Cardinal Newman greatly enriched both the Anglican and the Catholic traditions by his scholarship and his personal commitment to the one Lord of the church.

There are many editions of the *Apologia*. Requiring concentration and some knowledge of classics and patristics, the narrative makes slow going. Newman keeps inserting references to letters, records, and passages from his books and articles. The excerpts presented here attempt to gather together the main sequence of events without including the documentation. The text is from his *Apologia Pro Vita Sua: Being A History of His Religious Opinions*, ed. Martin J. Svaglic (Oxford: The Clarendon Press, 1967), 90-214. © Oxford University Press, 1967, and reprinted by permission.

And now that I am about to trace, as far as I can, the course of that great revolution of mind, which led me to leave my own home, to which I was bound by so many strong and tender ties, I feel overcome with the difficulty of satisfying myself in my account of it, and have recoiled from the attempt, till the near approach of the day, on which these lines must be given to the world, forces me to set about the task. For who can know himself, and the multitude of subtle influences which act upon him? . . .

These then were the *parties* in the controversy:—the Anglican *Via Media* and the popular religion of Rome. And next, as to the *issue,* to which the controversy between them was to be brought, it was this:—the Anglican disputant took his stand upon Antiquity or Apostolicity, the Roman upon Catholicity. The Anglican said to the Roman: "There is but One Faith, the Ancient, and you have not kept to it"; the Roman retorted: "There is but One Church, the Catholic, and you are out of it." The Anglican urged: "Your special beliefs, practices, modes of action, are nowhere in Antiquity"; the Roman objected: "You do not communicate with any one Church besides your own and its offshoots, and you have discarded principles, doctrines, sacraments, and usages, which are and ever have been received in the East and the West." The true Church, as defined in the Creeds, was both Catholic and Apostolic; now, as I viewed the controversy in which I was engaged, England and Rome had divided these notes or prerogatives between them: the cause lay thus, Apostolicity *versus* Catholicity.

However, in thus stating the matter, of course I do not wish it supposed that I allowed the note of Catholicity really to belong to Rome, to the disparagement of the Anglican Church; but I considered that the special point or plea of Rome in the controversy was Catholicity, as the Anglican plea was Antiquity. Of course I contended that the Roman idea of Catholicity was not ancient and apostolic. It was in my judgment at the utmost only natural, becoming, expedient, that the whole of Christendom should be united in one visible body; while such a unity might, on the other hand, be nothing more than a mere heartless and political combination. For myself, I held with the Anglican divines, that, in the Primitive Church, there was a very real mutual independence between its separate parts, though, from a dictate of charity, there was in fact a close union between them. I considered that each See and Diocese might be compared to a crystal, and that each was similar to the rest, and that the sum total of them all was only a collection of crystals. The unity of the Church lay, not in its being a polity, but in its being a family, a race, coming down by apostolical descent from its first founders and bishops. And I considered this truth brought out, beyond the possibility of dispute, in the Epistles of St. Ignatius, in which the Bishop is represented as the one supreme authority in the Church, that is, in his own place, with no one above him, except as, for the sake of ecclesiastical order and expedience, arrangements had been made by which one was put over or under another. So much for our own claim to Catholicity, which was so perversely appropriated by our opponents to themselves:—on the other hand, as to our special strong point, Antiquity, while, of course, by means of it, we were able to condemn most emphatically the novel claim of Rome to domineer over other Churches, which were in truth her equals, further than that, we thereby especially convicted her of the intolerable offence of having added to the Faith. This was the critical head of accusation urged against her by the Anglican disputant; and as he referred to St. Ignatius in proof that he himself was a true Catholic, in spite of being separated from Rome, so he triumphantly referred to the Treatise of Vincentius of Lerins upon the "Quod semper, quod ubique, quod ab omnibus," in proof that the controversialists of Rome, in spite of their possession of the Catholic name, were separated in their creed from the Apostolical and primitive faith.

It is plain, then, that at the end of 1835 or beginning of 1836, I had the whole state of the question before me, on which, to my mind, the decision between the Churches depended. It is observable that the question

of the position of the Pope, whether as the centre of unity, or as the source
of jurisdiction, did not come into my thoughts at all; nor did it, I think I
may say, to the end. I doubt whether I ever distinctly held any of his
powers to be *de jure divino,* while I was in the Anglican Church;—not that
I saw any difficulty in the doctrine; not that in connexion with the history
of St. Leo, of which I shall speak by and by, the idea of his infallibility did
not cross my mind, for it did,—but after all, in my view the controversy
did not turn upon it; it turned upon the Faith and the Church. This was
my issue of the controversy from the beginning to the end. There was a
contrariety of claims between the Roman and Anglican religions, and the
history of my conversion is simply the process of working it out to a
solution. . . .

I determined to be guided, not by my imagination, but by my reason.
And this I said over and over again in the years which followed, both in
conversation and in private letters. Had it not been for this severe resolve,
I should have been a Catholic sooner than I was. Moreover, I felt on
consideration a positive doubt, on the other hand, whether the suggestion
did not come from below. Then I said to myself, Time alone can solve that
question. It was my business to go on as usual, to obey those convictions
to which I had so long surrendered myself, which still had possession of
me, and on which my new thoughts had no direct bearing. That new conception of things should only so far influence me, as it had a logical claim
to do so. If it came from above, it would come again;—so I trusted,—and
with more definite outlines and greater cogency and consistency of proof.
I thought of Samuel, before "he knew the word of the Lord"; and there I
went, and lay down to sleep again. This was my broad view of the matter,
and my *primâ facie* conclusion. . . .

Anglicanism claimed to hold, that the Church of England was nothing else than a continuation in this country, (as the Church of Rome might
be in France or Spain,) of that one Church of which in old times Athanasius
and Augustine were members. But, if so, the doctrine must be the same;
the doctrine of the Old Church must live and speak in Anglican formularies,
in the 39 Articles. Did it? Yes, it did; that is what I maintained; it did in
substance, in a true sense. Man had done his worst to disfigure, to mutilate,
the old Catholic Truth; but there it was, in spite of them, in the Articles
still. It was there,—but this must be shown. . . .

I had in mind to remove all such obstacles as lay in the way of
holding the Apostolic and Catholic character of the Anglican teaching; to
assert the right of all who chose, to say in the face of day, "Our Church
teaches the Primitive Ancient faith." I did not conceal this: in Tract 90, it
is put forward as the first principle of all, "It is a duty which we owe both
to the Catholic Church, and to our own, to take our reformed confessions
in the most Catholic sense they will admit: we have no duties towards their
framers." And still more pointedly in my Letter, explanatory of the Tract,

addressed to Dr. Jelf, I say: "The only peculiarity of the view I advocate, if I must so call it, is this—that whereas it is usual at this day to make the *particular belief of their writers* their true interpretation, I would make the *belief of the Catholic Church such.* That is, as it is often said that infants are regenerated in Baptism, not on the faith of their parents, but of the Church, so in like manner I would say that the Articles are received, not in the sense of their framers, but (as far as the wording will admit or any ambiguity requires it) in the one Catholic sense." . . .

From the end of 1841, I was on my death-bed, as regards my membership with the Anglican Church, though at the time I became aware of it only by degrees. I introduce what I have to say with this remark, by way of accounting for the character of this remaining portion of my narrative. A death-bed has scarcely a history; it is a tedious decline, with seasons of rallying and seasons of falling back; and since the end is foreseen, or what is called a matter of time, it has little interest for the reader, especially if he has a kind heart. Moreover, it is a season when doors are closed and curtains drawn, and when the sick man neither cares nor is able to record the stages of his malady. I was in these circumstances, except so far as I was not allowed to die in peace,—except so far as friends, who had still a full right to come in upon me, and the public world which had not, have given a sort of history to those last four years. But in consequence, my narrative must be in great measure documentary, as I cannot rely on my memory, except for definite particulars, positive or negative. Letters of mine to friends since dead have come into my hands; others have been kindly lent me for the occasion; and I have some drafts of others, and some notes which I made, though I have no strictly personal or continuous memoranda to consult, and have unluckily mislaid some valuable papers.

And first as to my position in the view of duty; it was this:—1. I had given up my place in the Movement in my letter to the Bishop of Oxford in the spring of 1841; but 2. I could not give up my duties towards the many and various minds who had more or less been brought into it by me; 3. I expected or intended gradually to fall back into Lay Communion; 4. I never contemplated leaving the Church of England; 5. I could not hold office in its service, if I were not allowed to hold the Catholic sense of the Articles; 6. I could not go to Rome, while she suffered honours to be paid to the Blessed Virgin and the Saints which I thought in my conscience to be incompatible with the Supreme, Incommunicable Glory of the One Infinite and Eternal; 7. I desired a union with Rome under conditions, Church with Church; 8. I called Littlemore my Torres Vedras, and thought that some day we might advance again within the Anglican Church, as we had been forced to retire; 9. I kept back all persons who were disposed to go to Rome with all my might.

And I kept them back for three or four reasons; 1. because what I could not in conscience do myself, I could not suffer them to do; 2. because

I thought that in various cases they were acting under excitement; 3. because I had duties to my Bishop and to the Anglican Church; and 4. in some cases, because I had received from their Anglican parents or superiors direct charge of them.

This was my view of my duty from the end of 1841, to my resignation of St. Mary's in the autumn of 1843. . . .

The fact of the operation from first to last of that principle of development in the truths of Revelation, is an argument in favour of the identity of Roman and Primitive Christianity; but as there is a law which acts upon the subject-matter of dogmatic theology, so is there a law in the matter of religious faith. In the first chapter of this Narrative I spoke of certitude as the consequence, divinely intended and enjoined upon us, of the accumulative force of certain given reasons which, taken one by one, were only probabilities. Let it be recollected that I am historically relating my state of mind, at the period of my life which I am surveying. I am not speaking theologically, nor have I any intention of going into controversy, or of defending myself; but speaking historically of what I held in 1843–4, I say, that I believed in a God on a ground of probability, that I believed in Christianity on a probability, and that I believed in Catholicism on a probability, and that these three grounds of probability, distinct from each other of course in subject matter, were still all of them one and the same in nature of proof, as being probabilities—probabilities of a special kind, a cumulative, a transcendent probability but still probability; inasmuch as He who made us has so willed, that in mathematics indeed we should arrive at certitude by rigid demonstration, but in religious inquiry we should arrive at certitude by accumulated probabilities;—He has willed, I say, that we should so act, and, as willing it, He co-operates with us in our acting, and thereby enables us to do that which He wills us to do, and carries us on, if our will does but co-operate with His, to a certitude which rises higher than the logical force of our conclusions. And thus I came to see clearly, and to have a satisfaction in seeing, that, in being led on into the Church of Rome, I was not proceeding on any secondary or isolated grounds of reason, or by controversial points in detail, but was protected and justified, even in the use of those secondary or particular arguments, by a great and broad principle. But, let it be observed, that I am stating a matter of fact, not defending it; and if any Catholic says in consequence that I have been converted in a wrong way, I cannot help that now.

I have nothing more to say on the subject of the change in my religious opinions. On the one hand I came gradually to see that the Anglican Church was formally in the wrong, on the other that the Church of Rome was formally in the right; then, that no valid reasons could be assigned for continuing in the Anglican, and again that no valid objections could be taken to joining the Roman. Then, I had nothing more to learn; what still remained for my conversion, was, not further change of opinion, but to change opinion itself into the clearness and firmness of intellectual conviction. . . .

I could not continue in this state, either in the light of duty or of reason. My difficulty was this: I had been deceived greatly once; how could I be sure that I was not deceived a second time? I thought myself right then; how was I to be certain that I was right now? How many years had I thought myself sure of what I now rejected? how could I ever again have confidence in myself? As in 1840 I listened to the rising doubt in favour of Rome, now I listened to the waning doubt in favour of the Anglican Church. To be certain is to know that one knows; what inward test had I, that I should not change again, after that I had become a Catholic? I had still apprehension of this, though I thought a time would come, when it would depart. However, some limit ought to be put to these vague misgivings; I must do my best and then leave it to a higher Power to prosper it. So, at the end of 1844, I came to the resolution of writing an Essay on Doctrinal Development; and then, if, at the end of it, my convictions in favour of the Roman Church were not weaker, of taking the necessary steps for admission into her fold.

By this time the state of my mind was generally known, and I made no great secret of it. . . .

I had begun my Essay on the Development of Doctrine in the beginning of 1845, and I was hard at it all through the year till October. As I advanced, my difficulties so cleared away that I ceased to speak of "the Roman Catholics," and boldly called them Catholics. Before I got to the end, I resolved to be received, and the book remains in the state in which it was then, unfinished.

One of my friends at Littlemore had been received into the Church on Michaelmas Day, at the Passionist House at Aston, near Stone, by Father Dominic, the Superior. At the beginning of October the latter was passing through London to Belgium; and, as I was in some perplexity what steps to take for being received myself, I assented to the proposition made to me that the good priest should take Littlemore in his way, with a view to his doing for me the same charitable service as he had done to my friend. . . .

I left Oxford for good on Monday, February 23, 1846. On the Saturday and Sunday before, I was in my house at Littlemore simply by myself, as I had been for the first day or two when I had originally taken possession of it. I slept on Sunday night at my dear friend's, Mr. Johnson's, at the Observatory. Various friends came to see the last of me; Mr. Copeland, Mr. Church, Mr. Buckle, Mr. Pattison, and Mr. Lewis. Dr. Pusey too came up to take leave of me; and I called on Dr. Ogle, one of my very oldest friends, for he was my private Tutor, when I was an Undergraduate. In him I took leave of my first College, Trinity, which was so dear to me, and which held on its foundation so many who had been kind to me both when

I was a boy, and all through my Oxford life. Trinity had never been unkind to me. There used to be much snap-dragon growing on the walls opposite my freshman's rooms there, and I had for years taken it as the emblem of my own perpetual residence even unto death in my University. . . .

From the time that I became a Catholic, of course I have no further history of my religious opinions to narrate. In saying this, I do not mean to say that my mind has been idle, or that I have given up thinking on theological subjects; but that I have had no variations to record, and have had no anxiety of heart whatever. I have been in perfect peace and contentment; I never have had one doubt. I was not conscious to myself, on my conversion, of any change, intellectual or moral, wrought in my mind. I was not conscious of firmer faith in the fundamental truths of Revelation, or of more self-command; I had not more fervour; but it was like coming into port after a rough sea; and my happiness on that score remains to this day without interruption.

Charles H. Spurgeon
(1834–1892)

It would be difficult to calculate the impact on his own day and on later generations of the so-called "Prince of Preachers." Forced to occupy ever-larger lecture halls to accommodate the thousands who crowded to hear him preach, Spurgeon seems, in retrospect, a pulpit phenomenon. His published sermons and other biblical volumes are still in print, years after his death.

Charles Haddon Spurgeon was born into the British Baptist tradition of John Bunyan. Without formal theological training, Spurgeon based his preaching on the Bible and the doctrines of sin and salvation. Independent and aggressive, the emphasis of his ministry fell on preaching and conversion, rather than on liturgy or sacraments.

Distrustful of the emerging biblical criticism, he stuck to the great Old Testament narratives and the simple gospel of Jesus. He appealed primarily through human emotions to the individual conscience of his hearers. An eloquent orator, Spurgeon expounded endlessly on the degradation of sin and the glory of salvation.

During the height of his preaching fame, and long before electronic amplification, Spurgeon spoke twice a week in the huge six-thousand-seat Metropolitan Tabernacle in London. Preaching from a page of notes, his sermons were taken down by hand, revised the next day by Spurgeon himself, and then published and distributed, as it was said, "literally by the ton." A later edition of his printed sermons in *The Tabernacle Pulpit* filled nearly fifty volumes. His extensive expositions on the Psalms were published in seven volumes as *The Treasury of David*.

Everything Spurgeon put his hand to seemed large as life. Even his autobiography runs to four big folio volumes. We are not surprised, therefore, to find his conversion (Jan. 6, 1850) described on the grand scale. At the time, he considered it a simple surrender, but its subsequent influence on his life and especially on his preaching was clearly momentous.

The text for the conversion comes from *The Autobiography of Charles* H. *Spurgeon*, compiled from his diary, letters, and records by his wife and his private secretary (New York: Fleming H. Revell Co., 1898), I: 102-13.

In my conversion, the very point lay in making the discovery that I had nothing to do but to look to Christ, and I should be saved. I believe that I had been a very good, attentive hearer; my own impression about myself was that nobody ever listened much better than I did. For years, as a child, I tried to learn the way of salvation; and either I did not hear it set forth, which I think cannot quite have been the case, or else I was spiritually blind and deaf, and could not see it and could not hear it; but the good news that I was, as a sinner, to look away from myself to Christ, as much startled me, and came as fresh to me, as any news I ever heard in my life. Had I never read my Bible? Yes, and read it earnestly. Had I never been taught by Christian people? Yes, I had, by mother, and father, and others. Had I not heard the gospel? Yes, I think I had; and yet, somehow, it was like a new revelation to me that I was to "believe and live." I confess to have been tutored in piety, put into my cradle by prayerful hands, and lulled to sleep by songs concerning Jesus; but after having heard the gospel continually, with line upon line, precept upon precept, here much and there much, yet, when the Word of the Lord came to me with power, it was as new as if I had lived among the unvisited tribes of Central Africa, and had never heard the tidings of the cleansing fountain filled with blood, drawn from the Saviour's veins.

When, for the first time, I received the gospel to my soul's salvation, I thought that I had never really heard it before, and I began to think that the preachers to whom I had listened had not truly preached it. But, on looking back, I am inclined to believe that I had heard the gospel fully preached many hundreds of times before, and that this was the difference,—that I then heard it as though I heard it not; and when I did hear it, the message may not have been any more clear in itself than it had been at former times, but the power of the Holy Spirit was present to open my ear, and to guide the message to my heart. . . .

I sometimes think I might have been in darkness and despair until now had it not been for the goodness of God in sending a snowstorm, one Sunday morning, while I was going to a certain place of worship. When I could go no further, I turned down a side street, and came to a little Primitive Methodist Chapel. In that chapel there may have been a dozen or fifteen people. I had heard of the Primitive Methodists, how they sang so loudly that they made people's heads ache; but that did not matter to me. I wanted to know how I might be saved, and if they could tell me that, I did not care how much they made my head ache. The minister did not come that morning; he was snowed up, I suppose. At last, a very thin-looking man, a shoemaker, or tailor, or something of that sort, went up into the pulpit to preach. Now, it is well that preachers should be instructed; but this man was really stupid. He was obliged to stick to his text, for the simple reason that he had little else to say. The text was,—

"LOOK UNTO ME, AND BE YE SAVED, ALL THE ENDS OF THE EARTH."
He did not even pronounce the words rightly, but that did not matter. There was, I thought, a glimpse of hope for me in that text. The preacher began thus:—"My dear friends, this is a very simple text indeed. It says,

'Look.' Now lookin' don't take a deal of pains. It ain't liftin' your foot or
your finger; it is just, 'Look.' Well, a man needn't go to College to learn to
look. You may be the biggest fool, and yet you can look. A man needn't
be worth a thousand a year to be able to look. Anyone can look; even a
child can look. But then the text says, 'Look unto *Me.*' Ay!" said he, in
broad Essex, "many on ye are lookin' to yourselves, but it's no use lookin'
there. You'll never find any comfort in yourselves. Some look to God the
Father. No, look to Him by-and-by. Jesus Christ says, 'Look unto *Me.*'
Some on ye say, 'We must wait for the Spirit's workin'.' You have no
business with that just now. Look to *Christ.* The text says, 'Look unto *Me.*' "

Then the good man followed up his text in this way:—"Look unto
Me; I am sweatin' great drops of blood. Look unto Me; I am hangin' on
the cross. Look unto Me; I am dead and buried. Look unto Me; I rise again.
Look unto Me; I ascend to Heaven. Look unto Me; I am sittin' at the
Father's right hand. O poor sinner, look unto Me! look unto Me!"

When he had gone to about that length, and managed to spin out
ten minutes or so, he was at the end of his tether. Then he looked at me
under the gallery, and I daresay, with so few present, he knew me to be
a stranger. Just fixing his eyes on me, as if he knew all my heart, he said,
"Young man, you look very miserable." Well, I did; but I had not been
accustomed to have remarks made from the pulpit on my personal appearance before. However, it was a good blow, struck right home. He
continued, "and you always will be miserable—miserable in life, and miserable in death,—if you don't obey my text; but if you obey now, this
moment, you will be saved." Then, lifting up his hands, he shouted, as only
a Primitive Methodist could do, "Young man, look to Jesus Christ. Look!
Look! Look! You have nothin' to do but to look and live."

I saw at once the way of salvation. I know not what else he said,—
I did not take much notice of it,—I was so possessed with that one thought.
Like as when the brazen serpent was lifted up, the people only looked and
were healed, so it was with me. I had been waiting to do fifty things, but
when I heard that word, "Look!" what a charming word it seemed to me!
Oh! I looked until I could almost have looked my eyes away. There and
then the cloud was gone, the darkness had rolled away, and that moment
I saw the sun; and I could have risen that instant, and sung with the most
enthusiastic of them, of the precious blood of Christ, and the simple faith
which looks alone to Him. Oh, that somebody had told me this before,
"Trust Christ, and you shall be saved." . . .

It is not everyone who can remember the very day and hour of his
deliverance; but, as Richard Knill[1] said, "At such a time of the day, clang
went every harp in Heaven, for Richard Knill was born again," it was e'en
so with me. The clock of mercy struck in Heaven the hour and moment

---

[1] Richard Knill, 1787–1857, was a missionary contemporary.

of my emancipation, for the time had come. Between half-past ten o'clock, when I entered that chapel, and half-past twelve o'clock, when I was back again at home, what a change had taken place in me! I had passed from darkness into marvellous light, from death to life. Simply by looking to Jesus, I had been delivered from despair, and I was brought into such a joyous state of mind that, when they saw me at home, they said to me, "Something wonderful has happened to you;" and I was eager to tell them all about it. . . .

I have always considered, with Luther and Calvin, that the sum and substance of the gospel lies in that word *Substitution,*—Christ standing in the stead of man. If I understand the gospel, it is this: I deserve to be lost for ever; the only reason why I should not be damned is, that Christ was punished in my stead, and there is no need to execute a sentence twice for sin. On the other hand, I know I cannot enter Heaven unless I have a perfect righteousness; I am absolutely certain I shall never have one of my own, for I find I sin every day; but then Christ had a perfect righteousness, and He said, "There, poor sinner, take My garment, and put it on; you shall stand before God as if you were Christ, and I will stand before God as if I had been the sinner; I will suffer in the sinner's stead, and you shall be rewarded for works which you did not do, but which I did for you." I find it very convenient every day to come to Christ as a sinner, as I came at the first. "You are no saint," says the devil. Well, if I am not, I am a sinner, and Jesus Christ came into the world to save sinners. Sink or swim, I go to Him; other hope I have none. By looking to Him, I received all the faith which inspired me with confidence in His grace; and the word that first drew my soul—"Look unto Me,"—still rings its clarion note in my ears. There I once found conversion, and there I shall ever find refreshing and renewal.

Leo Tolstoy
(1828–1910)

Leo Tolstoy is one of the heroic figures in world literature, renowned primarily for his two powerful novels, War and Peace and Anna Karenina. He is also regarded as one of the most important religious and philosophical thinkers of the nineteenth century, and his understanding of history, human nature, and Christian discipleship had considerable influence during his lifetime and continue to affect people in the twentieth century.

He was born into a family of Russian aristocracy. His mother died before he was two, and he spent his life trying to remember her and to bring back the love that he idealized in her. After a dissolute life at the university and in the army, he married in 1862 and settled down to manage his estate and raise a family that eventually numbered thirteen children. His writings won acclaim from critics, and he enjoyed affluence and comfort; yet he still struggled for meaning and purpose in life. Despairing of the counsel of philosophers, theologians, and scientists, he considered suicide, but in 1879 he was converted.

The results of his conversion were not adherence to traditional Christianity, for Tolstoy sought a return to what he believed was the primitive Christianity of the Gospels. "For me," he wrote, "religion comes from life, not life from religion." He sought "the religion of Christ, but divested of faith and mysteries, a practical religion, not promising eternal bliss but providing bliss here on earth." Denying the divinity of Christ, he celebrated instead his understanding of the essence of Christ's teachings: the suppression of anger and the imperative of pacifism; love of one's enemies; nonresistance to evil and a refusal to exert force of any kind over others; the taking of oaths as morally wrong; and the sinfulness of sex outside of marriage.

This was a form of Christian and political anarchism — a repudiation of the supernatural dimensions of Christianity, the authority of the church and its sacraments, and the legitimacy of the state. In 1901 Tolstoy was excommunicated by the Russian Orthodox Church, and his religious writings were suppressed. He spent his last years trying to live out the practical implications of his creed by taking on the dress and life-style of a peasant.

After his conversion, Tolstoy refused to write what he considered mere fiction and tried to communicate his faith through religious articles and in what he hoped would be seen as moral works of art. These have not been judged to be his best work, but Tolstoy did become a symbol of Christian radicalism. In contrast to communist philosophy, Tolstoy believed that the perfect society would not be achieved by economic materialism but by increasing the goodness of human nature. His aspiration for a Kingdom of God without war, poverty, and oppression was not realized, and a different version of an earthly kingdom was implemented in Russia; yet his vision of Christian discipleship still beckons.

Excerpted from *My Confession, My Religion, The Gospel in Brief* (New York, 1899), 54-59, 72-75.

M<small>y</small> conviction of the error into which all knowledge based on reason must fall assisted me in freeing myself from the seductions of idle reasoning. The conviction that a knowledge of truth can be gained only by living, led me to doubt the justness of my own life; but I had only to get out of my own particular groove, and look around me, to observe the simple life of the real working-class, to understand that such a life was the only real one. I understood that, if I wished to understand life and its meaning, I must live, not the life of a parasite, but a real life; and, accepting the meaning given to it by the combined lives of those that really form the great human whole, submit it to a close examination.

At the time I am speaking of, the following was my position:—

During the whole of that year, when I was asking myself almost every minute whether I should or should not put an end to it all with a cord or a pistol, during the time my mind was occupied with the thoughts which I have described, my heart was oppressed by a tormenting feeling. This feeling I cannot describe otherwise than as a searching after God.

This search after a God was not an act of my reason, but a feeling, and I say this advisedly, because it was opposed to my way of thinking; it came from the heart. It was a feeling of dread, or orphanhood, of isolation amid things all apart from me, and of hope in a help I knew not from whom.

Though I was well convinced of the impossibility of proving the existence of God—Kant had shown me, and I had thoroughly grasped his reasoning, that this did not admit of proof—I still sought to find a God, still hoped to do so, and still, from the force of former habits, addressed myself to one in prayer, whom I sought, and did not find.

At times I went over in my mind the arguments of Kant and of Schopenhauer, showing the impossibility of proving the existence of the Deity; at times I began to test their arguments and refute them.

I would say to myself that causation is not in the same category of thought as space and time. If I am, there is a cause of my being, and that the cause of all causes. That cause of all things is what is called God; and

I dwelt on this idea, and strove with all my being to reach a consciousness of the presence of this cause.

As soon as I became conscious that there is such a power over me, I felt a possibility of living. Then I asked myself:—

"What is this cause, this power? How am I to think of it? What is my relation to what I call God?"

And only the old familiar answer came into my mind, "He is the creator, the giver of all."

This answer did not satisfy me, and I felt that what was necessary for life was failing me, a great horror came over me, and I began to pray to Him whom I sought, that He would help me. But the more I prayed, the clearer it became that I was not heard, that there was no one to whom one could turn. With despair in my heart that there was no God, I cried:—

"Lord, have mercy on me, and save! O Lord, my God, teach me!"

But no one had mercy on me, and I felt that my life had come to a standstill.

But again and again, from various other directions, I came back to the same conviction that I could not have appeared on earth without any motive or meaning,—that I could not be such a fledgling dropped from a nest as I felt myself to be. What if I cry, as the fallen fledgling does on its back in the high grass? It is because I know that a mother bore me, cared for me, fed me, and loved me. Where is she, where is that mother? If I have been thrown out, then who threw me? I cannot help seeing that some one who loved me brought me into being. Who is that some one? Again the same answer—God. He knows and sees my search, my despair, my struggle. "He is," I said to myself. I had only to admit that for an instant to feel that life re-arose in me, to feel the possibility of existing and the joy of it.

Then, again, from the conviction of the existence of God, I passed to the consideration of our relation toward Him, and again I had before me the triune God, our Creator, who sent His Son, the Redeemer. Again, this God, apart from me and from the world, melted from before my eyes as ice melts; again there was nothing left, again the source of life dried up. I fell once more into despair, and felt that I had nothing to do but to kill myself, while, worst of all, I felt also that I should never do it.

Not twice, not three times, but tens, hundreds, of times did I pass through these alternations,—now of joy and excitement, now of despair and of consciousness of the impossibility of life.

I remember one day in the early springtime I was alone in the forest listening to the woodland sounds, and thinking only of one thing, the same of which I had constantly thought for two years—I was again seeking for a God.

I said to myself:—

"Very good, there is no God, there is none with a reality apart from my own imaginings, none as real as my own life—there is none such. Nothing, no miracles can prove there is, for miracles only exist in my own unreasonable imagination."

And then I asked myself:—

"But my idea of the God whom I seek, whence comes it?"

And again at this thought arose the joyous billows of life. All around me seemed to revive, to have a new meaning. My joy, though, did not last long. Reason continued its work:—

"The idea of a God is not God. The idea is what goes on within myself; the idea of God is an idea which I am able to rouse in my mind or not as I choose; it is not what I seek, something without which life could not be."

Then again all seemed to die around and within me, and again I wished to kill myself.

After this I began to retrace the process which had gone on within myself, the hundred times repeated discouragement and revival. I remembered that I had lived only when I believed in a God. As it was before, so it was now; I had only to know God, and I lived; I had only to forget Him, not to believe in Him, and I died.

What was this discouragement and revival? I do not live when I lose faith in the existence of God; I should long ago have killed myself, if I had not had a dim hope of finding Him. I really live only when I am conscious of Him and seek Him. "What more, then, do I seek?" A voice seemed to cry within me, "This is He, He without whom there is no life. To know God and to live are one. God is life."

Live to seek God, and life will not be without God. And stronger than ever rose up life within and around me, and the light that then shone never left me again.

Thus I was saved from self-murder. When and how this change in me took place I could not say. As gradually, imperceptibly as life had decayed in me, till I reached the impossibility of living, till life stood still, and I longed to kill myself, so gradually and imperceptibly I felt the glow and strength of life return to me.

And strangely enough this power of life which came back to me was not new; it was old enough, for I had been led away by it in the earlier part of my life.

I returned, as it were, to the past, to childhood and my youth. I returned to faith in that Will which brought me into being and which required something of me; I returned to the belief that the one single aim of life should be to become better, that is, to live in accordance with that Will; I returned to the idea that the expression of that Will was to be found in what, in the dim obscurity of the past, the great human unity had fashioned for its own guidance; in other words, I returned to a belief in God, in moral perfectibility, and in the tradition which gives a meaning to life. The difference was that formerly I had unconsciously accepted this, whereas now I knew that without it I could not live.

The state of mind in which I then was may be likened to the following: It was as if I had suddenly found myself sitting in a boat which has been pushed off from some shore unknown to me, had been shown the direction of the opposite shore, had had oars put into my inexperienced hands, and had been left alone. I had used the oars as best I could and rowed on; but the farther I went toward the center, the stronger became the current which carried me out of my course, and the oftener I met other navigators, like myself, carried away by the stream. There were here and there solitary navigators who had continued to row hard, there were others who had thrown down their oars, there were large boats, and enormous ships crowded with men; some struggled against the stream, others glided on with it. The farther I got, the more, as I watched the long line floating down the current, I forgot the course pointed out to me as my own.

In the very middle of the stream, amid the crowd of boats and vessels floating down, I had altogether lost the course and thrown down my oars. From all sides the joyful and exulting navigators, as they rowed or sailed down-stream, with one voice assured me and one another that there could be no other direction. And I believed them, and let myself go with them. I was carried far, so far that I heard the roar of the rapids in which I was bound to perish, and I already saw boats that had been broken up within them.

Then I came to myself. It was long before I clearly comprehended what had happened. I saw before me nothing but the destruction toward which I was hurrying, which I dreaded, and I saw no salvation and knew not what I was to do! But on looking back, I saw a countless multitude of boats engaged in a ceaseless struggle against the force of the torrent, and then I remembered all about the shore, the oars, and the course, and at once I began to row hard up the stream and again toward the shore.

That shore was God, that course was tradition, those oars were the free will given me to make for the shore to seek union with the Deity. . . .

The above was written by me three years ago.

The other day, on looking over this part again, on returning to the train of thought and to the feelings through which I had passed while writing it, I saw a dream.

This dream repeated for me in a condensed form all that I had lived through and described, and I therefore think that a description of it may, for those who have understood me, serve to render clearer, to refresh the remembrance of, and to collect into one whole, all that has been described at so much length in these pages. The dream was as follows.

I see myself lying in bed, and I feel neither particularly well and comfortable, nor the contrary. I am lying on my back. I begin to think whether it is well for me to lie, and something makes me feel uncomfortable in the legs; if the bed be too short or ill-made, I know not, but something is not right. I move my legs about, and at the same time begin to think how and on what I am lying, a thing which previously had never troubled me. I examine my bed, and see that I am lying on a network of cords fashioned to the sides of the bedstead. My heels lie on one of these cords, my legs on another, and this is uncomfortable. I am somehow aware that the cords can be moved, and with my legs I push the cords away, and it seems to me that thus it will be easier.

But I had pushed the cord too far; I tried to catch it with my legs, but this movement causes another cord to slip from under me, and my legs hang down. I move my body to get right again, convinced that it will be easy, but this movement causes other cords to slip and change their places beneath me, and I perceive that my position is altogether worse; my whole body sinks and hangs, without my legs touching the ground. I hold myself up only by the upper part of the back, and I feel now not only discomfort, but horror. I now begin to ask myself what I had not thought of before. I ask myself where I am, and on what I am lying. I begin to look round, and first I look below, to the place toward which my body sank, and where I feel it must soon fall. I look below, and I cannot believe my eyes.

I am on a height far above that of the highest tower or mountain, a height beyond all my previous powers of conception. I cannot even make out whether I see anything or not below me, in the depths of that bottomless abyss over which I am hanging, and into which I feel drawn. My heart ceases to beat, and horror fills my mind. To look down is horrible. I feel that if I look down I shall slip from the last cord, and perish. I stop looking, but not to look is still worse, for then I think of what will at once happen to me when the last cord breaks. I feel that I am losing, in my terror, the last remnant of my strength, and that my back is gradually sinking lower and lower. Another instant, and I shall fall.

Then all at once comes into my mind the thought that this cannot be true—it is a dream—I will awake.

I strive to wake myself, and cannot. "What can I do? what can I do?" I ask myself, and as I put the question I look above.

Above stretches another gulf. I look into this abyss of heaven, and try to forget the abyss below, and I do actually forget it. The infinite depth repels and horrifies me; the infinite height attracts and satisfies me. I still hang on the last cords which have not yet slipped from under me, over the abyss; I know that I am hanging thus, but I look only upwards, and my terror leaves me. As happens in dreams, I hear a voice saying, "Look well; it is there!" My eyes pierce farther and farther into the infinity above, and I feel that it calms me. I remember all that has happened, and I remember how it happened—how I moved my legs, how I was left hanging in air, how I was horrified, and how I was saved from my horror by looking above. I ask myself, "And now, am I not hanging still?" and I feel in all my limbs, without looking, the support by which I am held. I perceive that I no longer hang, and that I do not fall, but have a fast hold. I question myself how it is that I hold on. I touch myself, I look around, and I see that under the middle of my body there passes a stay, and on looking up I find that I am lying perfectly balanced, and that it was this stay alone that held me up before.

As happens in dreams, the mechanism by which I am supported appears perfectly natural to me, a thing to be easily understood, and not to be doubted, although this mechanism has no apparent sense when I am awake. In my sleep I was even astonished that I had not understood this before. At my bedside stands a pillar, the solidity of which is beyond doubt, though there is nothing for it to stand on. From this pillar runs a cord, somehow cunningly and at the same time simply fixed, and if I lie across this cord and look upward, there cannot be even a question of my falling. All this was clear to me, and I was glad and easy in my mind. It seemed as if some one said to me, "See that you remember!"

And I awoke.

William Booth
(1829–1912)

The awesome urban poverty of nineteenth-century England spawned William Booth and his international revival and relief movement, the Salvation Army. Booth himself was born in poverty; fatherless by the age of thirteen, he was apprenticed to a pawnbroker, a position he detested. He later spoke repeatedly of his "blighted childhood." The wretched conditions of industrial cities in England made a profound impression on Booth, and he was particularly moved by the suffering of children. If it had not been for his conversion in 1844, he probably would have become a labor union leader in Britain.

Instead, he committed his life to the saving of souls and the alleviation of human misery. At the age of twenty, he went to London and worked as a pawnbroker, using all his free time for preaching and evangelistic work. In 1855, he met Catherine Mumford, a woman who redirected his life and focused his ministry. She persuaded him to become a full-time Methodist preacher, but soon Booth's violent tactics in the pulpit ran afoul of Methodist sensibilities. He organized the East London Revival Society in 1865, known as the Christian Mission, and in 1878 it became the Salvation Army with General William Booth in command. Catherine Booth became her husband's most valued ally, his most persistent critic, and the genius behind many of the Army's successes. She was largely responsible for guaranteeing equality for women in the Army, and her better education compensated for her husband's woeful lack of it.

In 1890, Catherine Booth died, and General Booth published *In Darkest England and the Way Out*, a manual for reform of English society in terms of evangelism and social relief. Booth never wavered from insisting that saving souls came first, but he did call for employment bureaus, vocational training programs, farm colonies for the poor, rehabilitation centers for "lost women," legal assistance and bank services for the poor, and other social programs.

His son Bramwell was the organizational force behind the Salvation Army in England, and his daughter Evangeline brought the Army to Canada and the United States, where it expanded rapidly during the early twentieth century. The striking Army uniforms, the stirring Army hymns, and the rich brass of the Army bands drew the curious, the scoffers, and the committed, and the Army reached out with a message of repentance and salvation as well as physical assistance.

Booth himself had practically no interest in theology. He said that people were responsible for their sins and God was responsible for their salvation. It was as simple as that, but behind it was also Christian compassion for the poor and a protest against the forces that degraded human life. "The first step in saving outcasts," Booth declared, "consists in making them feel that some decent human being cares enough for them to take an interest in the question of whether they are to rise or sink." To that end, the Salvation Army marched, a legacy of the man who vowed that "if I did go in for God I would do so with all my might."

Excerpted from G. S. Railton, *The Authoritative Life of General Booth: Founder of the Salvation Army* (New York, 1912), 9-12.

When as a giddy youth of fifteen I was led to attend Wesley Chapel, Nottingham, I cannot recollect that any individual pressed me in the direction of personal surrender to God. I was wrought upon quite independently of human effort by the Holy Ghost, who created within me a great thirst for a new life.

I felt that I wanted, in place of the life of self-indulgence, to which I was yielding myself, a happy, conscious sense that I was pleasing God, living right, and spending all my powers to get others into such a life. I saw that all this ought to be, and I decided that it should be. It is wonderful that I should have reached this decision in view of all the influences then around me. My professedly Christian master never uttered a word to indicate that he believed in anything he could not see, and many of my companions were worldly and sensual, some of them even vicious.

Yet I had that instinctive belief in God which, in common with my fellow-creatures, I had brought into the world with me. I had no disposition to deny my instincts, which told me that if there was a God His laws ought to have my obedience and His interests my service.

I felt that it was better to live right than to live wrong, and as to caring for the interests of others instead of my own, the condition of the suffering people around me, people with whom I had been so long familiar, and whose agony seemed to reach its climax about this time, undoubtedly affected me very deeply.

There were children crying for bread to parents whose own distress was little less terrible to witness.

One feeling specially forced itself upon me, and I can recollect it as distinctly as though it had transpired only yesterday, and that was the sense of the folly of spending my life in doing things for which I knew I must either repent or be punished in the days to come.

In my anxiety to get into the right way, I joined the Methodist

Church, and attended the Class Meetings, to sing and pray and speak with the rest. . . . But all the time the inward Light revealed to me that I must not only renounce everything I knew to be sinful, but make restitution, so far as I had the ability, for any wrong I had done to others before I could find peace with God.

The entrance to the Heavenly Kingdom was closed against me by an evil act of the past which required restitution. In a boyish trading affair I had managed to make a profit out of my companions, whilst giving them to suppose that what I did was all in the way of a generous fellowship. As a testimonial of their gratitude they had given me a silver pencil-case. Merely to return their gift would have been comparatively easy, but to confess the deception I had practised upon them was a humiliation to which for some days I could not bring myself.

I remember, as if it were but yesterday, the spot in the corner of a room under the chapel, the hour, the resolution to end the matter, the rising up and rushing forth, the finding of the young fellow I had chiefly wronged, the acknowledgment of my sin, the return of the pencil-case— the instant rolling away from my heart of the guilty burden, the peace that came in its place, and the going forth to serve my God and my generation from that hour.

It was in the open street that this great change passed over me, and if I could only have possessed the flagstone on which I stood at that happy moment, the sight of it occasionally might have been as useful to me as the stones carried up long ago from the bed of the Jordan were to the Israelites who had passed over them dry-shod.

Since that night, for it was near upon eleven o'clock when the happy change was realised, the business of my life has been not only to make a holy character but to live a life of loving activity in the service of God and man. I have ever felt that true religion consists not only in being holy myself, but in assisting my Crucified Lord in His work of saving men and women, making them into His Soldiers, keeping them faithful to death, and so getting them into Heaven.

I have had to encounter all sorts of difficulties as I have travelled along this road. The world has been against me, sometimes very intensely, and often very stupidly. I have had difficulties similar to those of other men, with my own bodily appetites, with my mental disposition, and with my natural unbelief.

Many people, both religious and irreligious, are apt to think that they are more unfavourably constituted than their comrades and neighbours, and that their circumstances and surroundings are peculiarly un-friendly to the discharge of the duties they owe to God and man.

I have been no exception in this matter. Many a time I have been tempted to say to myself, "There is no one fixed so awkwardly for holy living and faithful fighting as I am." But I have been encouraged to resist the delusion by remembering the words of the Apostle Paul: "There hath no temptation taken you but such as is common to man."

I am not pretending to say that I have worked harder, or practised more self-denial, or endured more hardships at any particular time of my life than have those around me; but I do want those who feel any interest in me to understand that faithfulness to God in the discharge of duty and the maintenance of a good conscience have cost me as severe a struggle as they can cost any Salvation Soldier in London, Berlin, Paris, New York, or Tokio to-day.

One reason for the victory I daily gained from the moment of my conversion was, no doubt, my complete and immediate separation from the godless world. I turned my back on it. I gave it up, having made up my mind beforehand that if I did go in for God I would do so with all my might. Rather than yearning for the world's pleasures, books, gains, or recreations, I found my new nature leading me to come away from it all. It had lost all charm for me. What were all the novels, even those of Sir Walter Scott or Fenimore Cooper, compared with the story of my Saviour? What were the choicest orators compared with Paul? What was the hope of money-earning, even with all my desire to help my poor mother and sisters, in comparison with the imperishable wealth of ingathered souls? I soon began to despise everything the world had to offer me.

In those days I felt, as I believe many Converts do, that I could willingly and joyfully travel to the ends of the earth for Jesus Christ, and suffer anything imaginable to help the souls of other men. Jesus Christ had baptised me, according to His eternal promise, with His Spirit and with Fire.

Yet the surroundings of my early life were all in opposition to this whole-hearted devotion. No one at first took me by the hand and urged me forward, or gave me any instruction or hint likely to help me in the difficulties I had at once to encounter in my consecration to this service.

Francis Thompson
(1859–1907)

Although he wrote many poems and essays on English literature, Francis Thompson today is known primarily for just one poem, "The Hound of Heaven." Written in a somewhat florid style, the poem's imagery shifts between the familiar and the strange. Yet there is no mistaking the meaning and the personal involvement of the poet himself.

The message of the lines reminds us that God seeks us out, even when we try to hide, and that the divine initiative cannot be ignored. As the Psalmist expressed it — "Whither shall I go from thy Spirit? Or whither shall I flee from thy presence?" (Ps. 139:7).

Speaking out of his disordered and often futile existence, Thompson's poem reveals to us not only his own inner spiritual experience but something of every person's struggle to find meaning. Born into a Catholic family that had been influenced by the conversion of John Henry Newman, Francis hoped to become an ordinand for the priesthood but was rejected. His physician father persuaded him to study medicine but he failed his exams.

Taking off for London to find a new life, Thompson was ill-suited physically and emotionally for life in the big city. His mind was full of images, pictures, and fantasies, some of which he transcribed as poems. But to live, he worked as a shoe-black, a match-seller, and a cab-caller. He neglected his health, became undernourished, and, following the example of Thomas De Quincey, whom he admired, Thompson became an opium addict.

At the depths of his depression, he was befriended by members of the literary and compassionate Meynell family. Restored to some degree of health, though never completely cured of his habit, he worked from time to time for one or more of the Meynell journals.

"The Hound of Heaven" was written in 1891, although not published until four years later. In the meantime, Thompson took up residence at the Franciscan Monastery at Pantasaph in Wales. Here for a time he was at ease, reading and writing. But restless as ever, he returned to London where he died alone and forlorn.

Speaking out of the depths of despair, Thompson's poem recalls the shepherd searching for the lost sheep. And near the close of the poem, we read the words: "Rise, clasp My hand, and come." Perhaps Francis

Thompson was thinking of the gracious invitation of Jesus — "Come unto me, all ye that labour and are heavy laden, and I will give you rest" (Matt. 11:28).

The edition of the poem quoted here is *The Hound of Heaven*, with a Biographical Sketch and Notes, by Michael A. Kelly (Philadelphia: Peter Reilly, Publisher, 1916), 23-31.

I fled Him, down the nights and down the days;
  I fled Him, down the arches of the years;
I fled Him, down the labyrinthine ways
  Of my own mind; and in the mist of tears
I hid from Him, and under running laughter.
      Up vistaed hopes, I sped;
      And shot, precipitated,
Adown Titanic glooms of chasmèd fears,
  From those strong Feet that followed, followed
    after.
      But with unhurrying chase,
      And unperturbèd pace,
  Deliberate speed, majestic instancy,
      They beat—and a Voice beat
      More instant than the Feet—
  "All things betray thee, who betrayest Me."
    I pleaded, outlaw-wise,
By many a hearted casement, curtained red,
  Trellised with intertwining charities;
  (For, though I knew His love Who followed,
      Yet was I sore adread
Lest, having Him, I must have naught beside)
But, if one little casement parted wide,
  The gust of His approach would clash it to.
  Fear wist not to evade as Love wist to pursue.
Across the margent of the world I fled,
  And troubled the gold gateways of the stars,
  Smiting for shelter on their clangèd bars;
    Fretted to dulcet jars
And silvern chatter the pale ports o' the moon.
I said to dawn: Be sudden; to eve: Be soon—
  With thy young skyey blossoms heap me over
    From this tremendous Lover!
Float thy vague veil about me, lest He see!
  I tempted all His servitors, but to find
My own betrayal in their constancy,

In faith to Him their fickleness to me,
    Their traitorous trueness, and their loyal deceit.
To all swift things for swiftness did I sue;
    Clung to the whistling mane of every wind.
        But whether they swept, smoothly fleet,
        The long savannahs of the blue;
            Or whether, Thunder-driven,
        They clanged His chariot 'thwart a heaven,
Plashy with flying lightnings round the spurn o'
        their feet:—
    Fear wist not to evade as Love wist to pursue.
        Still with unhurrying chase,
        And unperturbèd pace,
    Deliberate speed, majestic instancy,
        Came on the following Feet,
        And a Voice above their beat—
    "Naught shelters thee, who wilt not shelter
    Me."

I sought no more that, after which I strayed,
        In face of man or maid;
But still within the little children's eyes
        Seems something, something that replies,
They, at least, are for me, surely for me!
I turned me to them very wistfully;
But just as their young eyes grew sudden fair
        With dawning answers there,
Their angel plucked them from me by the hair.
"Come then, ye other children, Nature's—share
With me" (said I) "your delicate fellowship;
        Let me greet you lip to lip,
        Let me twine with you caresses,
            Wantoning
        With our Lady-Mother's vagrant tresses,
            Banqueting
        With her in her wind-walled palace,
        Underneath her azured daïs,
        Quaffing, as your taintless way is,
            From a chalice
Lucent-weeping out of the dayspring."
        So it was done:
I, in their delicate fellowship was one—
Drew the bolt of Nature's secrecies.
        I knew all the swift importings

On the wilful face of skies;
I knew how the clouds arise,
Spumèd of the wild sea-snortings;
    All that's born or dies
Rose and drooped with; made them shapers
Of mine own moods, or wailful or divine—
    With them joyed and was bereaven.
    I was heavy with the even,
When she lit her glimmering tapers
Round the day's dead sanctities.
I laughed in the morning's eyes.
I triumphed and I saddened with all weather,
    Heaven and I wept together,
And its sweet tears were salt with mortal mine;
Against the red throb of its sunset-heart
    I laid my own to beat,
    And share commingling heat;
But not by that, by that, was eased my human smart.
In vain my tears were set on Heaven's grey cheek.
For ah! we know not what each other says,
    These things and I; in sound *I* speak—
Their sound is but their stir, they speak in silences.
Nature, poor stepdame, cannot slake my drought;
    Let her, if she would owe me,
Drop yon blue bosom-veil of sky, and show me
    The breasts o' her tenderness:
Never did any milk of hers once bless
    My thirsting mouth.
    Nigh and nigh, draws the chase,
    With unperturbèd pace,
Deliberate speed, majestic instancy,
    And past those noisèd Feet
    A Voice comes yet more fleet—
"Lo! naught contents thee, who content'st
not Me."

Naked I wait Thy love's uplifted stroke!
My harness piece by piece Thou hast hewn from me,
    And smitten me to my knee;
    I am defenceless utterly.
    I slept, methinks, and woke,
And, slowly gazing, find me stripped in sleep.
In the rash lustihead of my young powers,
    I shook the pillaring hours

And pulled my life upon me; grimed with smears,
I stand amid the dust o' the mounded years—
My mangled youth lies dead beneath the heap.
My days have crackled and gone up in smoke,
Have puffed and burst as sun-starts on a stream.
      Yea, faileth now even dream
The dreamer, and the lute the lutanist;
Even the linked fantasies, in whose blossomy twist
I swung the earth a trinket at my wrist,
Are yielding; cords of all too weak account
For earth, with heavy griefs so overplussed.
      Ah! is Thy love indeed
A weed, albeit an amaranthine weed,
Suffering no flowers except its own to mount?
        Ah! must—
        Designer infinite!—
Ah! must Thou char the wood ere Thou canst limn with it?
My freshness spent its wavering shower i' the dust;
And now my heart is as a broken fount,
Wherein tear-drippings stagnate, spilt down ever
      From the dank thoughts that shiver
Upon the sighful branches of my mind.
      Such is; what is to be?
The pulp so bitter, how shall taste the rind?
I dimly guess what Time in mists confounds;
Yet ever and anon a trumpet sounds
From the hid battlements of Eternity,
Those shaken mists a space unsettle, then
Round the half-glimpsèd turrets slowly wash again;
      But not ere Him Who summoneth
      I first have seen, enwound
With glooming robes purpureal, cypress-crowned;
His Name I know, and what His trumpet saith.
Whether man's heart or life it be which yields
      Thee harvest, must Thy harvest fields
      Be dunged with rotten death?
      Now of that long pursuit
      Comes on at hand the bruit;
That Voice is round me like a bursting sea:
      "And is thy earth so marred,
      Shattered in shard on shard?
Lo, all things fly thee, for thou fliest Me!

Strange, piteous, futile thing!
Wherefore should any set thee love apart?
Seeing none but I makes much of naught" (He said),
"And human love needs human meriting:
How hast thou merited—
Of all man's clotted clay the dingiest clot?
Alack, thou knowest not
How little worthy of any love thou art!
Whom wilt thou find to love ignoble thee,
Save Me, save only Me?
All which I took from thee I did but take,
Not for thy harms,
But just that thou might'st seek it in My arms.
All which thy child's mistake
Fancies as lost, I have stored for thee at home:
Rise, clasp My hand, and come."

Halts by me that footfall;
Is my gloom, after all,
Shade of His hand, outstretched caressingly?
"Ah, fondest, blindest, weakest,
I am He Whom thou seekest!
Thou dravest love from thee, who dravest Me."

Thérèse of Lisieux
(1873–1897)

St. Thérèse of Lisieux is another example of a very short life that left an enduring imprint on the Christian church. Through her autobiography, Thérèse captured the affection and admiration of people throughout the world for her simple faith and piety in everyday life. Early in her own life, she declared, "I want to be a saint," and to that goal she devoted all her energies. Pope Pius X described her as "the greatest saint of modern times."

She was born Marie Françoise Thérèse Martin, the youngest of nine children, in Alencon, France. Her father was a prosperous watchmaker, her mother a craftswoman. Thérèse's mother died when she was four, a devastating experience for the little girl, but she soon demonstrated a precocious religiosity, as did two of her sisters, Marie and Pauline, who became Carmelite nuns. Always a sickly child, at 10 Thérèse was stricken with a disease that included a combination of convulsions, hallucinations, and comas. After three months, she was cured by what Thérèse believed was a miraculous intervention of the Virgin Mary.

She called the period between the death of her mother and her conversion her "winter of trial," and her conversion marked a new level of religious and emotional maturity. She wanted to enter the Carmelite convent at Lisieux, but she was initially turned down because of her youth. After a pilgrimage to Rome with her father and after entreating the bishop, Thérèse was finally admitted to the convent in 1888, two years after her conversion. In 1889 she was admitted to the order and in 1893 became assistant to the mistress of novices. She was persuaded to write her autobiography The Story of a Soul in 1895, which became after her death a worldwide best-seller.

The Lisieux convent was badly divided during her lifetime, but Thérèse remained distant from the political disputes, practicing what she called her "little Way," a childlike submission to the will of God in all things. She suffered from tuberculosis but continued her monastic regimen until six months before her death. Hospitalized in the infirmary, she endured great pain and confessed, "I did not think it was possible to suffer so much." Her last words were, "My God, I love you."

In the wake of her tremendously popular autobiography, Thérèse became an especially revered figure among ordinary Catholics. Calling her growing fame "a hurricane of glory," Pius XI waived the traditional fifty-year waiting period and canonized her in 1925. As he paid tribute to her, the Pope said that she had achieved sanctity "without going beyond the common order of things," and in this simple, direct, and practical piety lies the heart of Thérèse's appeal for the twentieth century.

Excerpted from The Autobiography of St. Thérèse of Lisieux: The Story of a Soul, trans. John Beevers (Garden City, N.Y.: Doubleday, 1957), 62-67. Reprinted by permission of Doubleday & Co.

It was on December 25, 1886, that I received the grace of emerging from childhood—the grace of my complete conversion. We went to midnight Mass where I had the joy of receiving almighty God. When we got home again, I was excited at the thought of my shoes standing, full of presents, in the fireplace. When we were small children, this old custom gave us such delight that Céline wanted to continue treating me like a baby as I was the youngest in the family. Daddy used to love to see my happiness and hear my cries of joy as I pulled out each surprise from the magic shoes, and the delight of my beloved King increased my own. But as Jesus wanted to free me from the faults of childhood, He also took away its innocent pleasures. He arranged matters so that Daddy was irritated at seeing my shoes in the fireplace and spoke about them in a way which hurt me very much: "Thank goodness it's the last time we shall have this kind of thing!" I went upstairs to take off my hat. Céline knew how sensitive I was. She said: "Thérèse, don't go downstairs again. Taking the presents out of your shoes will upset you too much." But Thérèse was not the same girl. Jesus had changed her. I suppressed my tears, ran downstairs, and picked up my shoes. I pulled out my presents with an air of great cheerfulness. Daddy laughed and Céline thought she was dreaming! But it was no dream. Thérèse had got back for good the strength of soul which she had lost when she was four and a half. On this glorious night the third period of my life began. It has been the loveliest of them all and the one richest with heavenly graces. Jesus, satisfied with my goodwill, accomplished in an instant what I had been unable to do in ten years. Like the apostles, we could say: "Master, I have toiled all the night, and caught nothing." Jesus was more merciful to me than to His disciples. He Himself took the net, cast it, and drew it up full of fishes. He made me a fisher of men. I longed to work for the conversion of sinners with a passion I'd never felt before. Love filled my heart, I forgot myself and henceforth I was happy.

One Sunday when I was looking at a picture of Our Lord on the Cross, I saw the Blood coming from one of His hands, and I felt terribly sad to think that It was falling to the earth and that no one was rushing forward to catch it. I determined to stay continually at the foot of the Cross and receive It. I knew that I should then have to spread It among other souls. The cry of Jesus on the Cross—"I am thirsty"—rang continually in my heart and set me burning with a new, intense longing. I wanted to quench the thirst of my Well-Beloved and I myself was consumed with a thirst for souls. I was concerned not with the souls of priests but with those of great sinners which I wanted to snatch from the flames of hell.

God showed me He was pleased with these longings of mine. I'd heard of a criminal who had just been condemned to death for some frightful murders. It seemed that he would die without repenting. I was determined at all costs to save him from hell. I used every means I could. I knew that by myself I could do nothing, so I offered God the infinite merits of Our Lord and the treasures of the Church. I was quite certain that my prayers would be answered, but to give me courage to go on praying for sinners I said to God: "I am sure You will forgive this wretched Pranzini. I shall believe You have done so even if he does not confess or give any other sign of repentance, for I have complete faith in the infinite mercy of Jesus. But I ask You for just one sign of his repentance to encourage me."

This prayer was answered. Daddy never allowed us to read any newspapers, but I thought I was justified in looking at the stories about Pranzini. On the day after his execution I eagerly opened *La Croix* and I had to rush away to hide my tears at what I read. Pranzini had mounted the scaffold without confessing and was ready to thrust his head beneath the guillotine's blade when he suddenly turned, seized the crucifix offered him by the priest, and thrice kissed the Sacred Wounds.

I had been given my sign, and it was typical of the graces Jesus has given me to make me eager to pray for sinners. It was at the sight of the Precious Blood flowing from the Wounds of Jesus that my thirst for souls had been born. I wanted to let them drink of this Immaculate Blood to cleanse them of their sins and the lips of my "first child" had pressed against the Sacred Wounds! What a wonderful reply to my prayers! After this striking favour my longing for souls grew greater every day. I seemed to hear Jesus say to me what He said to the Samaritan Woman: "Give me to drink." It was a real exchange of love: I gave souls the Blood of Jesus and offered Him these purified souls that His thirst might be quenched. The more I gave Him to drink, the more the thirst of my own poor soul increased, and He gave me this burning thirst to show His love for me.

In a short time God had lifted me out of the narrow circle in which I'd been going round and round, quite unable to escape from it. When I see the road He has made me tread, I am profoundly grateful, but it was essential that I should be fit for it, and though I'd made the first and greatest step along it, there still remained much for me to do. Now I was rid of my scruples and my excessive sensitiveness, my mind began to develop. All that was great and lovely had always appealed to me, but now I was gripped by an intense desire for learning. I wasn't satisfied with the lessons of Madame Papineau. I began working on my own at history and science. Other subjects didn't attract me at all, but I loved these two and I learnt more in a few months than in all the years before.

I was at the most dangerous time of life for young girls, but God did for me what Ezechiel recounts: Passing by me, Jesus saw that I was ripe for love. He plighted His troth to me and I became His. He threw His cloak about me, washed me with water and anointed me with oil, clothed me in fine linen and silk, and decked me with bracelets and priceless gems. He fed me on wheat and honey and oil and I had matchless beauty and He made me a great queen. Jesus did all that for me. I could go over every word of what I've just written and show how they applied to me, but the graces I've spoken about before are proof enough. All I'm going to write of now is the food Our Lord gave me so abundantly. For a long time I'd been fed on the wheat of *The Imitation*. It was the only book which did me any good, as I hadn't discovered the treasures of the Gospels. I knew every chapter by heart. I was never without this little book. My aunt often used to open it at random and I would recite whatever chapter appeared. When I was fourteen and had this passion for learning, God added honey and oil to the wheat of *The Imitation*. I found this honey and oil in Father Arminjon's book, *The End of this World and the Mysteries of the Future Life*. Reading it was one of the greatest graces I've known. All the great truths of religion and the secrets of eternity were there and filled my soul with a happiness not of this world. I saw already what God has in store for those who love Him. When I realised how trifling are the sacrifices of this life compared with the rewards of heaven, I wanted to love Jesus, to love Him passionately, and to give Him a thousand tokens of my love whilst I still could.

Céline shared my intimate thoughts. Since Christmas we understood each other perfectly. As Jesus wanted us to go forward together, He united us with bonds stronger than those of blood. He made us sisters in spirit, and we fulfilled those words of our Father, St. John of the Cross: "The young girls run gaily along the path in the track of Your footsteps. The touch of the spark and the spiced wine gives them longings for the Divine." We did indeed follow gaily in the footsteps of Jesus. The sparks of love He cast so generously into our souls and the strong, sweet wine He made us drink swept all the transient things of earth from our gaze and we breathed out words of love inspired by Him.

What wonderful talks we had every evening in our upstairs room! As we gazed out we saw the moon rise slowly above the trees and its silvery light pour over the sleeping world. The stars glittered in the dark blue of the sky and here and there a cloud drifted along blown by the night breeze. Everything drew our souls upwards to heaven. I think we were given many graces. As *The Imitation* says, God sometimes reveals Himself "in great light" or "appears veiled under signs and figures," and it was in this way that He disclosed Himself to us. But how light and transparent was the veil which hid Jesus from our eyes! Doubt wasn't possible and faith and hope were no longer needed, for love made us find on earth Him we sought: "When we were alone, He gave us His kiss, and now no one may despise us."

Such tremendous graces had to bear fruit and it was abundant. To be good became natural and pleasant for us. At first my face often betrayed the struggle I was having, but gradually spontaneous self-sacrifice came easily. Jesus said: "If ever a man is rich, gifts will be made to him, and his riches will abound." For every grace I made good use of, He gave me many more. He gave Himself to me in Holy Communion far oftener than I should have dared to hope. I had made it a rule to go very faithfully to every Communion allowed me by my confessor, but never to ask him to allow me more. In those days I hadn't the daring I have now, or I should have behaved quite differently, for I'm absolutely certain that people must tell their confessors of the longing they have to receive God. For He does not come down from heaven every day to lie in a golden ciborium: He comes to find another heaven which is infinitely dearer to Him—the heaven of our souls, created in His image, the living temples of the adorable Trinity!

Jesus, who saw what I wanted, moved my confessor to allow me to receive Holy Communion several times a week. I never said a word about what was going on in my soul. The path I trod was so bright and straight that I felt I needed no guide but Jesus. I considered spiritual directors were like mirrors which faithfully reflected the light of Jesus into souls, but I thought that God needed no intermediary where I was concerned. He dealt with me direct!

When a gardener takes trouble over fruit he wants to ripen early, it isn't because he wants to leave them hanging on the tree, but because he wants them to appear on a richly appointed table. It was the same reason that made Jesus shower His favours on His little flower. During His days on earth He exclaimed in a transport of joy: "I give thee praise that thou hast hidden all this from the wise and prudent, and revealed it to little children." As He wished to make His mercy evident through me and as I was small and weak, He stooped down to me and secretly taught me the secrets of His love. If scholars who had spent their lives in study had questioned me, I'm sure they'd have been amazed to come across a four-teen-year-old child who understood the secrets of perfection, secrets which all their learning couldn't reveal to them, for one has to be poor in spirit to understand them. As St. John of the Cross says: "I had neither guide nor light, except that which shone within my heart, and that guided me more surely than the midday sun to the place where He who knew me well awaited me." That place was Carmel, but before I could lie in the "shade cool to rest under" I had to go through many trials. Yet the divine call was so urgent that, if necessary, I'd have plunged through flames to follow Jesus.

Henrietta Gant

(1868?–?)

One of the least-known chapters of American religious history is the story of how African slaves and their descendants were converted to Christianity. But we have journals and diaries of ministers and missionaries who worked among the slaves, and there are some autobiographies and memoirs of black preachers and leaders, giving some evidence of the growth of Christianity among Afro-Americans.

The best recent account of the rise of Afro-American Christianity is contained in Albert J. Raboteau's *Slave Religion: The "Invisible Institution" in the Antebellum South* (New York: Oxford University Press, 1978). Raboteau makes extensive use of black sources, including a remarkable collection of interviews conducted under the Federal Writers' Project during the New Deal of the 1930s. These interviews, virtually ignored by historians until recently, provide a rich source for uncovering the life of black Americans during the nineteenth century.

The following conversion account concerns Henrietta Gant, who was interviewed in 1939 in Louisiana. At the conclusion of her account, the interviewer described her as follows: "Henrietta is small, rather stockily built, neatly dressed in black. She wore an old black hat and carried an old figured knitted bag. She wears glasses and looks to be well in her seventies, although she says she is sixty-one."

What is clear from Henrietta Gant's description of her conversion, and what emerges from the studies of black Christianity, is that Africans in America adopted Christianity but combined it with themes and traditions from their own tribal religions and culture. The final product was Afro-American Christianity, a faith clearly Christian but with emphases rooted in African religious life. It was also a faith that gave hope in the midst of despair, promising freedom despite enslavement and oppression. Too often the Christianity they heard about from whites emphasized the virtues of submission and obedience. Afro-American Christianity testifies to the power of the gospel to go beyond the expected and to break through the sinfulness and inadequacy of those who proclaim it.

The original text of this interview is located in the Federal Writers' Project Collection, Archives Division, Northwestern State University, Natchitoches, Louisiana, and is reprinted here with permission. The assistance

of Randall M. Miller, St. Joseph's University, Philadelphia, and of Carol
Wells, Archives Division of Northwestern State University, in securing the
text is hereby gratefully acknowledged. The text is reproduced as it was
transcribed by the interviewer.

It took me a long time to get religion. I said when ah got religion,
ah would be finished with the world, an' that there would be no backslidin'.
Ahm 61. Ah made 61 on the 6th of last month, an' Ahse only bin a member
of the church 22 years, but Ah ain't never fell away, an' Ah never bin called
up to the Board, or sot back, since Ah bin a christian.

Ah was born an raised here, but Ah got religion on Bayou Lafourche.
My husband was cuttin' cane in the field there, an' Ah went to Bayou
Lafourche to him. When Ah was there, ah started to pray for my religion.
Ah went off by myself an' Ah jest talked to God by myself. It took me a
long time to get religion but when He did give it to me, He did everything
but kill me. Ah prayed about 3 weeks, but Ah was converted in one week.
Ah wanted Him to come an' talk to me. Ah wanted Him to talk to me, to
sit down an' talk like we's talkin'. He didn't do that, but He appeared to
me. He came to me in a cloud, an' He jest kep bowin' to me an' welcomin'
me. The clouds opened an' it was jest like a little ball about that big (extending her hand showing the size of the ball) appeared in the clouds. He
was dressed in a little blue uniform with gold buttons, an' a blue girdle an'
sash. He looked at me jest like Ahm lookin' at you. Ah was so frightened,
Ah didn't know what to do. Did Ah cry? Ah wouldn't ask you those
words—Then he appeared to me again in a chariot. He had on that same
blue uniform an' He was in a gold chariot with diamonds in it. An' it was
pulled by six white horses. It looked like He had wings on his back. He
was sittin' on the edge of the chariot, an' He bowed an' beckoned to me,
to make me understand it was Him, an' He was callin' me. He was welcomin' me home, an' you know with all that, Ah didn't believe Ah was
converted. So Ah told the Lord, Ah sez, "If Ahm really a christian, make
the sun shout to me 3 times."

Well, Ah was by myself, my husband was out in the field yet, an'
Ah bin prayin' all day, an' it was about 6 o'clock in the evenin' an' the sun
had gone behind the clouds. An' Ah said, "Father, let the sun come out,
an' shout three times, an' shout three times, an' shout three times." Well,
do you know somethin', that whole day sun jest ris outa those clouds, an'
it shouted to me three times. It bowed to me, an' then it went back in the
clouds. That didn't convert me.

Den after that, Ah asked Him what He will have me to do. Ah was
sittin' down in the house jest like Ahm sittin' here, then Ah heard a knock
at the door, an' Ah went out, an' there was a nurse standin' at the door,
dressed like the ones at Tero. This lady come an' said, "Henrietta, you will
have to come on duty, an' you'll have to be in uniform." An' Ah sez to

her, "Ah can't go with you, 'cause where am Ah gonna get a uniform like you got?" She sez, "It's right here." Ah went in the back room, an' Ah looked in the mirror, an' Ah was all shrouded in white, shoes an' stockings an' everything, just like she has. She said, "Let's go," and we walked outa the house together an' we went to another house, an' there was a mother an' father in one bed, sick, an' the son and daughter in another bed, sick. She said, "Ah want you to heal these people, an' you got to stay here until you heals them. You gotta stay here an' heal them children in the bed." An when Ah turned around an' said, "With what?" she was gone. Ah didn't know what to do, 'cause Ah ain't never healed nobody in my life, so Ah jest rubbed them with my naked hands, an' they gotta outa bed an' walked. An' they said, "You got the most beautifullest talent that ever was seen."

That woman was my gospel-mother. Your gospel-mother is somebody God sends for you. Someone you travel with, in your visions. It's somebody in the church, but He sends them to you an' then they your gospel-mother. They pray with you an' take care of you. It took a long time for me to be converted, but Ah got it to stay, haven't Ah?

Well, when the Spirit really got on me, it was between half past 3 an' a quarter to 4 in the mornin'. Ah got up at 12 o'clock an' prayed an' ah said to God, "Convert me." At 4 o'clock, the minister of the Baptist Church in the country on Bayou Lafourche, came to my door with the Late Mole, the deacon of the church. He worked in the field, he was an overseer. They stopped in from of my doah with a gray mare, an' the minister said, "Ah come to get you to baptise you," they carried me to the bayou an' back, an' they put me under the water. No they didn't take me on the mare, they carried me in the buggy. The mare was hitched to the buggy. Ah screamed so, 'till Ah woke up the whole place. Ah woke up everybody in the quarters, even my husband. They didn't do nothing to me, they jest said, "She's got religion." Ah don't know how long the Spirit stayed on me, 'cause Ah never tried to minite myself, an' Ah jest don't know how long. When that Spirit hit me, Ah jest saw a light lit. You talk about shoutin'—when Ah told my conversion, that church really shouted for me. An' when they dipped me in that water, there was plenty more shoutin'.

Ah wasn't baptised in Bayou Lafourche, 'cause Ah told the Lord that whatever church Ah would be baptised in, Ah would join, an' Ahd stay with that church. An' Ah asked Him to show me, or to send someone to tell me, what church to jine. Well, it was one Sunday night in the month of December, an' it was cold. Ah was sittin' in the church an' Ah told the Lord, "If this is the church for me, take me outa my seat with your will power an' send me to the rostrum." You know what He did—He jest stood me up an' took me outa my seat, an' when Ah come to, Ah found myself standin' in the rostrum. They say that Ah shouted so much when the preacher was preachin' that Ah stopped the man from preachin'. Ah lost my handkerchief, an' haven't found it to this day. An' if my sister hadn't bin sittin' by me an' taken it for me, Ah wouldn't have it to this day. If you'd give me this world full of money to tell you where that handkerchief went that night, Ah wouldn't be able to tell you. Ah was baptised in St. John's Church on First between Ferret and Howard, an' Ah bin a member there since. An' that's 22 years ago. No Ah never bin on no Board. Rev. Taylor, that's our pastor, always says to me, "Ah don't see why you haven't bin on the Board." An' Ah sez, "Ah guards the meetin'." Ah don't wanta be on no Board, 'cause sometimes they provoke you so on those Boards, that they make you commit yourself. You got so much to contend with on the Board. Rev. Taylor is sho a good man. He's a wonderful minister. Ah says he's a child, 'cause Ahm so old, he's a child under me. You know he's good, 'cause we baptises every month in the year.

You gotta pray for something to get the spirit. An' when Ah prayed Ah wasn't near the church. You know the quarters on the plantation, well, the church is way aroun' on the front, an', of course, it was too far, an' Ah jest prayed in my house. Ah didn't sing no hymn when the Spirit hit me, Ah jest shouted. Ah screamed an' hollared, an' Ah sho' cried. You jest get so sorry you cry an' cry an' cry. The Spirit of God makes you jump benches, an' they never hurts themselves. Ah never jumps, Ah jests runs an' shouts an' hollars. But now, Ah stop runnin'.

Ah went to a white house on the hill an' the Host of Heaven sin, "Why should we start an' fear to die?" The doors of that white house on the hill opened an' the Lord was standin' there. He laid me on a table, jest like a doctor. The Father, the Son and the Mother were there an' they was all dressed in white. Her hair, was so shinin' gold, that you couldn't look at her. An' She put her hand out, an' it glittered like diamonds. It glittered so you couldn't look at it. She was beautiful. He's got a different resemblance to anyone Ahve ever seen. Ah don't know how to tell you how He looks. The Father, Son and Mother didn't say a word to me. The Lord jest put me on that table an' operated on me. He took my heart out, scraped it, put it back, an' it dripped 3 drops of blood. The 3 drops was the healin' power. The the Mother turned to me an' she said, "Why did you come?" Ah said, "Ah come to work." An' she said, "You could mind these little children, your work is finished. There is nothin' for you to do." She took me in another room an' it was filled with little children. They was all dressed in white with crowns on their heads. Dat was to show me that Ah was a teacher for Sabbath school. You see the Lord shows you what you cut out to be. Ah used to teach Sabbath school but Ah give it up since Ahm gettin' old. The only time Ah don't come to get my communion is when Ahm sick.

Ah bin sick since New Year's Eve night. Ah was comin' from work, Ah does washin' an' ironin' at 3018 Monroe Street, Ah was gettin' off the bus on Washington Ave. an' Ah was filled with bundles, an' somebody knocked me down an' took my purse. Ah had $25.19 in my purse an'

$15.19 belonged to the church. An' Ah gotta put the money that belonged to the church back. That was the drive money, not Sunday School money. Ahm jest able to go out now an' do some work, an' all Ah make Ahm savin' to pay back for the church. Ah don't know who knocked me down, but they took everythin' Ah had. Ah had to have the doctor, an' my sister thought Ah was gonna die. Ah still can't walk so good. The doctor said the reason Ah was so sick was Ah was sufferin' from shock, Ah was so nervous. Sunday was the first time Ah took communion in the church since before the New Year's 'cause Ah bin too sick to go. Ah got well, 'cause Ah trust the Lord.

If you trust the Lord, for one thing, you trust Him for all. An' Ah really trust Him, Ah really does that. If you don't trust him you don't have Faith. An' there's nothin' in life if you don't have Faith. Ahm tellin' you, religion is better felt than it ever was told. An' if you felt always like you does the day you baptise you would sho' die. When you baptise you jest sits an waits, an' when your time comes, they ties a band aroun' your haid, an' they tie you up aroun' your legs. You sho' feels funny. Jest so happy you can't wait for your time to come. You feels like you could leap over walls an' run through troops. Ah don't remember nothin' when Ah was baptised. Ah don't know a thing. They tells me Ah shouted so when they dipped me, they could hardly hold me. It was on the 31 of December an Ishickles was hangin' from the trees. An' Ah took my coat off an' Ah give it to my sister an' Ah walked home in that drippin' gown an' Ah never caught cold that Ah knows of. Ah didn't eat nothin' that whole day—Ah didn't even take coffee—an' Ahm crazy about coffee, coffee is my whiskey. An' that night when they welcomed you in the church, an' gives you the righthand fellowship, Ah shouted so that Ah had the whole church shoutin'. Ahm tellin' you religion is the most wonderfullest thin' in this world.

Wese havin' a revival at 12 o'clock every day to get souls for Easter. We sings in our church

He Will Understand

If when you give the best of your service
Telling the world that the Savior has gone
Be not desolate if men don't believe you
He will understand and say well done

If when you give, then enter my journey
Wearied of night and the battle is won
Carry the staff and cross of redemption
He will understand and say well done.

Ah got to go out an' get me somethin' to eat before Ah got to the revival so Ah can't talk to you any longer, but if you come back some other time Ahl be glad to talk with you, 'cause Ah always like to talk about religion. Ah never gets tired doin' that.

Billy Sunday
(1862–1935)

Some thought he should have stuck to baseball or gone into the circus. But others, maybe as many as one hundred million, listened and watched with rapt attention as Billy Sunday belted out the gospel, punched sin in the nose, and thundered against the saloons.

In an age of famous revivalists and mass evangelism in tents and tabernacles, Billy Sunday developed his own distinctive style. Born into poverty in farmland Iowa, William Ashley Sunday joined the Chicago White Sox baseball team when he was about twenty and almost immediately seemed on his way to stardom. He excelled as a base runner, reportedly making the trip around the bases in fourteen seconds. He once won a game by stealing second, third, and home plate on three successive pitches.

But Billy got religion, and his conversion not only changed his life but his career. The baseball evangelist became an itinerant revivalist known all across the country. With his musical accompanist, Homer Rodeheaver and his slide trombone, Billy Sunday tantalized enormous crowds, huddled together in hastily built wooden tabernacles. He was a born actor with an instinctive sense of the dramatic, a flair for local street-talk, and an uncanny ability to scare the daylights out of sinners. Lacking formal education, Billy Sunday invented his own down-to-earth preaching style, punctuated with lots of body language. "If the English language gets in my way," he said, "I tramp all over it." As for sin, he said he would "kick it as long as I've got a foot, and I'll fight it as long as I've got a fist. I'll butt it as long as I've got a head. I'll bite it as long as I've got a tooth."

There was a serious, no-nonsense side to Billy Sunday. He worked for the YMCA, was ordained a Presbyterian minister, made generous donations to charities, and advocated racial equality, women's suffrage, and sex education in the public schools.

A colorful figure, he made people laugh, and when they did, he said, he shoved the gospel down their throats when their mouths were open. If for some it seemed an unconventional method, for hundreds of others it worked.

This account of Billy Sunday's conversion is taken from a newspaper report of one of his sermons in The Boston Herald, Dec. 4, 1916.

Twenty-nine years ago I walked down a street in Chicago in company with some ball players who were famous in this world (some of them are dead now), and we went into a saloon.

It was Sunday afternoon and we got tanked up and then went and sat down on a corner. I never go by that street without thanking God for saving me. It was a vacant lot at that time.

We sat down on a curbing. Across the street a company of men and women were playing on instruments—horns, flutes and slide trombones—and the others were singing the gospel hymns that I used to hear my mother sing back in the old church, where I used to go to Sunday school.

And God painted on the canvas of my recollection and memory a vivid picture of the scenes of other days and other faces.

Many have long since turned to dust. I sobbed and sobbed, and a young man stepped out and said:

"We are going to the Pacific Garden Mission; won't you come down to the mission? I am sure you will enjoy it. You can hear drunkards tell how they have been saved and girls tell how they have been saved from the red light district."

I arose and said to the boys:

"I'm through. I am going to Jesus Christ. We've come to the parting of the ways," and I turned my back on them. Some of them laughed and some of them mocked me; one of them gave me encouragement, others never said a word.

Twenty-nine years ago I turned and left that little group on the corner of State and Madison streets and walked to the little mission and fell on my knees and staggered out of sin and into the arms of the Savior.

I went over to the West Side of Chicago, where I was keeping company with a girl, now my wife, Nell. I married Nell. She was a Presbyterian, so I am a Presbyterian. If she had been a Catholic I would have been a Catholic—because I was hot on the trail of Nell.

The next day I had to go out to the ball park and practice. Every morning at 10 o'clock we had to be out there and practice. I never slept that night. I was afraid of the horse-laugh that gang would give me because I had taken my stand for Jesus Christ.

I walked down to the old ball grounds. I will never forget it, I slipped my key into the wicket gate and the first man to meet me after I got inside was Mike Kelley.

Up came Mike Kelley. He said, "Bill, I'm proud of you. Religion is not my long suit, but I'll help you all I can."

Up came Anson, the best ball player that ever played the game; Pfeffer, Clarkson, Flint, Jimmy McCormick, Burns, Williamson, and Dalrymple. There wasn't a fellow in the gang who knocked; every fellow had a word of encouragement for me.

That afternoon we played the old Detroit club. We were neck and neck for the championship. That club had Thompson, Richardson, Rowe, Dunlap, Hanlon, and Bennett, and they could play ball.

I was playing right field. Mike Kelley was catching and John G. Clarkson was pitching. He was as fine a pitcher as ever crawled into a uniform. There are some pitchers today—O'Toole, Bender, Wood, Mathewson, Johnson, Marquard—but I do not believe any one of them stood in the class with Clarkson. . . .

We had two men out and they had a man on second and one on third, and Bennett, their old catcher, was at bat. Charley had three balls and two strikes on him. Charley didn't hit a high ball. I don't mean a Scotch highball; but he could kill them when they went about his knee.

I hollered to Clarkson and said: "One more and we got 'em."

You know every pitcher puts a hole in the ground where he puts his foot when he is pitching. John stuck his foot in the hole and he went clear to the ground.

Oh, he could make them dance. He could throw overhanded, and the ball would go down and up like that. He is the only man on earth I have seen do that. That ball would go by so fast that the batter could feel the thermometer drop two degrees as she whizzed by.

John went clear down, and as he went to throw the ball his right foot slipped and the ball went low instead of high.

I saw Charley swing hard and heard the bat hit the ball with a terrific boom. Bennett had smashed the ball on the nose. I saw the ball rise in the air and knew that it was going to clear over my head.

I could judge within 10 feet of where the ball would light. I turned my back to the ball and ran.

The field was crowded with people and I yelled; "Stand back!" and that crowd opened like the Red Sea opened for the rod of Moses.

I ran on and as I ran I made a prayer, it wasn't theological either, I tell you that. I said: "God, if you ever helped mortal man, help me to get that ball, and you haven't very much time to make up your mind, either."

I ran and jumped over the bench and stopped.

I thought I was close enough to catch it. I looked back and I saw it going over my head and I jumped and shoved out my left hand and the ball hit it and stuck.

At the rate I was going the momentum carried me on and I fell under the feet of a team of horses. I jumped up with the ball in my hand. Up came Tom Johnson. Tom used to be mayor of Cleveland.

"Here is $10, Bill. Buy yourself the best hat in Chicago. That catch won me $1500. Tomorrow go and buy yourself the best suit of clothes you can find in Chicago."

An old Methodist minister said to me a few years ago: "Why, William, you didn't take the $10 did you?" I said:

"You bet your life I did!"

Frank Flint, our old catcher, who caught for 19 years, drew $3200 a year on an average. He caught before they had chest protectors, masks and gloves.

I've seen old Frank Flint sleeping on a table in a stale beer joint, and I've turned my pockets inside out and said: "You're welcome to it, old pal."

He drank on and on and one day in winter he staggered out of a stale beer joint and stood on a corner, and was seized with a fit of coughing. The blood streamed out of his nose, mouth and eyes.

Down the street came a wealthy women. She took one look and said: "My God, is it you, Frank?" and his wife came up and kissed him. "They telephoned me and I came." He said: "There's nothing in the life of years ago I care for now. I can hear the bleachers cheer when I make a hit that wins the game. But there is nothing that can help me out now; and if the umpire calls me out now won't you say a few words over me, Bill?" Then he died.

He sat on the street corner with me drunk 29 years ago in Chicago, when I said: "Goodbye, boys, I'm through."

Men of Boston, did they win the game of life or did I?

W. T. Grenfell
(1865–1940)

College students on summer internships in Labrador used to quip about "non-sequitur Grenfell." Not one to bother about stringing two coherent sentences together, Sir Wilfred's life spoke consistently and eloquently for his unwavering commitment to the Christian gospel.

Born in Parkgate, Cheshire, England, Wilfred T. Grenfell went to Oxford and received a medical degree from the London Hospital. At a casual visit to an evangelistic meeting one night in 1885, he was much taken by a speaker who turned out to be the American evangelist Dwight L. Moody. Grenfell was converted and decided to devote his life to medical missions in the Labrador north seas area.

He established the Royal National Mission to Deep Sea Fishermen and launched the first hospital ship to serve that whole vast region of barren lands and stormy seas. The record of his mission reads like fiction. He founded homes and orphanages, hospitals and nursing stations, co-operative stores and agricultural farms. Knighted in 1927 and the recipient of numerous honorary degrees, Grenfell was known and loved all along the Labrador and Newfoundland coasts.

On furloughs to Britain and America, he rallied support for his northern missions and became a symbol everywhere of adventuresome Christian witness. His Christianity was a robust and athletic variety. A vigorously physical, outdoors type, Grenfell believed in rolling up his sleeves and going to work, whether it was deep sea fishing or preaching the gospel.

A prolific author of missionary stories, he also wrote two autobiographies, A *Labrador Doctor* (1920) and *Forty Years for Labrador* (1932). In a curious twist of geography, Wilfred Grenfell was doing in Labrador very much what Albert Schweitzer was doing at the same time in Lambaréné, Africa. In 1935, the two great medical missionaries of our time met in Edinburgh where Schweitzer was delivering the Gifford Lectures.

Grenfell's conversion is narrated in his book, *What Christ Means to Me* (Boston: Houghton Mifflin, 1930), 29-124. Copyright © 1927 by Wilfred T. Grenfell. Copyright renewed 1954 by K. Pascoe Grenfell, Rosamond Grenfell Shaw and Wilfred T. Grenfell. Reprinted by permission of Houghton Mifflin Co.

One evening in 1883, going down a dark street in Shadwell on my way from a maternity case, I passed a great tent, something like a circus.

A crowd had gathered and I looked in to see what was going on. An aged man was praying on the platform before an immense audience. The length of the prayer bored me, and I started to leave as he droned on. At that moment a vivacious person near him jumped up and shouted: "Let us sing a hymn while our brother finishes his prayer." Unconventionality, common sense, or humor in anything "religious" was new to me. Brawling, or disturbing the order or ritual is criminal in the Established Church. Someone said the interrupter was the speaker of the evening so I stayed to hear him. I did not know anything about the man, nor did I see him again till fourteen years later, but he left a new idea in my mind, the idea that loyalty to a living Leader was religion, and that knightly service in the humblest life was the expression of it. His illustrations were all from our own immediate environment, much as Christ's were, and the whole thing was so simple and human it touched everyone's heart. Religion, as the speaker put it, was chivalry, not an insurance ticket. Life was a field of honour calling for courage to face it, not a tragedy to escape from. Christ's call was to follow Him, not to recognize, much less to comprehend, Him. What Christ asked us for was reasonable service, or the service of our reason—but real hard service either way. His religion was a challenge, not a sop or dope. The whole talk was of a living Leader of men.

The preacher was an ordinary looking layman, and I listened all the more keenly because I felt he had no professional axe to grind. Someone, after the meeting ended, gave me a booklet entitled *How to Read the Bible,* by D. L. Moody, the man to whom we had been listening, and during the next few days as I got time, I followed the advice in it, and read the familiar legend with new interest and from a new view-point. I was searching for some guide to life in it, exactly as I sought in my medical textbooks a guide to physical treatment. I seemed to have suddenly waked up and to be viewing from outside the life which before I just took for granted as it came. . . .

Some time later, I forget how long, some famous athletes known to all the world interested in sports, were advertised to speak in East London—cricketers, oarsmen, athletes of national and international fame. I was intensely interested in hearing what they had to say. Seven of them a little later, known on both sides of the Atlantic as the "Cambridge Seven," all went to China. That their faith was no more an emotional flash in the pan than John's or Peter's or Paul's is proven by the fact that they are all still there in the field thirty-five years later, though all are men of ample means to live at home in comfort. The speaker whom I actually heard was a great cricketer. For the last forty years he has been the leader in boys' work in London through the Polytechnic Institute; and the last time I saw him, he was disguised in the gorgeous apparel of High Sheriff of London at a city banquet given to the Prince of Wales. After all these years I can still remember the whole drift of his talk. It was the old call of Joshua

"Choose to-day whom you will serve," self, fear of comrades and others, or Christ.

I felt then and I still believe to-day, that he was absolutely right. The advance in our ability to understand things, such as the constitution of matter or the realization of the definite limits of our understanding, makes religion more and more a matter of choice. The will to believe is essential. Experience alone will make it knowledge, or as Christ put it: "Follow me and you shall have the light of life." The increasing modesty of science after its marvellous discoveries during the past twenty-five years is permitting us ever more freely to accept this faith. The very conceit of Christ's challenge makes it seem divine. For His "Follow" meant "Do as I would do in every relation of life." No one is certain whether the atom is something or nothing moving around in an orbit. I am not sure I am sitting here, but I am so convinced that treading in the footsteps of the Christ explains the meaning of life, that even when I fail, not a shadow of doubt about it softens my sense of regret and self-condemnation.

A truth I learned then and one which the years have confirmed is that real religion involves real courage. The inefficiency which I had associated with it had not been its fault, but ours. We had not dreamt of taking Christ in earnest. At the close of that address, the speaker urged all present who had made a decision to stand up. There were a number of my friends in the meeting and I felt chained through fear to my seat. Sitting in the front semi-circle of seats were almost a hundred husky lads, all dressed alike in sailor suits. They were from a training ship in the harbour. Suddenly one smallish boy got up and stood there, the target of many astounded eyes. I knew well what it would mean to him, when the boys got back aboard, and it nerved me to stand up also. This step I have ever since been thankful for. It is invaluable to know where you stand. The decision to fairly try out that faith, which has challenged and stirred the ages, in the laboratory of one's own life, is, I am convinced, the only way to ever obtain a fixed heart on the matter. The prize is to be won, not swallowed, as must be everything else we know of that is of permanent value.

Whatever else was the result of so apparently ephemeral a thing as decision, it certainly entirely changed the meaning of life to me. I enjoyed everything in it more than ever, and the sneers of my fellows, which I honestly dreaded at first, wore down to a good humoured chaff, when they realized that religion made one do things. . . .

In the autumn of 1891, a friend suggested my visiting the fisheries on the Newfoundland Banks, so in 1892 I sailed in the 99-ton ketch *Albert* to the Newfoundland and Labrador Coasts. The conceit of the suggestion, the expense of it, and the question of qualifications for the undertaking worried me not a little. As a mere physical adventure, the opportunity seemed almost too good to be true. . . .

Even before I entered the work among the fishermen, I decided that for my part, I would never ask a man whether he believed exactly as I did before I could agree to work whole-heartedly with him. If we wait until our thinking machines are all in complete accordance before we co-operate, we shall never work together in that universal brotherhood which must precede the coming of the kingdom of God on earth. The emphasis on intellectual interpretation divides us—the willingness to work together draws men together. And it is wonderful how hard it is, looking at the manner in which men of diverse faiths have met their problems, and interpreted divine love in their deeds of every day, to judge as to the way in which they say their prayers or get their inspiration and strength, or what particular labels they should bear in the religious world, unless they insist on telling you.

Illustrations by the score leap to mind as this thought comes to me. To refuse the help of a surgeon, a nurse, a teacher, or an engineer, in a position where no interpretation of love is more needed than that which they can render, and as an alternative to allow one's fellow-creatures to suffer for lack of what they offer, just because I believed differently than they, would be to my mind not only criminal, but the very reverse of what Christ did. . . .

When first I visited Labrador, there was no lighthouse on its rock-bound coast, so a friend offered both the money to build one, and the salary of a keeper. However, the Government warned us that no private person may own a lighthouse, for possibly the man might let its light go out. Every year, with a thousand other vessels, I cruise along our rugged coastline. Each vessel sets out full of high hopes of a successful voyage, a full fare, and afterward a hearty "well done" from the satisfied owner of the craft, when at the end of the venture she has once more reached home. Alas! Our coast is strewn with wrecks. How many times have I sorely needed a pilot and guide myself to advise me what to do! . . .

The faith in Christ upon which I have based my life has given me a light on life's meaning which has satisfied my mind, body, and soul. The hope that through that faith, He would reveal a way of life here which justifies it, has been more than answered; and it seems to me ever more reasonable to hold that it will "carry on," just as gloriously when we have passed beyond the limits of what material machines can reveal to us. That the love which has made itself conscious to me through forty odd years, and has not failed even when I failed, should desert me when in the presence of God I shall need it most is to me unthinkable.

Sergius Bulgakov
(1871–1944)

Tracing his journey from Communism to Christianity, from Eastern Orthodoxy to the ecumenical movement, and from Moscow to Paris, one realizes
that the life and work of Sergius Bulgakov deserve to be kept alive for
later generations.

Counting several of his ancestors as Russian Orthodox priests, Bulgakov's first crisis came when he repudiated the religious teachings and
traditions of his church. For fifteen years, Bulgakov studied Marxist ideology in Berlin, Paris, and London, writing learned treatises with titles such
as *The Role of the Market in Capitalist Production* and *Capitalism and Agriculture*.
He was appointed as a professor of politics and law at the University of
Moscow, but his basic orientation underwent a significant change on reading Dostoyevsky. By 1918, at the time of the Russian Revolution, Bulgakov
was becoming increasingly involved in the Orthodox Church; and he even
helped toward the restoration of the Moscow Patriarchate.

When Bulgakov sought ordination to the priesthood, he was ousted
from his university post, and traveled as an exile to Istanbul, Prague, and
finally Paris. Here a small but influential group of Russian émigrés set up
an Orthodox Theological Academy, of which Bulgakov became Dean. His
colleagues included learned men such as Florovsky, Zernov, Berdyaev,
and Arseniev — all key figures in the developing ecumenical enthusiasm
of the time. Bulgakov himself attended the Lausanne Conference in 1927
and the Oxford Conference in 1937. His writings on the Orthodox tradition
gave new insight for Anglicans, Catholics, and Protestants for whom Eastern
Orthodoxy seemed a remote and aloof mystery. In many ways, this little
cluster of Russian exiles in Paris provided fresh theological excitement for
Orthodoxy much in the same fashion as Vatican II for Roman Catholicism
a full generation later.

A prolific writer and an original thinker, Bulgakov sought to interpret the Eastern notion of the divine Sophia as the cosmic ground for an
intelligible culture. Verging, as some thought, on a kind of Eastern Gnos-
ticism, Bulgakov stoutly maintained the Christian character of his theological system.

The account of Bulgakov's conversion is found in A *Bulgakov An-
thology*, ed. James Pain and Nicolas Zernov (London: SPCK; Philadelphia:
Westminster Press, 1976), 3-12. Reprinted by permission.

I was born in a priest's family, and Levite blood of six generations flowed in my veins. I grew up near the parish church of St. Sergius, in the gracious atmosphere of its prayers and within the sound of its bells. The aesthetic, moral, and everyday recollections of my childhood are bound up with the life of that parish church. Within its walls my heart rejoiced in prayer and mourned the departed. Until I was an adolescent I was faithful to my birth and upbringing as a son of the Church. I attended the parochial school in my native town, Livny, for four years and was then sent to the Theological Seminary in Oryol for three years.

In early adolescence, during my first or second year at the Seminary, I went through a religious crisis—painful but not tragic—which ended in my losing religious faith for many, many years. From the age of fourteen to about thirty the prodigal son withdrew into a far country to the sorrow and dismay of many, principally of his parents. I had a great deal to lose, and I gave it up with seeming ease, without any struggle (though in my godlessness I did think of suicide). . . .

In losing religious faith I naturally and, as it were, automatically adopted the revolutionary mood then prevalent among the intelligentsia. Without belonging to any particular party, I was bitterly opposed to the monarchism which was dominant in our clerical circles. In short, at that period in my life I went through the same experience as my predecessors in the Seminaries (Chernyshevsky, Dobrolyubov, and others). I fell victim to a gloomy revolutionary nihilism, though in my case it was always combined with a love of art and literature which saved me. The general atmosphere of the theological schools, based on tradition and compulsion, was impotent to combat this nihilism and grew more and more unendurable to a proud and independent boy who genuinely loved truth and freedom.

The Seminary authorities intended me for the Theological Academy, but I felt that my only hope of salvation was to escape from the Seminary at once, without looking back. Where might I escape? "To be useful," to serve mankind and progress by scientific thought—towards which I always had a leaning. It was not easy for me to carry out my plan. It demanded sacrifices, not only from me but from my family, and in the first place from my parents (whom, in my youthful egoism, I considered least of all). Nevertheless, in the summer of 1888 I left the Oryol Seminary. After attending the classical school at Yalets for two years, I entered Moscow University as a student in the Faculty of Law in the autumn of 1890.

In my choice of faculty I followed the herd of the intelligentsia against my personal inclination. I was attracted by philology, philosophy, and literature, but chose law, which did not appeal to me. I did this with the idea that I might help save my country from Tsarist tyranny. And to this end I had to take up the social sciences and bind myself to political economy like a galley slave chained to his bench. I doomed myself voluntarily to go through this purgatory that I might redeem my sin as a prodigal son.

I entered the University with the firm intention of devoting myself to a discipline alien to me, and I carried out my decision. After graduation I was called by Moscow University to be a lecturer in political economy. My appointment was made by Professor A. I. Chuprov, the kindest and nicest man imaginable, whose fate was similar to mine: he too had been a theological student and recalled his past as a lost-paradise, but he was not destined to reach the promised land beyond the "intellectualistic wilderness." I can well fancy how perturbed he would have been at seeing me in a cassock; but he did not live to see such a shocking thing.

My mind developed along the lines of social and socialistic thought. Consecutively, and almost automatically, I then passed from one form of thought to another until finally I appeared enslaved by Marxism, which suited me about as well as a saddle fits a cow. In the years 1898 to 1900 the University sent me to study abroad. Naturally, I went first to Germany—the land of Marxism and Social Democracy. But there, contrary to all my expectation, I soon met with disappointment, and my *Weltanschauung* began to disintegrate all along the line.

At last I returned to Russia to occupy the chair of political economy I had longed for. By that time I was in a state of complete spiritual resignation, through which the voice of religious faith sounded, at first timidly and uncertainly but then more and more victoriously. I began to profess this faith in my writings from 1901 and 1902 onwards, much to the surprise and indignation of my former comrades in thought. But basically, even as a Marxist in a state of spiritual barbarism, I always longed for religion and I was never indifferent to faith. Initially, I had a passionate emotional belief in an earthly paradise. Then, after a certain moment when I gave myself permission to do so, I took a sharp turn and went quickly and decidedly straight from the far country to my spiritual fatherland. Having regained faith in a "personal" God, instead of the impersonal idol of progress, I accepted Christ—whom I had loved and carried in my heart as a child. And finally, I returned to Orthodoxy.

I was irresistibly drawn to my native Church. However, for years the thought of returning to my Father's house and the longing to do so remained unrealized. Secret suffering was the price I had to pay for my return. I was returning, of course, not only in heart but in mind as well. From a sociologist I was turning into a theologian (I note with gratitude the spiritual influence of Dostoyevsky and Vladimir Solovyov upon me in those years). At the same time there arose within me a desire, which secretly indeed had never left me, to return to my Father's house completely and become a priest. In those years I sometimes spoke of myself to my friends as a "traitor to the altar." It was not enough that I should have changed my philosophy of life. My Levite blood asserted itself more and more: my soul longed for priesthood and the altar. Prince E. N. Trubetskoy said to me once that he felt as though I "had been born in a cassock." . . .

How did I come to lose my faith? I lost it without noticing it myself. It occurred as something self-evident and unavoidable when the poetry of my childhood was squeezed out of my life by the prose of seminary education. As soon as I experienced my first doubts, and my critical faculty was early awakened, I realized that I could not be satisfied with the apologetics of the text-books. Instead of helping me, they further undermined my faith. My seminary education constantly raised before me many religious problems, but I was unable to cope with them, and the instructions given to me by my teachers only confused my mind. This conflict was further aggravated by compulsory attendance at the long services. Orthodox piety only irritated me, for its mystical side had ceased to exist for me.

I was twenty-four years old. For a decade I had lived without faith and, after early stormy doubts, a religious emptiness reigned in my soul. One evening we were driving across the southern steppes of Russia, and the strong-scented spring grass was gilded by the rays of a glorious sunset. Far in the distance I saw the blue outlines of the Caucasus. This was my first sight of the mountains. I looked with ecstatic delight at their rising slopes. I drank in the light and the air of the steppes. I listened to the revelation of nature. My soul was accustomed to the dull pain of seeing nature as a lifeless desert and of treating its surface beauty as a deceptive mask. Yet, contrary to my intellectual convictions, I could not be reconciled to nature without God.

Suddenly, in that evening hour, my soul was joyfully stirred. I started to wonder what would happen if the cosmos were not a desert and its beauty not a mask or deception—if nature were not death, but life. If he existed, the merciful and loving Father, if nature was the vesture of his love and glory, and if the pious feelings of my childhood, when I used to live in his presence, when I loved him and trembled because I was weak, were true, then the tears and inspiration of my adolescence, the sweetness of my prayers, my innocence and all those emotions which I had rejected and trodden down would be vindicated, and my present outlook with its emptiness and deadness would appear nothing more than blindness and lies, and what a transformation it would bring to me!

In 1898 a new wave of intoxication with this world came upon me. I experienced "personal happiness." I met the West for the first time. My admiration of its culture, its comfort, and its social democracy was boundless; and then suddenly a wonderful encounter with Raphael's Sistine Madonna took place in Dresden. It was a foggy autumn morning. I went to the art gallery in order to do my duty as a tourist. My knowledge of European painting was negligible. I did not know what to expect. The eyes of the Heavenly Queen, the Mother who holds in her arms the Eternal Infant, pierced my soul. I cried joyful and yet bitter tears, and with them the ice melted from my soul, and some of my psychological knots were loosened. This was an aesthetic emotion, but it was also a new knowledge; it was a miracle. I was then still a Marxist, but I was obliged to call my contemplation of the Madonna by the name of "prayer." I went to the Zwinger gallery early in the mornings in order to be there before others arrived. I ran there every day to pray and weep in front of the Virgin, and few experiences in my life were more blessed than those unexpected tears.

One sunny autumn day in 1908 I made my way to a solitary hermitage lost in the forest, where I was surrounded by the familiar sights of northern nature. I was still in the clutches of doubt and hesitation. I had come there as a companion of a friend; secretly I hoped that I might meet God. But my determination deserted me, and while I was at Vespers I remained cold and unfeeling. When the prayers for those preparing for confession began, I almost ran out of the church. I walked in deep distress towards the guest house, seeing nothing around me, and suddenly found myself in front of the elder's cell. I had been led there. I intended to go in another direction but absent-mindedly made a wrong turn in the confusion of my distress.

A miracle had happened to me. I realized it then without any doubt. The Father, seeing his prodigal son, ran to meet me. I heard from the elder that all human sin was like a drop of water in comparison with the ocean of divine love. I left him, pardoned and reconciled, trembling and in tears, feeling myself returned as on wings within the precincts of the Church. At the door of the chapel I met my surprised and delighted companion, who had seen me leave in a state of acute distress. He was the witness of this conversion in my life.

It was another evening and another sunset, but this time a northern and not a southern one. The bells were calling to prayer. I listened to them as if I heard them for the first time in my life, for they invited me also to join the fellowship of believers. I looked on the world with new eyes. The next morning at the Eucharist I knew that I was a participant in the Covenant, that our Lord hung on the cross and shed his blood for me and because of me; that the most blessed meal was being prepared by the priest for me, and that the gospel narrative about the feast in the house of Simon the leper and about the woman who loved much was addressed personally to me. It was on that day when I partook of the blessed body and blood of my Lord.

C. F. Andrews
(1871–1940)

Friend and biographer of three of the most distinguished Indians of the time, Rabindranath Tagore, Sadhu Sundar Singh, and Mahatma Gandhi, C. F. Andrews provided a mediating ministry between the Christian West and India through his writings, his example, and his living presence among all sorts and conditions of people.

Born at Newcastle-on-Tyne in 1871, Charles Freer Andrews went to school in Birmingham and then attended Cambridge University. His father was a minister of the Catholic Apostolic Church, founded by Edward Irving and the "Irvingites." It was an independent group who sought to return to the simplicity of the early church and who discerned the signs of the time for Christ's second coming. But Andrews never felt comfortable in any denominational structure, and he moved from the church of his father to the Church of England and then, in India and elsewhere, he was satisfied to call himself simply a follower of Jesus Christ.

A reflective and highly gifted person, Andrews carried himself with saintly bearing, and his Christian witness in many parts of the world commanded instant acceptance and respect. Modest and gentle, he was a vigorous and aggressive advocate for social justice and the rights of the oppressed.

Among his many interests, Andrews sought to relate the Christian church to the problems of labor. An essay written while at Cambridge and later published bore the title *The Relation of Christianity to the Conflict between Capital and Labour* (1896). In India, he became deeply involved in the struggle for the abolition of so-called "indentured" labor. This brought him in touch with Gandhi, and the two became friends and associates in the wider struggle for freedom and independence.

In connection with his ministry on behalf of the Indian laborer, Andrews traveled to South Africa, Fiji, the West Indies, and British Guiana. During this time he was writing continuously, and his bibliography runs to about two dozen books. Best known of his writings were his biographical accounts of Gandhi (1930, 1931) and his own autobiography, *What I Owe to Christ* (1932), an immensely popular and influential testimony at the time, especially among young people. When he died in 1940, tributes to his life and work came from many friends and admirers from various religious traditions all over the world.

The account of Andrews' conversion comes from his chapter "A Pilgrim's Progress," in *Religion in Transition*, ed. Vergilius Ferm (London: Allen & Unwin, 1937), 60-79. Another version, very much the same in content, appears in *What I Owe to Christ* (New York: Abingdon Press, 1932), 77-92. Reprinted by permission.

M y mother was by far the most potent influence in my religious life when I was a child. Her love was the one pre-eminent factor in my infancy and early boyhood. It was not so much what she said, or even what she did for me, but rather what she was.

There were Scotch ancestors on my mother's side, though she came directly from a Wessex family with the surname Cartwright. The Highland blood had mingled with the Saxon, and this gave her a mystical vein of character which could be recognized in her face and in her eyes.

The place where I was born was Newcastle-on-Tyne in the north of England. The year of my birth was 1871, and the date February 12th. But when I was still a child my father moved to the Midlands, and I was educated at King Edward VI School, Birmingham, and then on to Cambridge in the year 1890.

When I was between four and five years old, a very severe attack of rheumatic fever nearly proved fatal. For many months my life was almost despaired of and the suffering was very great. But this long illness drew me to my mother with an intense affection, for she nursed me in my pain with a tenderness that created a new bond of affection between us.

My first conscious thoughts about God and Christ were implanted in me at this time by my mother, for I was very close to death, and she used to tell me of the love of Christ for little children and how He took them in His arms and blessed them.

There was a picture of Jesus, the Good Shepherd, which had a great attraction for me. The face of Jesus in the picture used to look at me with the same look of love which I could see in my mother's eyes.

One incident I have told at length in a book called *What I Owe to Christ*. It has always clung to my mind during the many years that have passed since it occurred.

For a long time my spirit had been hovering between life and death. Then, one morning, when I opened my eyes, I saw a flower which my mother had put by my bedside while I was asleep. Its fresh beauty seemed to revive me and bring back an interest in life again. From that day recovery was rapid.

The loving care and forethought of my mother had placed that flower beside me, and her unceasing prayers to God had been answered in that way. For He, by whom the very hairs of our head are all numbered and who cares for the fall of a sparrow, had used that tiny event in His good providence to bring me back to health and strength.

It was this illness in childhood that first brought me into touch with the world of spirit, while I hovered near the border of the unseen and almost passed to the other side. There has often come to me a wonder, why, amid all the changes in my inner thinking, the one fundamental faith in God and Christ and immortality has ever remained unshaken. Surely, my mother's silent influence over me, at such an impressionable age, during the climax of this long illness, must have had very much to do with this. . . .

The long line of ancestors from which my father was descended were hardy Puritans, who had often endured persecution for conscience' sake. Some had left home and all that they held dear in order to maintain their religious freedom. Men and women, such as these, had sought across the sea in North America a religious liberty which they could not find in England.

While my father had a passionate love of freedom very deeply implanted in him, this did not, in his case, lead on to a hardness and severity of character associated with a Puritan faith. For he was the tenderest of men, and a lover of little children. His Christian faith seemed to reveal itself in an unworldly character, which made him an idealist—generous to the last degree.

When my father was a child his own father, who was a Baptist minister in Essex, had left his congregation to follow certain saintly men who had received, as they believed, wonderful gifts of the Spirit through the ministry of a Scotch Presbyterian minister, named Edward Irving. This young preacher had shaken London society by his sermons upon the Book of Revelation. He declared that the last days of human history had arrived after the downfall of Napoleon. Out of the movement which had thus originated, apostolic gifts of healing and speaking with tongues and prophesying were declared to have been restored to the Christian Church.

As he grew up to manhood, my father himself became a fervent believer. He was quite convinced that he had found the key to the prophetic books in Holy Scripture and could read the "signs of the times." He himself spoke in prophecy, under the guidance of the Holy Spirit; he had also laid hands on the sick and they had recovered. Therefore he was as certain of the truth of the doctrines which he had learnt to believe as he was of his own existence.

It was in this strange, emotional atmosphere of prophesying and speaking with tongues and ecstasy in the Spirit that my own boyhood was passed. Every chapter in the Book of Revelation was explained to me as certain to come to pass in our own days. The solemnity of the religious services was awe-inspiring for a young child, and sometimes the awe was so overwhelming that it brought with it nervous reactions. The Second Coming of the Lord was daily expected. Christ was immediately coming "as a thief in the night" to take away His elect. This phrase, "The Second Coming," was continually upon my father's lips and he lived in expectation of the Advent.

At first my own appreciation of these things which my father taught me was vivid and strong. I had a keenly sensitive imagination, as a boy, and the imagery of the Book of Revelation used to haunt me. But an evil form of impurity crept into my life while I was at school, and gradually I fell away from this earlier belief which had filled my boyhood with awe and wonder.

In the midst of this decline, the inner consciousness of sin made me painfully aware that I was not ready to meet Christ at His Second Coming, if He should suddenly appear. Outwardly, I was leading a strictly religious life, in the bosom of our family, going regularly with my father and mother to church; but inwardly a conflict was going on deep down in the subconscious part of my being, and for a long time this remained unresolved.

Then came a wonderful conversion of my heart to God at the age of nineteen, when I was just about to enter college at Cambridge. So wonderful was it that it changed my whole inner life and released me from the bondage of sin which had bound me fast. Let me tell here very briefly what happened; for it was the great turning-point of my life.

One night the burden of the extreme evil of what I was doing came quite unexpectedly upon me as I knelt down at my bedside to say my prayers. For long hours of darkness I cried out in agony of my spirit. Then, out of my utter need and helplessness, came a marvellous sense of pardon and release. From that moment the new life in Christ began, which was veritably a new birth. His grace and love flooded my whole being.

The days that followed were like a glorious dream. I seemed to be living in a different world of light and love and peace. It illuminated the glory of Nature, and made me love every one I met.

The effect of this inflow of the Spirit, which came from Christ, was immediately to send me among the poor. Though, up to that time, I was quite unacquainted with that work of service in Christ's name, an inner compulsion seemed to drive me towards it; and all through my life the impulse to surrender all for Christ's sake and to find Him among those who are in need has been present with me so strongly that sooner or later everything has had to give way before it. Although I have never been able literally to obey Christ's command, as St. Francis did, I can well understand the joy which he and his young followers felt in their first love for their Lord and Master, Jesus Christ, when they left all that they had to follow Him. For the happiest moments I have known have always been those when I have been able to find my active work, not in university centres, or among the rich, or even among the middle class, but among the suffering poor. To say this is not to value lightly those other aspects of human society which I have mentioned, but rather to state a fact in my own individual life which has been verified again and again. For Christ's presence has drawn me towards those who are down-trodden and oppressed; and among these I have found all my love for Him grow deeper. . . .

After a long university course at Cambridge had been completed, I was ordained in 1896 to the Pembroke College Mission, in Walworth, which is one of the poorest parts of South-East London. There some of the happiest years of my life were spent among the poor. The joy of Christ's own service of love was so great that no labour seemed too hard for me at that time.

But after some years, while actively engaged in this work, I over-strained myself and was obliged in the end, under doctor's orders, to sur-render it. An invitation to go back as a teacher to Cambridge came at this critical juncture, and I was induced to accept it. There, too, in the Uni-versity, years of great happiness were spent, mingled with great sorrows. For I came face to face with death, among those I loved most dearly, not once only but again and again. During those solemn days, when death was my constant companion, the Christian faith became rooted and grounded in me with a new intensity of conviction. I seemed to be continually living with Christ on the very border of the unseen world.

Yet in spite of great inward happiness and renewed spiritual vision, which followed my ordination, the difficulties which I had to face in my own intellectual life did not seem to decrease. New questionings arose. The recitation, in a Christian act of worship, of the imprecatory Psalms, calling down vengeance on enemies, who were not only hated, but cursed, became almost intolerable to me. The Athanasian Creed with its damnatory clauses was an even greater stumbling block. The Thirty-nine Articles, to which I had subscribed, began also to trouble me; and however much I might try to ease my conscience by regarding mere assent to them as al-lowing latitude of acceptance, it was difficult to be quite clear in my own mind that I was not again deceiving myself just as I had done before.

Although I was still a long way off from coming to conclusions on these and other matters, I began more and more to realize that the only solution of all my intellectual troubles was to get back to the simplicity of the Gospel in my daily life. This was my one dominating thought during my second period at Cambridge as a teacher, and in my heart I knew that I must be ready to follow Christ still more completely and not shrink from any sacrifice which He called upon me to make in His name.

The call came at last in a very sudden and tragic manner. My friend Basil Westcott died at Delhi of cholera, while trying to save the life of another. His death made a very deep impression on me, and I sailed for India as soon as ever I could be set free to do so, in order to take his place. . . .

The joy came into my life, at this time, of a great transforming friendship with Susil Kumar Rudra, the principal of my own college. He used to go, each year, up into the mountains with me, beyond Simla. His two sons used to accompany us and sometimes students from college were

with us also. Susil had lost his wife, owing to an illness after the birth of
his youngest child, and he had never married again.

There, at Kotgarh, we met Samuel Stokes of Germanstown, Philadelphia, who was living a Franciscan life along with Sadhu Sundar Singh.
About the Sadhu I have written very fully in a memoir which has been
published in America and England. He is also referred to in other books
which I have written. His love for Christ was so ardent that my own love
was kindled by it. I found in him, also, one who had not ceased to reverence
that which was pure and noble and of good report in his old religious faith.
He felt that he had received the consummation of it all in his Lord and
Master, Jesus Christ.

It was in this atmosphere of the glorious mountains, with their snows
reaching up into the blue sky, that the narrowness of the boundaries of my
former religious faith was made clear to me, and the decision was slowly
formed within me to seek a wider sphere of work.

The break actually came when, in 1913, I was asked by Mr. Gokhale
to go out to South Africa in order to help in the Indian cause at a time of
great anxiety and danger.

A form of servile labour called "indenture" had been in operation
for many years. Villagers from India had been induced to leave India and
go out to the sugar-plantations. The whole system of recruiting was corrupt
beyond description.

The moral conditions on these plantations were deplorable. Mahatma Gandhi had started a passive resistance movement in order to bring
to an end, once and for all, these widespread evils.

He had suffered imprisonment with more than two thousand of his
followers and the struggle had reached a very critical point. General Smuts
represented the South African Government.

It was in order to help in this passive resistance struggle that Mr.
Gokhale invited me to go out to Natal. Willie Pearson, the son of the great
Congregational minister of Manchester, Dr. Samuel Pearson, went with
me. In the end the passive resistance struggle was won and Mahatma Gandhi was able to return to India.

But the vicious system of Indian indenture still existed in other parts
of the world, such as Fiji, Trinidad, British Guiana, etc. In order to obtain
its abolition, further journeys were necessary and I had to go twice to Fiji.

At last, in 1920, this form of Indian indentured labour was altogether abolished. The day, January 1st, will go down in Indian history as
parallel to the date on which slavery was abolished in the British dominions
and later on in the United States. Now, in India, all recruiting for such a
purpose abroad has been entirely prohibited.

This experience in South Africa and elsewhere widened my outlook
upon life and gave me a new world vision of the Christian faith. When I
went back to India from South Africa, it soon became clear to me that I

could no longer remain in the more confined sphere of the Cambridge Brotherhood at Delhi. With the kindliest recognition of the larger field of work which had opened out for me, the Head of the Mission, the Rev. Canon Allnutt, bade me God speed, and allowed me to depart.

But something still further happened almost at the same time, though I had not expected it to come about in this way. All these earlier questionings about subscription to the Prayer-book and Thirty-nine Articles now came to a head; and at last it was clear to me that I ought no longer to exercise my full Orders in the Anglican ministry under a bishop's licence. . . .

Rabindranath Tagore had invited me to join his institution at Santiniketan. In his magnanimity he had agreed to take me just as I was, an ordained clergyman. He wished me to continue all my religious duties as far as possible, while at the same time working with him, at Santiniketan, in his great educational work.

But when Trinity Sunday came and I was faced with the recital of the Athanasian Creed, I suddenly found that I could not repeat it, with its damnatory clauses. It came home to me with a shock that I could not lead an Indian Christian congregation in the recitation of that Creed and then go back lightheartedly to Santiniketan as if nothing had happened. So I omitted the Creed altogether. But at once I recognized that I was playing a coward's part in thus trifling with my conscience.

When I returned and saw the pure face of the poet Rabindranath looking into my own, I knew at once that I had been living a life of untruth. So there and then I confessed to him with shame all that had happened and how from henceforth I must be truthful.

He urged me earnestly to take no hasty step. But when I showed him how near to the brink of the precipice of falsehood I had been, he said no more to dissuade me.

Thus, the inner struggle, that had gone on for so many years, had suddenly come to an end. But bitter wounds had been left behind which took many years to heal.

Nevertheless, it soon became clear that this action meant to me not only a release from bondage, but also a greater power of Christian service. The blessing of God had been with me, leading me forward.

Since that step was taken I have gradually come to recognize that Christ Himself in His Gospel has given us His own definition of discipleship and also of membership in His Body, which is called the Household of faith. For He has said plainly: "He that doeth the will of God, the same is my brother and my sister and my mother."

If this is Christ's own definition it is not for us to draw boundaries more narrowly than our Lord Himself had drawn them. Where this will lead me ultimately is not yet clear. But it will certainly make a vast difference in my own conception of what a Christian is and what he ought to be.

E. Stanley Jones
(1884–1973)

A born evangelist, Stanley Jones was twice-born, and when he caught a vision of his missionary ministry, he was ever on the move.

Eli Stanley Jones began his evangelistic career with high castes in India. He developed the so-called Christian Ashram, a kind of discussion commune to which church leaders were invited to live together for a time of shared experiences. His Round Table Conference plan extended the format to include representatives of other religions, and his later interest in America in the "Federated" church proposal was still another attempt at innovative dialogue.

In 1925, he wrote *The Christ of the Indian Road*, a widely popular book that was translated into twenty languages and has sold over a million copies. Fiercely independent and somewhat of a loner in private, Jones made his own programs and was in constant demand as a speaker, especially to young people in college. Self-effacing and modest, he magnified Christ and always spoke with enthusiasm about the power of the gospel.

In later years, he became more involved in the social witness of Christianity, arranging in India for mobile dispensary trucks. He believed that Christianity was "the answer" to communism and wrote a much-read book called *Christ's Alternative to Communism* (1934). A pacifist and an advocate for home rule for India, Jones was often criticized by British government officials and even by American missionaries who felt uncomfortable with his free-wheeling methods. But his influence on behalf of a native and indigenous Indian Christianity was decisive and substantial at the time.

Surprised to be elected a Methodist bishop in 1928, Stanley Jones resigned in favor of his missionary vocation. Those who knew him felt he would make a good church administrator. But he thought otherwise, and the gospel was heard in many strange and unusual places because of his decision.

This account of his conversion is taken from E. Stanley Jones, A *Song of Ascents: A Spiritual Autobiography* (Nashville: Abingdon Press, 1968), 26-33. Copyright © 1968 by Abingdon Press and reprinted by permission.

I am an ordinary man doing extraordinary things because I'm linked with the extraordinary. But apart from this I am very ordinary. And worse. A woman put it this way: "Apart from the Holy Spirit, Brother Stanley would be a mess." She was right. But with the Holy Spirit I am not a mess, but a message, for I have a message. This is not boasting. It is witnessing, witnessing to Another. To say anything else would be a false humility which is concealed pride.

How did it all begin? My first remembered contact with religion was when, as a little boy, I went to the Sunday school at Frederick Avenue Methodist Church, South, in Baltimore, dressed in a brand new suit. To call attention to my new suit, and me, I took a collection plate and began to pass it around before the grown-ups standing chatting. I didn't hope to get any money. I hoped to collect compliments for my new suit and incidentally for myself. Hardly an auspicious beginning with religion. And yet I had unwittingly run into the central problem in religion—the problem of the self-assertive self.

My second crisis contact with religion was when, about ten years later, at the age of fifteen, I was in the gallery of the Memorial Church, with a group of boys, mostly my chums. The speaker was an Englishman from John Bunyan's church in England. He was a man of God, and at the close of his address he pointed his finger to where we were seated and said, "Young men, Jesus said, 'He that is not with me is against me.' " It went straight to my heart. I knew I wasn't with him, but I didn't want to be against him. It shook me. I turned to my chum and said: "I'm going to give myself to Christ. Will you?" He replied: "No, I'm going to see life first." Then I saw that I would have to go alone, and did. I climbed over the young men, went down the steps and up the aisle to the altar, and took my place among the seekers. I felt undone and wept—wept because I was guilty and estranged. I fumbled for the latchstring of the Kingdom of God, missed it, for they didn't tell me the steps to find. I stood up at the close when they asked if it was all right with us. I wanted the Kingdom of God, wanted reconciliation with my heavenly Father, but took church membership as a substitute. My mother came into my room next morning and silently kissed me before I got out of bed. Her son was a Christian. But I soon found I wasn't. I felt religious for a few weeks, and then it all faded out and I was back again exactly where I was before, the springs of my character and my habit formation unchanged. I had been horizontally converted, but not vertically. I was outwardly in, but not inwardly in. It was a sorry impasse. I could have lived out my life on that level the balance of my days, a cancelled-out person, neither here nor there.

But as I look back, I am not sorry I went through that half-conversion which was a whole failure. For the fact that I got out of that failure into the real thing may be used to encourage those who have settled down to a compromised stalemate, dull, listless, and with no note of victory.

They, too, can get into the real things. So my failure can be used to help others to victory.

The real thing came two years later. An evangelist, Robert J. Bateman, came to Memorial Church. Through his rough exterior I saw there was reality within. He was a converted alcoholic, on fire with God's love. I said to myself, "I want what he has." This time I was deadly serious. I was not to be put off by catch phrases and slogans. I wanted the real thing or nothing. No halfway houses for me; I wanted my home. For three days I sought. During those three days I went to the altar twice. On one of those times my beloved teacher, Miss Nellie Logan, knelt alongside me and repeated John 3:16 this way: "God so loved Stanley Jones, that he gave his only begotten Son, that if Stanley Jones will believe on him he shall not perish, but have everlasting life." I repeated it after her, but no spark of assurance kindled my darkened heart. The third night came; before going to the meeting I knelt beside my bed and prayed the sincerest prayer I had prayed so far in my life. My whole life was behind that simple prayer: "O Jesus, save me tonight." And he did! A ray of light pierced my darkness. Hope sprang up in my heart. I found myself saying, "He's going to do it." I now believe he had done it, but I had been taught that you found him at an altar of prayer. So I felt I must get to the church to an altar of prayer. I found myself running the mile to the church. The eagerness of my soul got into my body. I was like Christian running from the City of Destruction to the Celestial City. I went into the church and took the front seat, a thing I had never done before. But I was all eagerness for the evangelist to stop speaking, so I could get to that altar of prayer. When he did stop, I was the first one there. I had scarcely bent my knees when Heaven broke into my spirit. I was enveloped by assurance, by acceptance, by reconciliation. I grabbed the man next to me by the shoulder and said: "I've got it." "Got it?" What did I mean? I see now it was not an "it": it was a him. I had him—Jesus—and he had me. We had each other. I belonged. My estrangement, my sense of orphanage were gone. I was reconciled. As I rose from my knees, I felt I wanted to put my arms around the world and share this with everybody. Little did I dream at that moment that I would spend the rest of my life literally trying to put my arms around the world to share this with everybody. But I have. This was a seed moment. The whole of my future was packed into it.

Crude? No, creative. Emotional? It took an emotional upheaval to carry me across from a self-preoccupied life to a Christ-preoccupied life. The center of being was changed from self to Savior. I didn't try by an act of will to give up my sins—they were gone. I looked into his face and was forever spoiled for anything that was unlike him. The whole me was converted. There was nothing the same except my name. It was the birthday of my soul. Life began there. Note I say "began"—the whole of my life has been an unfolding of what was infolded in that moment. . . .

So a sense of the deepest gratitude a human is capable of knowing takes possession of me when I think of what I would have been had conversion not intervened and turned life into new channels. When the Memorial Church moved farther out the Frederick Road to a new site, they cut the altar rail where I knelt and was converted and made it into a prayer desk with an inscription on it: "At this spot Stanley Jones knelt and gave himself to Christ," and invited others to do the same. Tradition says that Zacchaeus used to go and water the sycamore tree in which he first met the Lord. I can understand that; I go periodically to that spot and water it with my tears of gratitude, for there "I first saw the light, and the burden of my heart rolled away."

He put a Song in my heart, for I had something to sing about. Many undertones and overtones have enriched that Song, but there I caught the standard note—"Jesus," a Savior—from what I didn't want to be to what I wanted to be. The United States Government strikes a standard note in Washington every day to let people tune their off-tune instruments again. From the day I was given the standard note to this day, sixty-six years later, I have been sounding that "note" through all the world. And I hope my last gasp will be, "I commend my Savior to you."

Evelyn Underhill
(1875–1941)

Behind the typical British reserve and formality in religion and theology, as in everything else, there has always been a mystical strain of inner spiritual questing.

Especially after the devastation of World War I, which decimated a whole British generation, there emerged here and there distinctive figures who looked for a peace that "passes understanding." Names like Dean Inge, Olive Wyon, Hywel Hughes, Baron Friedrich von Hügel, Charles Williams, and Evelyn Underhill became widely known among a select company of spiritual seekers.

Evelyn Underhill, "to the manor born" but with a nonreligious family background, came under the influence of the Austrian-born Baron Friedrich von Hügel. "The Baron," as she always referred to him, moved to England as a young boy and later was a recognized authority on the religious philosophy of spiritual experience. An ecumenical Catholic, he was eagerly read by Protestant theologians, and his major writings, such as *The Mystical Element of Religion* (2 vols., 1908; 1923), *Eternal Life* (1912), and *Philosophy of Religion* (1921; 1926), anticipated later theological trends. He insisted that the mystical, the institutional, and the intellectual spheres of religion be maintained in creative tension.

Under "the Baron's" gentle leading, Evelyn Underhill decided to profess her Christian faith by becoming a member of the Roman Catholic Church. She understood the formal ceremony to be an outward sign of her inner quest. But when, in 1907, Pope Pius X issued the decree against "Modernism" in the Catholic Church, she felt that her intelligence would be offended, and she joined the Church of England.

Through a series of intensely personal but scholarly volumes such as *Mysticism* (1911) and *Worship* (1936), she became a leader, in spite of herself, of the spirituality movement both within and outside the churches. A self-contained person and something of a solitary contemplative, she was much in demand as a spiritual counselor and as a speaker at religious retreats.

The letters of Evelyn Underhill were edited after her death by the well-known writer Charles Williams. They reveal an alert mind at work and a sensitive spirit as critical of herself as of religious ideas. It is characteristic

of her wry and witty side that among her "recreations" noted in the British
Who's Who she listed "talking to cats."

In June 1923, Evelyn Underhill wrote an extended letter to Baron
Friedrich von Hügel, detailing the steps in her own spiritual pilgrimage.
The letter is printed in the biography, Evelyn Underhill, by Margaret Cropper
(London: Longmans, Green and Co., 1958), 105-10. Reprinted by permission.

General. I feel quite different from last year: but in ways rather
difficult to define. Deeper in. More steady on my knees though not yet
very steady on my *feet.* Not so rushing up and down between blankness
and vehement consolations. Still much oscillation, but a kind of steady line
persists instead of zigzags.

I have been trying all the time to shift the focus from feeling to will,
but have not yet fully done it, and shall not feel safe till I have. The
Christocentric side has become so much deeper and stronger—it nearly
predominates. I never dreamed it was like this. It is just beginning to dawn
on me what the Sacramental life really does involve: but it is only in flashes
of miraculous penetration I can realize this. On the whole, in spite of
blanks, times of wretched incapacity, and worse . . . I have never known
such deep and real happiness, such a sense of at last having got my real
permanent life, and being able to love without stint, where I am meant to
love. It is as if one were suddenly liberated and able to expand all round.
Such joy that it sometimes almost hurts. All this, humanly speaking, I owe
entirely to you. Gratitude is a poor dry word for what I feel about it. I can't
say anything.

The moral struggle is incessant, but there is a queer joy in it. I don't
think I need bother much about that. Small renunciations are easier, but
real ones still mean a fight. Nervous tension or exhaustion means a renewed
attack of all my old temptations at full strength and I feel invaded by hard,
exasperated, critical, hostile, gloomy, and unloving inclinations.

Of course my will does not consent to these horrors: I do struggle
with them: all the same they creep into my mind, and stick for days, another
proof at bottom I am un-Christian still (for surely mere nervous tension
should not mean these odious feelings?). And that lovely gentle suppleness
and radiance I see in all my real Christian friends, and long for, I can't get.
I don't think I have ever seen the deepest roots in myself of pride and self-
love.

Many religious practices I still can't do, e.g. self-examination. I did
make myself do a long written one at my retreat. . . . It looked horrid—
but somehow I can't feel much interest in it, or that these curry combings
matter much. So much more worth while and far more humbling, just to
keep on trying to look at Christ. I know instantly by that when I do anything

odious. Even before Holy Communion I don't do much else but, as it were, let that love flow over and obliterate everything. There is so little difference between one's best and worst. . . .

Last October, one day when I was praying, quite suddenly a Voice seemed to speak to me—with tremendous staccato sharpness and clearness. It only said one short thing, first in Latin and then in English! Please don't think I am going in for psychic automatisms or horrors of that sort. It has never happened again, and I don't want it to. Of course I know all about the psychological aspect and am not *hallucinated*. All the same, I simply cannot believe that there was not something deeper, more real, not me at all, behind. The effect was terrific. Sort of nailed me to the floor for half an hour, which went as a flash. I felt definitely called out and settled, once for all—that any falling back or leaving off, after that, will be an unpardonable treason. That sense has persisted—it marked a sort of turning point and the end of all the remorse and worry, and banging about. I feel now if all consolations went, it ought not to matter very much; though as a matter of fact derelictions are more painful and trying than they used to be, but have their purifying side. I feel a total, unconditioned dedication is what is asked, and it is so difficult. I shall never do it—one fails at every corner.

There have been other things since from time to time, but quite formless, and unspeakably sacred, penetrating, intimate, abasing. Now and then new lights, too, sort of intellectual intuitions, and quite clear of "sensible devotion"; but they are so quick and vast one can only retain about half. I would like to get away from the more vividly emotional feelings: I don't altogether trust them—but how can one help feeling pretty intensely. One has only one soul and body to do one's feelings with after all.

Prayer, at good times though still mixed, is more passive: a sort of inarticulate communion, or aspirations, often merely one word, over and over. Sometimes I wonder whether this is not too much taking the line of least resistance; but it is so wonderful, sweeps one along into a kind of warm inhabited darkness and blind joy—one lives in Eternity in that— can't keep at this pitch long, twenty minutes or so.

I do try to say a few psalms each day and do Intercessions, but one forgets everything then. Of course it's not always like this, often all distraction and difficulty.

As to Intercession, if I ask myself whether I would face complete Spiritual deprivation for the good of another: e.g. to effect a conversion, I can't do that yet. So I have not got real Christian love: and the question is, can one intercede genuinely for anyone, unless ready to pay, if necessary, this price.

Special points (a) A terrible, overwhelming suspicion that after all, my whole "invisible experience" may be only subjective. There are times (of course when one has got it) when it seems incredible that these things could happen to me, considering what I have been. All the books say in unmortified beginners they are very suspicious, so what is one to think?

And further, there is the obvious fact that consolation and deprivation are somehow closely connected with the ups and downs of one's nervous and even bodily life. There is no real test: I may have deceived myself right through, and always studying these things, self-suggestion would be horribly easy. These doubts are absolute torture after what has happened. They paralyse one's life at the roots, once they lodge in the mind. I do not want to shirk *any* pain, but this does not seem a purifying kind. . . .

So far I have struggled through all right, generally by deliberate forced prayer—but this only shelves the problem, does not solve it—and it makes one feel horribly unsafe. The return to peace and certitude is wonderful; but how am I to know for certain this is not just some psychic mechanism? There are times when I wish I had never heard of psychology.

(*b*) Sometimes an even more terrifying visitation, when not *only* my own inner experience, but the whole spiritual scheme seems in question. The universe seems cast iron and the deterministic view the obvious one. All the old difficulties come back: and especially that chasm between the universal and the historic experience of Christ. I see clearly that for me religious realism is the only thing that is any use. Generally I seem to have it with an increasingly vivid sense of real approach to, or communion with God and Christ as objective facts, completely other than myself. I can't love on any other basis than this: even human love can't be spun from one's dreams, and this is far, far beyond that. But in these black times of doubt, it seems possible that one's hours of prayer and adoration simply react on oneself and produce the accompanying experiences. I have no guarantee of genuineness. It is not the awful moral struggle I knew I should have once I gave in; that has a sort of joy in it; those mental conflicts are just pure horror. . . .

Psycho-physical tangles. The parallels between nervous states and spiritual sensitiveness worry me: nerves and soul seem hopelessly mixed up; one thinks one is out of grace and finds it was only mental fatigue and impotence. Don't know how best to run my devotional life in nervous exhaustion. Often too stupefied to think, will, or love at all. I do keep my whole rule somehow—merely kneeling on a hard floor the proper time seems better than nothing—but the struggle to pray is fruitless then. This rule keeping tends to a sort of rigidity. I am restless and starved when my particular routine is upset. And during holidays, or when travelling, lecturing, etc., approximately a quarter of the year—I can't rely on keeping it. Often no privacy, no certain free time, safe from interruption: and the desperate struggle to get it at all costs induces a strain which is hostile to prayer. Lately, in fact, "holidays" have been periods of misery on this account. Of course, I never sacrifice Communions unless they are quite impossible—even these I cannot be sure of when we are yachting. What I want here is permission to be more flexible about the external rule and make up by taking every opportunity of quietude or of short aspirations, for any irregularity in long recollections. I believe I should do better like this and am sure it would not mean slackness. And there must be some way of super-naturalizing one's active life when one can't have one's usual solitude and fixed adoration. After all it's not my choice that I have to be at other people's disposal the whole time. Could not one turn these conditions into something worth offering? . . .

Vocation. I feel great uncertainty as to what God chiefly wants of me. Selection has become inevitable. I can't meet more than half the demands made. I asked for more opportunity of personal service and have thoroughly been taken at my word! But there is almost no time or strength left now for study for its own sake; always giving or preparing addresses, advice, writing articles, trying to keep pace with work, going on committees and conferences—and with so little mental food I risk turning into a sort of fluid clergyman! More serious the conflict between family claims and duties and work is getting acute. My parents are getting old: they don't understand, and are a bit jealous of the claims on my life (especially as it's all unpaid work). I feel perhaps I ought to have more leisure for them, though I do see them nearly every day. But this could only be done by reducing what seems like direct work for God, or my poor people or something. I confess the work and the poor people are congenial: and idling about chatting and being amiable, when there is so much to be done, a most difficult discipline—so I can't judge the situation fairly. It is not a case of being needed in any practical sense: just of one's presence being liked, and one's duties slightly resented!

Albert Schweitzer
(1875–1965)

Early in his life, Albert Schweitzer realized that he had been graced much beyond his deserving. In fact, he did not yet know how gifted he was or how versatile his career would be. "Every one to whom much is given, of him will much be required" (Luke 12:48). Whether or not he had such a text in mind, Schweitzer's life was a deliberately dedicated payment of a debt as he tried to live his own version of the Christ-life.

Born in the Alsace region on the border between France and Germany, Schweitzer graduated from the University of Strasbourg, having specialized in philosophy and theology. He became principal of a theological college affiliated with the university and immediately plunged into several writing projects that were soon published.

The most important and controversial of all his works appeared in 1906 and was translated into English in 1910 as The Quest of the Historical Jesus. Upsetting the nineteenth-century liberal view of Jesus as a teacher of religious truths and a moral leader of humanitarian ideals, Schweitzer insisted on taking seriously the messianic eschatology of the Gospels.

For Schweitzer, the conclusion of the Christ story remained ambiguous. In giving himself, as the suffering servant, for the fulfillment of the kingdom, Jesus as the "One unknown" can only be known by those who respond to his invitation to "Follow me." Schweitzer was not given to work out a constructive Christology except in the one way that perhaps counts most, namely by giving himself to serve others less fortunate.

In the meantime, Schweitzer was pursuing another career as a musicologist and an authority on Bach. He studied the organ in Paris and wrote a definitive edition on the music and religious meaning of Bach's chorales and cantatas.

In the same year, 1905, Schweitzer startled his friends and associates by announcing his intention to study medicine to become a missionary doctor in equatorial Africa. This decision emerged out of his early sense of gratitude and feeling of indebtedness. He was deeply disturbed by the radical difference between the gifts of civilization which the white peoples of the earth enjoyed and the abysmal poverty and disease of "the Black Continent."

The rest of the story is familiar, for it is one of the thrilling sagas of modern heroism and self-dedication. The hospital at Lambaréné, primitive but humane, became a symbol for all the world to see.

In 1928, Albert Schweitzer received the Goethe Prize, and in 1952, the Nobel Peace Prize. His last significant writing project involved a philosophy of civilization using "reverence for life" as his guiding principle.

Theologians and biblical scholars have continued to debate his views of the Christian gospel. The Paris Mission Society had doubts about his orthodoxy. But no one could question that this gifted and magnetic jungle doctor came closer than most to fulfilling the words of Jesus — ". . . I was hungry and you gave me food, I was thirsty and you gave me drink, I was a stranger and you welcomed me, I was naked and you clothed me, I was sick and you visited me . . ." (Matt. 25:35-36).

The passage describing his decision to go to Africa comes from the chapter, "I Resolve to Become a Jungle Doctor," in his *Out of My Life and Thought: An Autobiography*, trans. C. T. Campion (New York: Henry Holt & Co., 1933), 102-18.

O n October 13th, 1905, a Friday, I dropped into a letter-box in the Avenue de la Grande Armée in Paris letters to my parents and to some of my most intimate acquaintances, telling them that at the beginning of the winter term I should enter myself as a medical student, in order to go later on to Equatorial Africa as a doctor. In one of them I sent in the resignation of my post as Principal of the Theological College of S. Thomas's, because of the claim on my time that my intended course of study would make.

The plan which I meant now to put into execution had been in my mind for a long time, having been conceived so long ago as my student days. It struck me as incomprehensible that I should be allowed to lead such a happy life, while I saw so many people around me wrestling with care and suffering. Even at school I had felt stirred whenever I got a glimpse of the miserable home surroundings of some of my schoolfellows and compared them with the absolutely ideal conditions in which we children of the parsonage at Günsbach lived. While at the University and enjoying the happiness of being able to study and even to produce some results in science and art, I could not help thinking continually of others who were denied that happiness by their material circumstances or their health. Then one brilliant summer morning at Günsbach, during the Whitsuntide holidays—it was in 1896—there came to me, as I awoke, the thought that I must not accept this happiness as a matter of course, but must give something in return for it. Proceeding to think the matter out at once with calm deliberation, while the birds were singing outside, I settled with myself before I got up, that I would consider myself justified in living till I was thirty for science and art, in order to devote myself from that time forward to the direct service of humanity. Many a time already had I tried to settle what meaning lay hidden for me in the saying of Jesus! "Whosoever would save his life shall lose it, and whosoever shall lose his life for My sake and the Gospels shall save it." Now the answer was found. In addition to the outward, I now had inward happiness.

What would be the character of the activities thus planned for the future was not yet clear to me. I left it to circumstances to guide me. One thing only was certain, that it must be directly human service, however inconspicuous the sphere of it.

I naturally thought first of some activity in Europe. I formed a plan for taking charge of abandoned or neglected children and educating them, then making them pledge themselves to help later on in the same way children in similar positions. When in 1903, as Warden of the theological hostel, I moved into my roomy and sunny official quarters on the second floor of the College of S. Thomas, I was in a position to begin the experiment. I offered my help now here, now there, but always unsuccessfully. The constitutions of the organizations which looked after destitute and abandoned children made no provision for the acceptance of such voluntary co-operation. For example, when the Strassburg Orphanage was burnt down, I offered to take in a few boys, for the time being, but the Superintendent did not even allow me to finish what I had to say. Similar attempts which I made elsewhere were also failures. . . .

One morning in the autumn of 1904 I found on my writing-table in the College one of the green-covered magazines in which the Paris Missionary Society reported every month on its activities. A certain Miss Scherdlin used to put them there knowing that I was specially interested in this Society on account of the impression made on me by the letters of one of its earliest missionaries, Casalis by name, when my father read them aloud at his missionary services during my childhood. That evening, in the very act of putting it aside that I might go on with my work, I mechanically opened this magazine, which had been laid on my table during my absence. As I did so, my eye caught the title of an article: "Les besoins de la Mission du Congo" ("The needs of the Congo Mission").

It was by Alfred Boegner, the President of the Paris Missionary Society, an Alsatian, and contained a complaint that the Mission had not enough workers to carry on its work in the Gaboon, the northern province of the Congo Colony. The writer expressed his hope that his appeal would bring some of those "on whom the Master's eyes already rested" to a decision to offer themselves for this urgent work. The conclusion ran: "Men and women who can reply simply to the Master's call, 'Lord, I am coming,' those are the people whom the Church needs." The article finished, I quietly began my work. My search was over.

My thirtieth birthday a few months later I spent like the man in the parable who "desiring to build a tower, first counts the cost whether he have wherewith to complete it." The result was that I resolved to realize my plan of direct human service in Equatorial Africa.

With the exception of one trustworthy friend no one knew of my intention. When it became known through the letters I had sent from Paris, I had hard battles to fight with my relations and friends. Almost more than with my contemplated new start itself they reproached me with not having shown them so much confidence as to discuss it with them first. With this side issue they tormented me beyond measure during those difficult weeks. That theological friends should outdo the others in their protests struck me as all the more preposterous, because they had, no doubt, all preached a fine sermon—perhaps a very fine one—showing how S. Paul, as he has recorded in his letter to the Galatians, "conferred not with flesh and blood" beforehand about what he meant to do for Jesus.

My relatives and my friends all joined in expostulating with me on the folly of my enterprise. I was a man, they said, who was burying the talent entrusted to him and wanted to trade with false currency. Work among savages I ought to leave to those who would not thereby be compelled to leave gifts and acquirements in science and art unused. Widor, who loved me as if I were his son, scolded me as being like a general who wanted to go into the firing-line—there was no talk about trenches at that time—with a rifle. A lady who was filled with the modern spirit proved to me that I could do much more by lecturing on behalf of medical help for natives than I could by the action I contemplated. That saying from Goethe's *Faust* ("In the beginning was the Deed"), was now out of date, she said. To-day propaganda was the mother of happenings.

In the many verbal duels which I had to fight, as a weary opponent, with people who passed for Christians, it moved me strangely to see them so far from perceiving that the effort to serve the love preached by Jesus may sweep a man into a new course of life, although they read in the New Testament that it can do so, and found it there quite in order. I had assumed as a matter of course that familiarity with the sayings of Jesus would produce a much better appreciation of what to popular logic is non-rational, than my own case allowed me to assert. Several times, indeed, it was my experience that my appeal to the act of obedience which Jesus' command of love may under special circumstances call for, brought upon me an accusation of conceit, although I had, in fact, been obliged to do violence to my feelings to employ this argument at all. In general, how much I suffered through so many people assuming a right to tear open all the doors and shutters of my inner self!

As a rule, too, it was of no use allowing them, in spite of my repugnance, to have a glimpse of the thoughts which had given birth to my resolution. They thought there must be something behind it all, and guessed at disappointment at the slow growth of my reputation. For this there was no ground at all, seeing that I had received, even as a young man, such recognition as others usually get only after a whole life of toil and struggle. Unfortunate love experiences were also alleged as the reason for my decision.

I felt as a real kindness the action of persons who made no attempt to dig their fists into my heart, but regarded me as a precocious young man, not quite right in his head, and treated me correspondingly with affectionate mockery.

I felt it to be, in itself, quite natural that relations and friends should put before me anything that told against the reasonableness of my plan. As one who demands that idealists shall be sober in their views, I was conscious that every start upon an untrodden path is a venture which only in unusual circumstances looks sensible and likely to be successful. In my own case I held the venture to be justified, because I had considered it for a long time and from every point of view, and credited myself with the possession of health, sound nerves, energy, practical common sense, toughness, prudence, very few wants, and everything else that might be found necessary by anyone wandering along the path of the idea. I believed myself, further, to wear the protective armour of a temperament quite capable of enduring an eventual failure of my plan. . . .

What seemed to my friends the most irrational thing in my plan was that I wanted to go to Africa, not as a missionary, but as a doctor, and thus when already thirty years of age burdened myself as a beginning with a long period of laborious study. And that this study would mean for me a tremendous effort, I had no manner of doubt. I did, in truth, look forward to the next few years with dread. But the reasons which determined me to follow the way of service I had chosen, as a doctor, weighed so heavily that other considerations were as dust in the balance.

I wanted to be a doctor that I might be able to work without having to talk. For years I had been giving myself out in words, and it was with joy that I had followed the calling of theological teacher and of preacher. But this new form of activity I could not represent to myself as being talking about the religion of love, but only as an actual putting it into practice. Medical knowledge made it possible for me to carry out my intention in the best and most complete way, wherever the path of service might lead me. In view of the plan for Equatorial Africa, the acquisition of such knowledge was especially indicated because in the district to which I thought of going a doctor was, according to the missionaries' reports, the most needed of all needed things. They were always complaining in their magazine that the natives who visited them in physical suffering could not be given the help they desired. To become one day the doctor whom these poor creatures needed, it was worth while, so I judged, to become a medical student. Whenever I was inclined to feel that the years I should have to sacrifice were too long, I reminded myself that Hamilcar and Hannibal had prepared for their march on Rome by their slow and tedious conquest of Spain.

There was still one more point of view from which I seemed directed to become a doctor. From what I knew of the Parisian Missionary Society, I could not but feel it to be very doubtful whether they would accept me as a missionary. . . .

The kindly Director of the Mission, Monsieur Boegner, was much moved at finding that someone had offered to join the Congo Mission in answer to his appeal, but at once confided to me that serious objections would be raised to my theological standpoint by members of the Committee, and that these would have to be cleared away first. My assurance that I wanted to come "merely as a doctor" lifted a heavy weight from his mind, but a little later he had to inform me that some members objected even to the acceptance of a mission-doctor, who had only correct Christian love, and did not, in their opinion, hold also the correct Christian belief. However, we both resolved not to worry about the matter too much so long beforehand, and relied on the fact that the objectors still had some years to wait during which they might be able to attain to a truly Christian reasonableness.

No doubt the more liberal Allgemeine Evangelische Missionsverein (General Union of Evangelical Missions) in Switzerland would have accepted me without hesitation either as missionary or doctor. But as I felt my call to Equatorial Africa had come to me through the article in the Paris Mission magazine, I felt I ought to try to join that Mission, if possible, in its activities in that colony. Further, I was tempted to persist in getting a decision on the question whether, face to face with the Gospel of Jesus, a missionary society could justifiably arrogate to itself the right to refuse to the suffering natives in their district the services of a doctor, because in their opinion he was not sufficiently orthodox.

But over and above all this, my daily work and daily worries, now that I was beginning my medical course, made such demands upon me, that I had neither time nor strength to concern myself about what was to happen afterwards.

Samuel M. Shoemaker
(1893–1963)

Sam Shoemaker was one of a very few in his time who sensed the importance of the life of inner spirituality. Theologians, church leaders, and preachers tended not to be very personal or disclosive about their devotional life or conversion experience, if any. It was a blasé, aloof generation following World War I, and religion became perfunctory and formalized. Sam knew all about this first-hand as an undergraduate at Princeton University and later as the director of the Student Christian Association on campus.

After college, Shoemaker signed up for a "short term" missionary teaching stint at a Chinese boys' school sponsored by a group of interested Princeton alumni. This was a popular and adventuresome post-graduate option for those who felt some Christian or humanist concern for the peoples of Asia. While in Peking, as he tells the story, Sam was himself reconverted in the process of trying to convert a Chinese friend. The experience stuck; it changed Sam's life by providing direction and purpose for his future brilliant ministry.

Returning to New York, Shoemaker attended General Theological Seminary and became the assistant minister at Grace Episcopal Church. In 1925, he was appointed Rector of Calvary Episcopal Church, and in 1952 he moved to the Calvary Episcopal Church in Pittsburgh. He was a dynamic preacher, a compassionate pastor, and an intellectual and literary innovator. The author of a dozen popular books, he also edited a series of religious magazines, the best known of which, with a worldwide circulation, was Faith at Work.

While in Peking, Shoemaker met Frank Buchman, the founder of the so-called Oxford Group Movement which later became known as Moral Re-Armament. He had launched his religious program at Princeton University with mixed and controversial results. Sam was apparently deeply moved by the movement but never identified himself as a "Buchmanite."

Shoemaker took the best out of the Oxford Group and put it back into the full-time ministry of his mainline church. This meant a vigorous program of evangelism among all sorts of people, open and honest religious self-appraisal, cell groups and prayer fellowships of all kinds. The effect of this emphasis was to bring personal religious experience out into the open, unashamedly, for all to see. Sam Shoemaker, a no-nonsense, Ivy

League, articulate Episcopalian rector, was just the man to do it — ahead of his time.

The account of the conversion episode comes from "The Turning Point," in his book *Faith at Work* (New York: Hawthorn Books, Inc., 1958), 80-84. Reprinted by permission.

 An experience in Peking . . . in January of 1918 changed the course of my life and ministry. It was war-time. I had gone out to China on short-term because I had agreed to go before the war began and was free to do so, having drawn a high number in the draft; but also because I had heard Dr. W. E. Orchard, then of King's Weigh House, London, say that "foreign missions are the one indisputably Christian flag flying at this moment."

Princeton University maintained then a business school where Chinese boys learned the rudiments of English and business methods. It was lodged in the Peking Christian Association.

Soon after my arrival, I was given a Bible class of young businessmen who were enquirers into the Christian faith. We gathered in my room around the stove. The first time there were about twenty, the next about fourteen, and the third about seven! I was aware that something was the matter with the Bible class, and with the methods I was using. But this was not all that was the matter. *God cannot use a channel that is not open.*

I had been brought up in a responsible, church-going Episcopalian family. I thank God for all those early associations and for what I learned. It had turned me towards religion and decided me on the ministry. But this is not enough. In China I found I did not have sufficient power to communicate my faith to other people. (I had learned that at home, too, but it was sharpened by the new experience.)

About that time a group of people came into the city who brought with them spiritual power. They seemed to know how to make faith live for other people, how to win them for Christ and set them on fire. Frank Buchman was the leader of this company, and I listened to what he told, and then went round to see him, asking him if he wouldn't help a young Chinese businessman who had been in my class, was not satisfied with Buddhism, and was seeking.

I have parted company with Frank Buchman for various reasons, but till my dying day I shall be thankful to him for what he did for me in those early times. He was the first, older religious leader who did not pat me on the back and say how fine it was I was going into the ministry. He said instead, "Why don't you win this man yourself?"

I replied that I had not been brought up in just that way and that we didn't do it quite that way in my Church. Then he said, "Now, what is the real reason?"

I countered by asking what he thought it was and he said, "Might be sin—resentment kept me from this kind of work for a whole year." He put before me "four absolutes" which Dr. Robert E. Speer distilled out as the essence of the Sermon on the Mount—absolute honesty, purity, unselfishness, and love. That night, when trying to say my prayers, everything jammed. I knew I was up against my Waterloo. Either I would or would not "let go."

Then I made my surrender to God's will so far as I could see it at the time. The crux of it was the willingness to stay in China for life if God willed it. Some of us have wills like a bar of iron, and it is hard to break them and let God's will come into their place. I faced as honestly as I could my sins and got down on my knees and gave them to God, and my will with them. I felt no emotion about this and saw no stars nor bright lights; but afterwards I felt light and at ease, as if life had slipped into its right groove at last.

Next morning I wakened with an uneasy sense that I must go and talk to my young Chinese business friend myself. That afternoon I got into a ricksha and drove over to the East City where he lived. I paced up and down outside his door, almost prayed he wouldn't be home, for I did not yet know what I would say to him. I don't know what would have happened if he had been out that day—but he wasn't!

Crossing his threshold I prayed God to tell me what to say. And it seemed to come to me, "Tell him what happened to you last night."

My Chinese friend asked me to sit down, and in a pair of creaky wicker chairs we began to talk.

"I believe you have been interested in my class," I began, "but not satisfied with it. The fault has been mine. May I tell you something that happened to me last night?" He listened to my story intently and when I had finished surprised me with, "I wish that could happen to me."

"It can if you will let God in completely."

And that day he made his decision and found Christ.

This is the way I began to be interested in one person at a time. After this I sought out individual after individual and asked each one to accept Christ and surrender himself to Him. Every day I would try to see one of the schoolboys after hours, and every evening a young man in business or government service.

I soon saw that there were four elements in the initial decision:

(1) *The break with conscious wrong.* Either sin controls us, or God controls us. And pride is the root sin—the pride that fundamentally wants to get on in its own way, even if one calls on God to help.

Many Christians do not make this step decisive enough and it accounts for their falling by the wayside later. Nothing can be tolerated that interferes with God's pouring His power into and through us.

(2) *Daily time for personal devotions.* I had struggled with the old

"morning watch," and found prayer dry and the Bible like sawdust. Somehow my new experience made prayer live, for prayer became seeking God's will afresh, not trying to change it.

The Bible opened up as a living record of those who tried to live in obedience to God's will. I shall never forget how it helped me to read every reference I could find to Simon Peter; he had so many weaknesses, yet God greatly used him.

(3) *The need to put life's major decisions in God's hands.* It was not enough to have decided to be a minister; where did God want me, how must I serve Him, would I go anywhere if He said so? So many of us want to keep matters of vocation, and marriage, too, purely private, as our own choice and decision. But marriage also must be entered into in accordance with God's will, so far as we can find it. Christian marriage *is* a vocation.

(4) *The need to learn how to witness.* Most Christians are tongue-tied, and most Communists are articulate—that is the most serious fact in our world. If faith is real to us, we should be able to make it real to others.

Many of us cannot witness, because we have no real experience of conversion, of prayer, of experienced power, to witness to. We call it shyness, but it is really spiritual poverty. We can learn to make friends, to help people to talk about themselves, to bring Christ to bear upon the situations they reveal, to help them accept Him and begin living with Him, in Him, for Him.

We are not saved by our experiences; we are saved by the "mighty acts" of Christ for us—the Crucifixion and the Resurrection. But for many, these vast truths will only begin to be real as they come to see how He can help them with their immediate problems and situations.

These have been wonderful years. There have been bad failures and old Satan comes back always along familiar paths. But I would not take anything for the initial experience that launched me out in faith and flung me into the lives of individual persons, and taught me something of the small group wherein this new life is best conserved.

Thanks be to God Who giveth us the victory.

C. S. Lewis
(1898 — 1963)

It is probably true that C. S. Lewis has in our time instructed more people in the reasonableness of Christian faith than all the theological faculties in the world. The curious thing is that he has done this almost entirely through the written word, while he himself has been content to remain mostly hidden and inconspicuous.

Like Thomas Aquinas, the "dumb ox" who roared like a lion, the quiet, scholarly Oxford and Cambridge professor, immersed in his books and his writing, became the foremost Christian apologist of the twentieth century.

Without pen and paper, we would likely not have heard of Clive Staples Lewis. Today there are more books and articles about him than he himself produced. And his literary output was substantial, including poetry, literary criticism, allegory, science fiction, novels, children's books, as well as a whole series of volumes on theology and Christian doctrine.

The so-called space trilogy, which consists of *Out of the Silent Planet* (1938), *Perelandra* (1943), and *That Hideous Strength* (1946), predated the current immensely popular science fiction craze. But Lewis's stories are parables as well as fantasies, and they are devoured by old as well as young readers. *The Screwtape Letters* (1942), best known and in some ways symbolic of his literary signature, combines all his talents for story-telling with a serious purpose.

The genius of Lewis's impact rests, no doubt, with the fact that he speaks to all kinds of people, the agnostic and the seeker, the child and the adult, the liberal and the conservative. Perhaps his classical training has something to do with his ability to convey meaning for us today out of the collective treasury of Greece and Rome and the whole of Western culture.

C. S. Lewis has told of his conversion experience in his book entitled *Surprised by Joy* (1955). The word "joy" is used by him in a special way and is not the same as happiness, gladness, or pleasure. In fact, for Lewis it includes a measure of agony and grief, but if once experienced it is eagerly sought for again and again. As would be expected, this personal account is closely reasoned, deliberate, and reflective. And it rings true.

The odd thing was that before God closed in on me, I was in fact
offered what now appears a moment of wholly free choice. In a sense. I
was going up Headington Hill on the top of a bus. Without words and (I
think) almost without images, a fact about myself was somehow presented
to me. I became aware that I was holding something at bay, or shutting
something out. Or, if you like, that I was wearing some stiff clothing, like
corsets, or even a suit of armour, as if I were a lobster. I felt myself being,
there and then, given a free choice. I could open the door or keep it shut;
I could unbuckle the armour or keep it on. Neither choice was presented
as a duty; no threat or promise was attached to either, though I knew that
to open the door or to take off the corslet meant the incalculable. The
choice appeared to be momentous but it was also strangely unemotional.
I was moved by no desires or fears. In a sense I was not moved by anything.
I chose to open, to unbuckle, to loosen the rein. I say, "I chose," yet it did
not really seem possible to do the opposite. On the other hand, I was aware
of no motives. You could argue that I was not a free agent, but I am more
inclined to think that this came nearer to being a perfectly free act than
most that I have ever done. Necessity may not be the opposite of freedom,
and perhaps a man is most free when, instead of producing motives, he
could only say, "I am what I do." Then came the repercussion on the
imaginative level. I felt as if I were a man of snow at long last beginning
to melt. The melting was starting in my back—drip-drip and presently
trickle-trickle. I rather disliked the feeling. . . .

Really, a young Atheist cannot guard his faith too carefully. Dangers
lie in wait for him on every side. You must not do, you must not even try
to do, the will of the Father unless you are prepared to "know of the
doctrine." All my acts, desires, and thoughts were to be brought into har-
mony with universal Spirit. For the first time I examined myself with a
seriously practical purpose. And there I found what appalled me; a zoo of
lusts, a bedlam of ambitions, a nursery of fears, a hareem of fondled hatreds.
My name was legion.

Of course I could do nothing—I could not last out one hour—
without continual conscious recourse to what I called Spirit. But the fine,
philosophical distinction between this and what ordinary people call "prayer
to God" breaks down as soon as you start doing it in earnest. Idealism can
be talked, and even felt; it cannot be lived. It became patently absurd to
go on thinking of "Spirit" as either ignorant of, or passive to, my ap-
proaches. Even if my own philosophy were true, how could the initiative
lie on my side? My own analogy, as I now first perceived, suggested the
opposite: if Shakespeare and Hamlet could ever meet, it must be Shake-

speare's doing.[1] Hamlet could initiate nothing. Perhaps, even now, my Absolute Spirit still differed in some way from the God of religion. The real issue was not, or not yet, there. The real terror was that if you seriously believed in even such a "God" or "Spirit" as I admitted, a wholly new situation developed. As the dry bones shook and came together in that dreadful valley of Ezekiel's, so now a philosophical theorem, cerebrally entertained, began to stir and heave and throw off its gravecloths, and stood upright and became a living presence. I was to be allowed to play at philosophy no longer. It might, as I say, still be true that my "Spirit" differed in some way from "the God of popular religion." My Adversary waived the point. It sank into utter unimportance. He would not argue about it. He only said, "I am the Lord"; "I am that I am"; "I am."

People who are naturally religious find difficulty in understanding the horror of such a revelation. Amiable agnostics will talk cheerfully about "man's search for God." To me, as I then was, they might as well have talked about the mouse's search for the cat. The best image of my predicament is the meeting of Mime and Wotan in the first act of *Siegfried; hier brauch' ich nicht Spärer noch Späher, Einsam will ich* . . . (I've no use for spies and snoopers. I would be private. . . .)

Remember, I had always wanted, above all things, not to be "interfered with." I had wanted (mad wish) "to call my soul my own." I had been far more anxious to avoid suffering than to achieve delight. I had always aimed at limited liabilities. The supernatural itself had been to me, first, an illicit dram, and then, as by a drunkard's reaction, nauseous. Even my recent attempt to live my philosophy had secretly (I now knew) been hedged round by all sorts of reservations. I had pretty well known that my ideal of virtue would never be allowed to lead me into anything intolerably painful; I would be "reasonable." But now what had been an ideal became a command; and what might not be expected of one? Doubtless, by definition, God was Reason itself. But would He also be "reasonable" in that other, more comfortable, sense? Not the slightest assurance on that score was offered me. Total surrender, the absolute leap in the dark, were demanded. The reality with which no treaty can be made was upon me. The demand was not even "All or nothing." . . .

You must picture me alone in that room in Magdalen, night after night, feeling, whenever my mind lifted even for a second from my work, the steady, unrelenting approach of Him whom I so earnestly desired not to meet. That which I greatly feared had at last come upon me. In the Trinity Term of 1929 I gave in, and admitted that God was God, and knelt and prayed: perhaps, that night, the most dejected and reluctant convert

---

[1] I.e. Shakespeare could, in principle, make himself appear as Author within the play, and write a dialogue between Hamlet and himself. The "Shakespeare" within the play would of course be at once Shakespeare and one of Shakespeare's creatures. It would bear some analogy to Incarnation.

in all England. I did not then see what is now the most shining and obvious thing; the Divine humility which will accept a convert even on such terms. The Prodigal Son at least walked home on his own feet. But who can duly adore that Love which will open the high gates to a prodigal who is brought in kicking, struggling, resentful, and darting his eyes in every direction for a chance of escape? The words *compelle intrare,* compel them to come in, have been so abused by wicked men that we shudder at them; but, properly understood, they plumb the depth of the Divine mercy. The hardness of God is kinder than the softness of men, and His compulsion is our liberation. . . .

It must be understood that the conversion . . . was only to Theism, pure and simple, not to Christianity. I knew nothing yet about the Incarnation. The God to whom I surrendered was sheerly non-human.

It may be asked whether my terror was at all relieved by the thought that I was now approaching the source from which those arrows of Joy had been shot at me ever since childhood. Not in the least. No slightest hint was vouchsafed me that there ever had been or ever would be any connection between God and Joy. If anything, it was the reverse. I had hoped that the heart of reality might be of such a kind that we can best symbolise it as a place; instead, I found it to be a Person. For all I knew, the total rejection of what I called Joy might be one of the demands, might be the very first demand, He would make upon me. There was no strain of music from within, no smell of eternal orchards at the threshold, when I was dragged through the doorway. No kind of desire was present at all.

My conversion involved as yet no belief in a future life. I now number it among my greatest mercies that I was permitted for several months, perhaps for a year, to know God and to attempt obedience without even raising that question. . . .

The last stage in my story, the transition from mere Theism to Christianity, is the one on which I am now least informed. Since it is also the most recent, this ignorance may seem strange. I think there are two reasons. One is that as we grow older we remember the more distant past better than what is nearer. But the other is, I believe, that one of the first results of my Theistic conversion was a marked decrease (and high time, as all readers of this book will agree) in the fussy attentiveness which I had so long paid to the progress of my own opinions and the states of my own mind. For many healthy extroverts self-examination first begins with conversion. For me it was almost the other way round. Self-examination did of course continue. But it was (I suppose, for I cannot quite remember) at stated intervals, and for a practical purpose; a duty, a discipline, an uncomfortable thing, no longer a hobby or a habit. To believe and to pray were the beginning of extroversion. I had been, as they say, "taken out of myself." If Theism had done nothing else for me, I should still be thankful that it cured me of the time-wasting and foolish practice of keeping a diary.

(Even for autobiographical purposes a diary is nothing like so useful as I had hoped. You put down each day what you think important; but of course you cannot each day see what will prove to have been important in the long run.[2])

As soon as I became a Theist I started attending my parish church on Sundays and my college chapel on weekdays; not because I believed in Christianity, nor because I thought the difference between it and simple Theism a small one, but because I thought one ought to "fly one's flag" by some unmistakable overt sign. I was acting in obedience to a (perhaps mistaken) sense of honour. The idea of churchmanship was to me wholly unattractive. I was not in the least anti-clerical, but I was deeply anti-ecclesiastical. . . .

But though I liked clergymen as I liked bears, I had as little wish to be in the Church as in the zoo. It was, to begin with, a kind of collective; a wearisome "get-together" affair. I couldn't yet see how a concern of that sort should have anything to do with one's spiritual life. To me, religion ought to have been a matter of good men praying alone and meeting by twos and threes to talk of spiritual matters. And then the fussy, time-wasting botheration of it all! the bells, the crowds, the umbrellas, the notices, the bustle, the perpetual arranging and organising. Hymns were (and are) extremely disagreeable to me. Of all musical instruments I liked (and like) the organ least. I have, too, a sort of spiritual *gaucherie* which makes me unapt to participate in any rite. . . .

I was by now too experienced in literary criticism to regard the Gospels as myths. They had not the mythical taste. And yet the very matter which they set down in their artless, historical fashion—those narrow, unattractive Jews, too blind to the mythical wealth of the Pagan world around them—was precisely the matter of the great myths. If ever a myth had become fact, had been incarnated, it would be just like this. And nothing else in all literature was just like this. Myths were like it in one way. Histories were like it in another. But nothing was simply like it. And no person was like the Person it depicted; as real, as recognisable, through all that depth of time, as Plato's Socrates or Boswell's Johnson (ten times more so than Eckermann's Goethe or Lockhart's Scott), yet also numinous, lit by a light from beyond the world, a god. But if a god—we are no longer polytheists—then not a god, but God. Here and here only in all time the myth must have become fact; the Word, flesh; God, Man. This is not "a religion," nor "a philosophy." It is the summing up and actuality of them all. . . .

---

[2] The only real good I got from keeping a diary was that it taught me a just appreciation of Boswell's amazing genius. I tried very hard to reproduce conversations, in some of which very amusing and striking people had taken part. But none of these people came to life in the diary at all. Obviously something quite different from mere accurate reporting went to the presentation of Boswell's Langton, Beauclerk, Wilkes, and the rest.

I know very well when, but hardly how, the final step was taken. I was driven to Whipsnade one sunny morning. When we set out I did not believe that Jesus Christ is the Son of God, and when we reached the zoo I did. Yet I had not exactly spent the journey in thought. Nor in great emotion. "Emotional" is perhaps the last word we can apply to some of the most important events. It was more like when a man, after long sleep, still lying motionless in bed, becomes aware that he is now awake. . . .

Freedom, or necessity? Or do they differ at their maximum? At that maximum a man is what he does; there is nothing of him left over or outside the act. As for what we commonly call Will, and what we commonly call Emotion, I fancy these usually talk too loud, protest too much, to be quite believed, and we have a secret suspicion that the great passion or the iron resolution is partly a put-up job.

They have spoiled Whipsnade since then. Wallaby Wood, with the birds singing overhead and the bluebells underfoot and the Wallabies hopping all round one, was almost Eden come again.

But what, in conclusion, of Joy? for that, after all, is what the story has mainly been about. To tell you the truth, the subject has lost nearly all interest for me since I became a Christian. I cannot, indeed, complain, like Wordsworth, that the visionary gleam has passed away. I believe (if the thing were at all worth recording) that the old stab, the old bittersweet, has come to me as often and as sharply since my conversion as at any time of my life whatever. But I now know that the experience, considered as a state of my own mind, had never had the kind of importance I once gave it. It was valuable only as a pointer to something other and outer. While that other was in doubt, the pointer naturally loomed large in my thoughts. When we are lost in the woods the sight of a signpost is a great matter. He who first sees it cries, "Look!" The whole party gathers round and stares. But when we have found the road and are passing signposts every few miles, we shall not stop and stare. They will encourage us and we shall be grateful to the authority that set them up. But we shall not stop and stare, or not much; not on this road, though their pillars are of silver and their lettering of gold. "We would be at Jerusalem."

Lin Yutang

(1895–1976)

Although missionaries can usually relate fascinating stories of converts to Christianity from other faiths, the story of Lin Yutang must be unusual. Born in China to Christian parents and educated in Christian schools, he renounced his Christian faith and became an ardent Confucianist.

After further study at Harvard and in Germany, Lin Yutang served in several academic positions in China — as professor of English at Peking National University, Dean of Peking's Women's Normal University, the English editor of *Academia Sinica*, editor of several Asian journals, Chancellor of Nanyang University, Singapore, and Head of the Arts and Letters Division of UNESCO, to name a few.

In 1937, Lin Yutang published *The Importance of Living*, the best known of his many books and a runaway best-seller. In one chapter, "Relationship to God," he headed one section — "Why I Am a Pagan." Christian theology, he said, repelled him with its "presumptuous arrogance" that it could know and define God. And so far as ethics goes, he preferred Confucianism as a better guide to life than Christianity.

Other books followed, most of them interpreting aspects of Chinese and Indian culture and philosophy. He invented a Chinese typewriter and became a symbol of the sophisticated, cosmopolitan Asian scholar. For the last decade of his life, he lived in New York. His wife attended the Madison Avenue Presbyterian Church, and one Sunday she persuaded Lin Yutang to accompany her.

The rest of the story is contained in an article, "Why I Came Back to Christianity," in *Presbyterian Life* (April 15, 1959): 13-15. Reprinted by permission.

Many people have asked me, some with great joy, some with great disappointment, why I, a self-declared pagan, have returned to Christianity. I have returned to Christianity and have rejoined the Christian church because I wish to re-enter that knowledge of God and love of God which Jesus revealed with such clarity and simplicity.

The question of paramount importance is, Can man survive without religion? For over thirty years, my only religion was humanism or the Confucian concept of the self-perfectibility of man through education—the belief that humanity is sufficient unto itself. I now believe that mankind cannot survive without religion; that humanity is not, and never has been, sufficient unto itself; that, for man's very survival, a religion of self-perfectibility is not religion enough. Man needs contact with a Power outside himself that is greater than himself. I believe that Christianity, because of what Christ revealed, offers man incomparably the best way to God. I have also been compelled to conclude that, as irreligion and materialism advance, the spirit of man decays and weakens, for I have witnessed the doings of a nation living without God.

A few words about my background are necessary. I was a third-generation Chinese Christian. My father was a Presbyterian minister in an inland village far back in the mountains from the port of Amoy on China's southeast coast. The valley where I lived, Paoa, was so completely closed in by mountains that it was called a "lake." I had a wonderful childhood, near to God and his greatness, filled with the beauty of the clouds on the jagged peaks, the gray-blue tints on the pastures at sunset, the sound of a brook's laughter. These memories have a close relation to my religion. They made me hate what is artificial and complicated and small.

In my childhood family life we had simplicity and love. We children were not supposed to quarrel, and we didn't. The quest for learning was implicit in our home. It was fantastic, but in that inland village of the early nineteen hundreds, when the Empress Dowager was still ruling China, my father talked to us of the Universities of Berlin and Oxford and, half jokingly, half seriously, expressed the hope that I might study there. We were a family of dreamers.

One incident influenced my life deeply. My second sister, gifted and good, wanted to go to college. But education in China in those days was for sons, seldom for daughters. My father could not afford to educate both. Instead, at twenty-one, she married, for Chinese girls were not supposed to reach that age and not be married. We came down on the same river boat—she for her wedding, I to go to Shanghai for my first year of college. After her wedding she took forty Chinese pennies from the pocket of her bridal dress and gave them to me and said, with tears in her eyes:

"You have your chance to go to college. Being a girl, your sister can't. Do not waste your opportunity. Make up your mind to be a good man, a useful man, and a famous man."

Two years later, she died of bubonic plague. The forty pennies were soon spent. Her words have remained with me.

In college in Shanghai, I studied for the ministry by my own choice. Then, what seemed to me the theological hocus-pocus discouraged me. As a matter of intellectual honesty, I dropped my intention of becoming a minister. While still believing in God, I turned from the church.

But other forces were at work to turn me toward paganism. After college I went to teach in Peking. Like many graduates of mission schools

I was backward in Chinese. I had scant acquaintance with Chinese folklore because, as a Christian, I was not supposed to listen to the songs of street minstrels. When we passed a theatrical performance in the square, we were supposed to look straight ahead and not loiter. In my childhood I had known how Joshua's trumpets blew down the walls of Jericho, but no one had told me how the tears of Chi-Liang's widow had melted down and washed away a section of the Great Wall of China. Coming into contact with an authentic Chinese society and the glories of Peking, I burned with shame at my ignorance and plunged into the study of Chinese literature and philosophy.

But the break was not easy for one brought up in a deeply religious home. I feared the leap from a God-sheltered world into stark paganism. Then one of my colleagues, a modern-educated man, made an appeal to me on the basis of the Confucian ideal of human dignity: "We should be good men because we are human beings." Confucius, I found, had bred men who dared death in order to do right. Mencius had said: "I love life, but I also love righteousness. If I cannot have both, I would sacrifice life to do what is right."

This was humanism: the belief in human reason and in man's power, lifting himself by his own bootstraps, to better himself and make a better world. Such was the doctrine—inspired, in part, by Confucius—of the 18th century rationalists: Voltaire, Diderot, Leibnitz. Theirs was called the Age of Enlightenment.

That doctrine appealed to me for many years as sufficient. Then below the surface of my life a disquiet, born of both reflection and experience, began to set in. I saw that the fruit of the humanistic age of enlightenment was an age of materialism. Man's increasing belief in himself as God did not seem to be making him more godlike. He was becoming more clever. But he had less and less of the sober, uplifting humility of one who has stood in the presence of God. Much of contemporary history seemed to me to indicate how dangerously near the savage state that man, lacking that humility, may be even while he is most advanced materially and technologically.

As the satisfactions of humanism declined, I increasingly asked myself: Is there a satisfying religion for the modern, educated man?

Like humanism, Confucianism, for all the high morality of its teachings, was not good enough simply because man on his own had so often and so disastrously shown he was not that good. Buddhism, though a religion of mercy, is based on the philosophy that all this sensuous world is only an illusion. The best the Buddhist has to say to humans and the most he has to offer to the world is, "The pity of it all." The teachings of Taoism come very near to the Sermon on the Mount. But the back-to-nature and beware-of-progress appeal inherent in Taoism is neither congenial to the modern soul nor helpful in solving man's modern problems.

Perhaps in this period the faith of my childhood was subconsciously reviving. Wherever we traveled during these years my wife always went to church. Sometimes I accompanied her. More often than not I came away discouraged rather than inspired. I could not stand a second-rate sermon. I squirmed in my seat at the rantings I heard about sin, hellfire, and brimstone. I would resolve not to go again.

Then one Sunday in New York City my wife again asked me to accompany her to church. She took care to point out that though I might or might not agree with the content of the sermon, I was certain to be impressed by its literary quality and the eloquence of the preacher. I was then at the crossroads, and I went. The church to which she took me was the Madison Avenue Presbyterian Church; the minister, Dr. David Read.

I did like the beauty of Dr. Read's English and his delivery, but that was not the point. His subject that morning was eternal life. I was more than curious as to what he would say. A heaven where we go on and on spending eternity praising God, where we do not falter or thirst or hunger from morning to night, day after day, had no attraction for me. The pearly gates were to me like a pawnbroker's dream. Many people who never set foot inside Tiffany's in this life hoped to do so in the next.

"What is eternal life?" asked the minister. It is certainly more, he said, than just going on living. It is more than continuance of life on the animal level of food, sleep, and reproduction; more than life on the secular level—the level on which we make our living, pay our debts, send our children to school.

There is, however, a higher level where man has a yearning for spiritual values and can be moved to unselfish sacrifice. That higher life concerned with spiritual values and conscious of the mysteries of the moral law within and the starry heavens above is the "life plus." That life deserves eternity, and on that level eternity will be eternally satisfying.

I returned again and again to that church. I returned also to a study of the awe-inspiring simplicity and beauty of the teachings of Jesus. The scales began to fall from my eyes.

I found—as though I had never read of him before—that no one ever spoke like Jesus. He spoke of God the Father as one who knew him and was identified with him in the fullness of knowledge and love. No other teacher of men revealed such personal knowledge or such a sense of personal identity with God. The result was his astounding claim: "He that hath seen me hath seen the Father."

It was astounding, too, that God, as Jesus revealed him, is so different from what men had thought him to be. There is a totally new order of love and compassion in Jesus' prayer from the cross, "Father, forgive them; for they know not what they do." That voice, unknown in history before, reveals God as forgiving, not in theory, but visibly forgiving as revealed in Christ. No other teacher said with such meaning, "Inasmuch as ye have done it unto one of the least of these my brethren, ye have done it unto me." The "me" in this context is God sitting on the Day of Judgment with a first concern for the downtrodden poor, the humble widow, the crippled orphan. There, I said to myself, Jesus speaks as the Teacher who is Master over both life and death. In him, this message of love and gentleness and compassion becomes incarnate. That, I saw, is why men have turned to him, not merely in respect but in adoration. That is why the light which blinded St. Paul on the road to Damascus with such a sudden impact continues to shine unobscured and unobscurably through the centuries.

I know, of course, that the teaching that God is Love and the consequent compulsion to make ours a better world must be derided and scoffed at by the materialists of our generation who believe that the world is only a whirl of blind atoms obeying blind mechanical laws. Such a gospel, too, must be despised and feared by the Marxists who preach hatred and violence. I do not know of anything, certainly not humanism, which will deter man from hatred and violence and cunning and deceit except these very opposite teachings and assumptions and compulsions of Christianity. In order to achieve a materially successful godless society, the Communists must first destroy man's fear of God. A good Christian makes a poor Communist and vice versa. The conflict between a godless society and one in which God is allowed room in the hearts of men is instinctive and elemental.

I no longer ask, "Is there a satisfying religion for the modern educated man?" I know there is. Returning to the Bible, I have found in it not merely a record of historical events but an authentic revelation that brings God, through Christ, within my reach. I have returned to the church. I am happy in my accustomed pew on Sunday morning. I believe we go to church not because we are sinners, and not because we are paragons of Christian virtue, but because we are conscious of our spiritual heritage, aware of our higher nature and equally conscious of our human failings and of the slough of self-complacency into which, without help from this greater power outside ourselves, we so easily fall back.

He who would reach out to see the incomparable beauty and soul-charging power of the teachings of Christ must often struggle against the "religious" claptrap that tends to obscure it. But it was Jesus himself who simplified for us the essence of Christianity and its adequacy above any other faith: Upon the two commandments, to love God and to love one's neighbor, "hang all the law and the prophets." That Person and that Gospel I have found sufficient—a sufficiency which is joyously renewed each day. Nothing less than that Person and Gospel can be sufficient for the world.

Looking back on my life, I know that for thirty years I lived in this world like an orphan. I am an orphan no longer. Where I had been drifting, I have arrived. The Sunday morning when I rejoined the Christian church was a homecoming.

Dorothy Day
(1897–1980)

By her own admission, Dorothy Day was "different." Throughout her life, she combined an intense commitment to social justice with an unwavering allegiance to the Roman Catholic Church. With Peter Maurin, she became associated with the Catholic Worker Movement, and through its newspaper, *The Catholic Worker*, she spoke out tirelessly for renewed religious dedication and alleviation of the plight of the poor.

Political radicals considered Dorothy Day's religiosity odd, and fellow Catholics often questioned her politics. But she asked her own question: "Where are the saints to call the masses to God?" Her answer was that all must seek to be saints, for in that, she emphasized, "is the Revolution."

Day's beginnings did not point toward sainthood. In fact, her biographer, William Miller, observed, "If anyone, in the first twenty-five years of life, seemed headed for despair, it was she, yet she turned away from that fate and, having set her vision on eternity, she never looked back."

Coming from an ostensibly religious home, she was attracted to leftist politics and alienated intellectuals. Settling for a time in New York, she began nurse's training, endured an unhappy love affair, and entered upon a painful, short-lived marriage. Turning to writing, she published a novel and settled down to live with her common-law husband, Foster Batterham. In June 1926, she was overjoyed to find she was pregnant. But her desire that her daughter, Tamar, be baptized in the church conflicted with Batterham's disgust with all religion, and they separated.

The following account chronicles Day's struggle to become a Catholic and to have her baby baptized, and it concludes with her "postscript" on the purpose of the Catholic Worker Movement and her witness of "a harsh and dreadful love." The concern for baptism can be misinterpreted, for Dorothy Day was not seeking respectability or absolution for her "sin." Writing in her "notes," she said, "It was the glories of creation, the tender beauty of flowers and shells, the songs of birds, the smile of my baby, these things brought such exultation, such joy to my heart that I could not but cry out in praise of God."

Dorothy Day was haunted, as many have been, by Francis Thompson's poem "The Hound of Heaven," and eventually through a series of retreats she achieved serenity of purpose. "So I will not be afraid," she wrote, "and I will talk of love and write of love, and God will help me, I will suffer from it too – the humiliations, the degradations, the misunderstandings because 'what is it I love when I love my God?' "

She became the dominant and outstanding figure of the Catholic left, deeply influencing Thomas Merton, Daniel Berrigan, Michael Harrington, John Cogley, Cesar Chavez, and many others. She wrote constantly, traveled and spoke across the country, and when she returned "home," it was to the Catholic Worker soup kitchen on the lower East Side. She combined her radical politics for the poor with pacifism and a conservative, nonquestioning view of liturgy and the sacraments. The church was the center of her life; "she taught me the crowning love of the life of the Spirit."

Despite her dedication and devotion, she felt that "we have scarcely begun to be Christian, to deserve the name Christian," and that sometimes one lived "on blind and naked faith." And yet "God sends intimations of immortality. We believe that if the will is right, God will take us by the hair of the head, as he did Habakkuk, who brought food to Daniel in the lions' den, and will restore us to the Way and no matter what our wandering, we can still say, 'All is Grace.' "

Excerpted from Dorothy Day, *The Long Loneliness* (New York: Harper & Row, 1952), 132-51; 285-86. The autobiography was reprinted in 1981 with an introduction by Daniel Berrigan. Copyright, 1952, by Harper & Row and reprinted by permission of the publisher.

I was surprised that I found myself beginning to pray daily. I could not get down on my knees, but I could pray while I was walking. If I got down on my knees I thought, "Do I really believe? Whom am I praying to?" A terrible doubt came over me, and a sense of shame, and I wondered if I was praying because I was lonely, because I was unhappy.

But when I walked to the village for the mail, I found myself praying again, holding in my pocket the rosary that Mary Gordon gave me in New Orleans some years before. Maybe I did not say it correctly but I kept on saying it because it made me happy.

Then I thought suddenly, scornfully, "Here you are in a stupor of content. You are biological. Like a cow. Prayer with you is like the opiate of the people." And over and over again in my mind that phrase was repeated jeeringly, "Religion is the opiate of the people."

"But," I reasoned with myself, "I am praying because I am happy, not because I am unhappy. I did not turn to God in unhappiness, in grief, in despair—to get consolation, to get something from Him."

And encouraged that I was praying because I wanted to thank Him, I went on praying. No matter how dull the day, how long the walk seemed, if I felt sluggish at the beginning of the walk, the words I had been saying insinuated themselves into my heart before I had finished, so that on the trip back I neither prayed nor thought but was filled with exultation.

Along the beach I found it appropriate to say the *Te Deum.* When

I worked about the house, I found myself addressing the Blessed Virgin and turning toward her statue.

It is so hard to say how this delight in prayer grew on me. The year before, I was saying as I planted seeds in the garden, "I *must* believe in these seeds, that they fall into the earth and grow into flowers and radishes and beans. It is a miracle to me because I do not understand it. Neither do naturalists understand it. The very fact that they use glib technical phrases does not make it any less of a miracle, and a miracle we all accept. Then why not accept God's mysteries?"

I began to go to Mass regularly on Sunday mornings. . . .

It was pleasant rowing about in the calm bay with Forster. The oyster boats were all out, and far on the horizon, off Sandy Hook, there was a four-masted vessel. I had the curious delusion that several huge holes had been stove in her side, through which you could see the blue sky. The other vessels seemed sailing in the air, quite indifferent to the horizon on which they should properly have been resting. Forster tried to explain to me scientific facts about mirages and atmospheric conditions, and, on the other hand, I pointed out to him how our senses lie to us.

But it was impossible to talk about religion or faith to him. A wall immediately separated us. The very love of nature, and the study of her secrets which was bringing me to faith, cut Forster off from religion.

I had known Forster a long time before we contracted our common-law relationship, and I have always felt that it was life with him that brought me natural happiness, that brought me to God.

His ardent love of creation brought me to the Creator of all things. But when I cried out to him, "How can there be no God, when there are all these beautiful things," he turned from me uneasily and complained that I was never satisfied. We loved each other so strongly that he wanted to remain in the love of the moment; he wanted me to rest in that love. He cried out against my attitude that there would be nothing left of that love without a faith.

I remembered the love story in Romain Rolland's *Jean Christophe,* the story of his friend and his engrossing marriage, and how those young people exhausted themselves in the intensity of their emotions.

I could not see that love between man and woman was incompatible with love of God. God is the Creator, and the very fact that we were begetting a child made me have a sense that we were made in the image and likeness of God, co-creators with him. I could not protest with Sasha about "that initial agony of having to live." Because I was grateful for love, I was grateful for life, and living with Forster made me appreciate it and even reverence it still more. He had introduced me to so much that was beautiful and good that I felt I owed to him too this renewed interest in the things of the spirit. . . .

Our child was born in March at the end of a harsh winter. In December I had come in from the country and taken an apartment in town. My sister came to stay with me, to help me over the last hard months. It was good to be there, close to friends, close to a church where I could pray. I read the *Imitation of Christ* a great deal during those months. I knew that I was going to have my child baptized, cost what it may. I knew that I was not going to have her floundering through many years as I had done, doubting and hesitating, undisciplined and amoral. I felt it was the greatest thing I could do for my child. For myself, I prayed for the gift of faith. I was sure, yet not sure. I postponed the day of decision.

A woman does not want to be alone at such a time. Even the most hardened, the most irreverent, is awed by the stupendous fact of creation. Becoming a Catholic would mean facing life alone and I clung to family life. It was hard to contemplate giving up a mate in order that my child and I could become members of the Church. Forster would have nothing to do with religion or with me if I embraced it. So I waited.

Those last months of waiting I was too happy to know the unrest of indecision. The days were slow in passing, but week by week the time came nearer. I spent some time in writing, but for the most part I felt a great stillness. I was incapable of going to meetings, of seeing many people, of taking up the threads of my past life.

When the little one was born, my joy was so great that I sat up in bed in the hospital and wrote an article for the *New Masses* about my child, wanting to share my joy with the world. I was glad to write this joy for a workers' magazine because it was a joy all women knew, no matter what their grief at poverty, unemployment and class war. The article so appealed to my Marxist friends that the account was reprinted all over the world in workers' papers. Diego Rivera, when I met him some four years afterward in Mexico, greeted me as the author of it. And Mike Gold, who was at that time editor of the *New Masses,* said it had been printed in many Soviet newspapers and that I had rubles awaiting me in Moscow. . . .

One of the disconcerting facts about the spiritual life is that God takes you at your word. Sooner or later one is given a chance to prove his love. The very word "diligo," the Latin word used for "love," means "I prefer." It was all very well to love God in His works, in the beauty of His creation which was crowned for me by the birth of my child. Forster had made the physical world come alive for me and had awakened in my heart a flood of gratitude. The final object of this love and gratitude was God. No human creature could receive or contain so vast a flood of love and joy as I often felt after the birth of my child. With this came the need to worship, to adore. I had heard many say that they wanted to worship God in their own way and did not need a Church in which to praise Him, nor a body of people with whom to associate themselves. But I did not agree to this. My very experience as a radical, my whole make-up, led me to want to associate myself with others, with the masses, in loving and praising

God. Without even looking into the claims of the Catholic Church, I was
willing to admit that for me she was the one true Church. She had come
down through the centuries since the time of Peter, and far from being
dead, she claimed and held the allegiance of the masses of people in all the
cities where I had lived. They poured in and out of her doors on Sundays
and holy days, for novenas and missions. What if they were compelled to
come in by the law of the Church, which said they were guilty of mortal
sin if they did not go to Mass every Sunday? They obeyed that law. They
were given a chance to show their preference. They accepted the Church.
It may have been an unthinking, unquestioning faith, and yet the chance
certainly came, again and again, "Do I prefer the Church to my own will,"
even if it was only the small matter of sitting at home on a Sunday morning
with the papers? And the choice was the Church. . . .

From the time Tamar Teresa was born I was intent on having her
baptized. There had been that young Catholic girl in the bed next to me
at the hospital who gave me a medal of St. Thérèse of Lisieux.

"I don't believe in these things," I told her, and it was another
example of people saying what they do not mean.

"If you love someone you like to have something around which
reminds you of them," she told me.

It was so obvious a truth that I was shamed. Reading William James'
Varieties of Religious Experience had acquainted me with the saints, and I had
read the life of St. Teresa of Ávila and fallen in love with her. She was a
mystic and a practical woman, a recluse and a traveler, a cloistered nun and
yet most active. She liked to read novels when she was a young girl, and
she wore a bright red dress when she entered the convent. Once when she
was traveling from one part of Spain to another with some other nuns and
a priest to start a convent, and their way took them over a stream, she was
thrown from her donkey. The story goes that our Lord said to her, "That
is how I treat my friends." And she replied, "And that is why You have so
few of them." She called life a "night spent at an uncomfortable inn." Once
when she was trying to avoid that recreation hour which is set aside in
convents for nuns to be together, the others insisted on her joining them,
and she took castanets and danced. When some older nuns professed themselves shocked, she retorted, "One must do things sometimes to make life
more bearable." After she was a superior she gave directions when the
nuns became melancholy, "to feed them steak," and there were other delightful little touches to the story of her life which made me love her and
feel close to her. I have since heard a priest friend of ours remark gloomily
that one could go to hell imitating the imperfections of the saints, but these
little incidents brought out in her biography made her delightfully near to
me. So I decided to name my daughter after her. That is why my neighbor
offered me a medal of St. Thérèse of Lisieux, who is called the little
Teresa. . . .

"How can your daughter be brought up a Catholic unless you become one yourself?" Sister Aloysia kept saying to me. But she went resolutely ahead in making arrangements for the baptism of Tamar Teresa.

"You must be a Catholic yourself," she kept telling me. She had no
reticence. She speculated rather volubly at times on the various reasons
why she thought I was holding back. She brought me pious literature to
read, saccharine stories of virtue, emasculated lives of saints young and old,
back numbers of pious magazines. William James, agnostic as he was, was
more help. He had introduced me to St. Teresa of Avila and St. John of
the Cross.

Isolated as I was in the country, knowing no Catholics except my
neighbors, who seldom read anything except newspapers and secular magazines, there was not much chance of being introduced to the good Catholic
literature of the present day. I was in a state of dull content—not in a state
to be mentally stimulated. I was too happy with my child. What faith I had
I held on to stubbornly. The need for patience emphasized in the writings
of the saints consoled me on the slow road I was traveling. I would put all
my affairs in the hands of God and wait.

Three times a week Sister Aloysia came to give me a catechism
lesson, which I dutifully tried to learn. But she insisted that I recite word
for word, with the repetition of the question that was in the book. If I had
not learned my lesson, she rebuked me, "And you think you are intelligent!" she would say witheringly. "What is the definition of grace—actual
grace and sanctifying grace? My fourth-grade pupils know more than you
do!". . .

I had no particular joy in partaking of these three sacraments, Baptism, Penance and Holy Eucharist. I proceeded about my own active par-
ticipation in them grimly, coldly, making acts of faith, and certainly with
no consolation whatever. One part of my mind stood at one side and kept
saying, "What are you doing? Are you sure of yourself? What kind of an
affectation is this? What act is this you are going through? Are you trying
to induce emotion, induce faith, partake of an opiate, the opiate of the
people?" I felt like a hypocrite if I got down on my knees, and shuddered
at the thought of anyone seeing me.

At my first communion I went up to the communion rail at the
Sanctus bell instead of at the *Domine, non sum dignus,* and had to kneel there
all alone through the consecration, through the *Pater Noster,* through the
Agnus Dei—and I had thought I knew the Mass so well! But I felt it fitting
that I be humiliated by this ignorance, by this precipitance.

I speak of the misery of leaving one love. But there was another
love too, the life I had led in the radical movement. That very winter I was
writing a series of articles, interviews with the workers, with the unemployed. I was working with the Anti-Imperialist League, a Communist af-
filiate, that was bringing aid and comfort to the enemy, General Sandino's

forces in Nicaragua. I was just as much against capitalism and imperialism as ever, and here I was going over to the opposition, because of course the Church was lined up with property, with the wealthy, with the state, with capitalism, with all the forces of reaction. This I had been taught to think and this I still think to a great extent. "Too often," Cardinal Mundelein said, "has the Church lined up on the wrong side." "Christianity," Bakunin said, "is precisely the religion par excellence, because it exhibits, and manifests, to the fullest extent, the very nature and essence of every religious system, which is the impoverishment, enslavement, and annihilation of humanity for the benefit of divinity."

I certainly believed this, but I wanted to be poor, chaste and obedient. I wanted to die in order to live, to put off the old man and put on Christ. I loved, in other words, and like all women in love, I wanted to be united to my love. Why should not Forster be jealous? Any man who did not participate in this love would, of course, realize my infidelity, my adultery. In the eyes of God, any turning toward creatures to the exclusion of Him is adultery and so it is termed over and over again in Scripture.

I loved the Church for Christ made visible. Not for itself, because it was so often a scandal to me. Romano Guardini said the Church is the Cross on which Christ was crucified; one could not separate Christ from His Cross, and one must live in a state of permanent dissatisfaction with the Church.

The scandal of businesslike priests, of collective wealth, the lack of a sense of responsibility for the poor, the worker, the Negro, the Mexican, the Filipino, and even the oppression of these, and the consenting to the oppression of them by our industrialist-capitalist order—these made me feel often that priests were more like Cain than Abel. "Am I my brother's keeper?" they seemed to say in respect to the social order. There was plenty of charity but too little justice. And yet the priests were the dispensers of the Sacraments, bringing Christ to men, all enabling us to put on Christ and to achieve more nearly in the world a sense of peace and unity. "The worst enemies would be those of our own household," Christ had warned us.

We could not root out the tares without rooting out the wheat also. With all the knowledge I have gained these twenty-one years I have been a Catholic, I could write many a story of priests who were poor, chaste and obedient, who gave their lives daily for their fellows, but I am writing of how I felt at the time of my baptism.

Not long afterward a priest wanted me to write a story of my conversion, telling how the social teaching of the Church had led me to embrace Catholicism. But I knew nothing of the social teaching of the Church at that time. I had never heard of the encyclicals. I felt that the Church was the Church of the poor, that St. Patrick's had been built from the pennies of servant girls, that it cared for the emigrant, it established hospitals, orphanages, day nurseries, houses of the Good Shepherd, homes for the aged, but at the same time, I felt that it did not set its face against a social order which made so much charity in the present sense of the word necessary. I felt that charity was a word to choke over. Who wanted charity? And it was not just human pride but a strong sense of man's dignity and worth, and what was due to him in justice, that made me resent, rather than feel proud of so mighty a sum total of Catholic institutions. Besides, more and more they were taking help from the state, and in taking from the state, they had to render to the state. They came under the head of Community Chest and discriminatory charity, centralizing and departmentalizing, involving themselves with bureaus, building, red tape, legislation, at the expense of human values. By "they," I suppose one always means the bishops, but as Harry Bridges once pointed out to me, "they" also are victims of the system.

*   *   *

We were just sitting there talking when Peter Maurin came in.

We were just sitting there talking when lines of people began to form, saying, "We need bread." We could not say, "Go, be thou filled." If there were six small loaves and a few fishes, we had to divide them. There was always bread.

We were just sitting there talking and people moved in on us. Let those who can take it, take it. Some moved out and that made room for more. And somehow the walls expanded.

We were just sitting there talking and someone said, "Let's all go live on a farm."

It was as casual as all that, I often think. It just came about. It just happened.

I found myself, a barren woman, the joyful mother of children. It is not easy always to be joyful, to keep in mind the duty of delight.

The most significant thing about *The Catholic Worker* is poverty, some say.

The most significant thing is community, others say. We are not alone any more.

But the final word is love. At times it has been, in the words of Father Zossima, a harsh and dreadful thing, and our very faith in love has been tried through fire.

We cannot love God unless we love each other, and to love we must know each other. We know Him in the breaking of bread, and we know each other in the breaking of bread, and we are not alone any more. Heaven is a banquet and life is a banquet, too, even with a crust, where there is companionship.

We have all known the long loneliness and we have learned that the only solution is love and that love comes with community.

It all happened while we sat there talking and it is still going on.

Ethel Waters
(1900–1977)

"I never was a child. I never was coddled, or liked, or understood by my family. I never felt I belonged. I was always an outsider. I was born out of wedlock, but that had nothing to do with all this. To people like mine a thing like that just didn't mean much. Nobody brought me up."

This is the way Ethel Waters began her best-selling autobiography, the story of a black girl of the urban ghetto who rose to stardom and acclaim, not only on stage and in film but also within the church. Born in Chester, Pennsylvania, Ethel Waters described herself as "a real dead-end kid": "I just ran wild as a little girl. I was bad, always a leader of the street gang in stealing and general hell-raising." She believed that her mixed blood was partly responsible; her maternal great-grandfather was a native of India, and her paternal grandmother was Dutch. She stole for food and earned $4.75 a week as a maid before she sought out the stage, first in Philadelphia, then in Baltimore, finally finding success in Harlem.

She became known for her renditions of "St. Louis Blues" and "Stormy Weather" in particular, but also for "Dinah," "Takin' a Chance on Love," "Cabin in the Sky," and "Am I Blue." For her the blues were her autobiography: "I sang them out of the depths of the private fire in which I was brought up," she said. "Only those who are being burned know what fire is like." Of her singing, The New Yorker wrote, "There is every reason (voice, technique, originality) to believe" that Ethel Waters "is the one truly great, compleat, popular singer this country has produced."

Her dramatic career began on Broadway in 1927 when she appeared in the all-black musical "Africana," and her last Broadway production was "Evening with Ethel Waters" in 1959. Her most famous role was Berenice Sadie Brown in "Member of the Wedding." In addition, she appeared in nine films and received an Academy Award nomination for her performance in "Pinky" in 1959.

She preferred acting to singing, and she regretted the "ungodly raw" songs that she had to sing in her youth; but, she said, "they didn't come up to Harlem to go to church. I wanted to sing decent things, but they wouldn't let me. They didn't even know I could." In the late 1950s, she joined the Billy Graham Crusade and sang at numerous Graham evangelistic meetings. She particularly loved to sing one black spiritual that she learned from her grandmother, and she made it the title of her autobiography, His Eye Is on the Sparrow:

> Why should I feel discouraged
> Why should the shadows come
> Why should my heart be lonely
> And long for heaven and home
> When Jesus is my portion
> My constant friend is He
> His eye is on the sparrow
> And I know He watches me.

Ethel Waters was never particular about her denominational affiliation, and late in life she stated her faith simply: "I don't say I'm a religious person. I say I'm a born-again Christian. And that is the most important thing in my life because I've found my living Saviour."

T hough dancing, being chased by the boys, and mysteries of human birth all fascinated me, my greatest interest, when I was eleven, lay in the Church. Though I was a Catholic, I recognized, as I said, that Louise's little Protestant churches had something. I'd watch the grownups praying and would get the same feeling they had of elation, exaltation, of being carried above and beyond oneself.

The beauty that came into the tired faces of the very old men and women excited me. All week long so many of them were confused and inarticulate. But on Sunday, in the church, they had no difficulty expressing themselves both in song and talk. The emotion that had invaded them was so much bigger than they. Some would rock. Some would cry. Some would talk with eloquence and fire, their confusions and doubts dispelled. And, oh, those hymns!

It began to dawn on me that if sordidness left a deep and lasting mark, so could the goodness in life. The big thing in my life was the feeling that I was getting close to God. Not that I could accept all the doctrine preached. My logic, my reasoning powers made me question much of the doctrine.

For example, as a little girl I was told to ask God to forgive my sins. But what sins could a little girl commit?

My search for God and my finding of Him were to begin in one of those Protestant churches where they were having a children's revival. It was there that I came truly to know and to reverence Christ, the Redeemer.

All my girl friends in the neighborhood were going to this children's revival. I went religiously, every day. When the preacher, the Reverend

R. J. Williams, called those who wished to repent and be saved, all my gang would go up there to the mourners' bench and kneel down—but not for long. They would pop up quick as hot cakes and as though they had brand-new souls. But we stout hearts in the back knew they hadn't been cleansed of sin but were just trying to attract attention.

"Come up and shake my hand," the Reverend R. J. Williams would say in his booming voice. "Don't you want to be little soldiers of the Lord?"

Two or three times I did go up to shake his hand. Then I'd return to my seat. I wasn't sure I wanted to be saved. "What can I ask God?" I kept thinking. "What have I got to say to Him?"

One night there were only three of us youngsters still left unsaved in the whole congregation. All the rest had gone to the mourners' bench and been redeemed.

"Come!" cried the Reverend Williams, an inspired and fiery preacher. "Get down on your knees and pray to our Lord!"

So I thought, "I will get down on my knees and pray just to see what happens." I prayed, "O Lord! I don't know what to ask of You!"

I did this every night. Every night I was on my knees—and nothing happened. I didn't feel purged of sin or close to the Lord. I didn't feel what some of the others felt so sincerely. It was this way with me right through the last night of the children's revival meeting.

I was the only one left who was still unsaved, and the preacher looked at me. He looked at me and announced he would continue the revival, if necessary, for three more nights—just to save me. I like to think that the Reverend R. J. Williams saw something special and fervent in me, something deep and passionate struggling toward salvation and spiritual expression.

On the last of the three extra nights of the meeting I got down on the mourners' bench, down on my knees once more. And I told myself, "If nothing happens tonight, I'll not come back again."

Nobody had come that night to the meeting, nobody but the very old people who were always there. I was praying hard and hopefully, asking God, "What am I seeking here? What do I want of You? Help me! If nothing happens, I can't come back here any more!"

And then it happened! The peace of heart and of mind, the peace I had been seeking all my life.

I know that never again, so long as I live, can I experience that wonderful reaction I had that night in the little church. Love flooded my heart and I knew I had found God and that now and for always I would have an ally, a friend close by to strengthen me and cheer me on.

I don't know exactly what happened or when I got up. I don't even know whether I talked. But the people who were there that night were astounded. Afterward they told me that I was radiant and like one transfixed. They said that the light in my face electrified the whole church. And I did feel full of light and warmth.

The preacher, the Reverend R. J. Williams, had some compelling force in him that enabled him to contact people. Great actresses and statesmen and other popular idols have that same force, but great preachers most of all. He could soothe you and calm you and also stir you to the depths of your soul with what lay in his eyes, his voice, and his heart.

Somehow, after that, it seemed more quiet in the house. Or perhaps things did not trouble me so much. I was no longer alone and knew now that I could never be alone anywhere, no matter what I did.

I started to go to church every Sunday. Any church to me has always been the House of God, whatever the denomination. I was a Catholic, but I didn't think He would mind whether I went to that church, a Protestant church, a synagogue, or a Hindu temple.

I was not made more grave and solemn by what had happened. I remained the same as before. Everybody smiled and said, "It is wintertime religion that Ethel has. When summertime comes it will wear off."

I smiled back at them. I didn't have to answer. I knew it was not just wintertime religion with me and that my feeling of being watched over and protected would never leave me.

Evelyn Waugh
(1903–1966)

Novels, histories, and satires, the writings of Englishman Evelyn Waugh have won him wide popularity and acclaim on both sides of the Atlantic. Born into a middle-class publisher's family, he aspired to be an aristocrat, which he eventually became, and yet his writings were acidly satirical of upper-class manners and stemmed from a severe moralistic vision of life.

Waugh is best known for *Brideshead Revisited* (1948), a devastating description of life at Oxford during the 1920s. The TV series based on the book (1982) attained a remarkably high audience rating. His portrayal of bizarre funeral practices in *The Loved One* (1948) was a comic best-seller and a provocative film. Edmund Wilson, the renowned literary critic, said that Waugh "is likely to figure as the only first-rate comic genius that has appeared in England since Bernard Shaw."

Waugh's description of his conversion contains the same wit, self-deprecation, and biting criticism that characterizes all his work. His conversion to Catholicism came in 1930 when he was twenty-six, and the moral tone of his books reflected his deep commitment to Christianity. When Edmund Wilson criticized him for dealing with God in *Brideshead Revisited*, Waugh retorted:

> He was outraged (quite legitimately by his standards) at finding God introduced into my story. I believe that you can only leave God out by making your characters pure abstractions.... They [modern novelists] try to represent the whole human mind and soul and yet omit its determining character — that of being God's creature with a defined purpose. So in my future books there will be two things to make them unpopular: a preoccupation with style and the attempt to represent man more fully, which to me means only one thing, man in his relation to God.

Waugh knew periods of despair and doubt in his youth, for in his autobiography, *A Little Learning* (1961), he described himself swimming out to sea, intending never to return. But even then, the comic element of life and his native wit saved him. As he swam, he was attacked by a school of jellyfish, and to escape the pain he worked his way back to shore. "Then," he said, "I climbed the sharp hill that led to all the years ahead."

His first marriage ended in divorce, but by his second wife he had six children. He ferociously guarded his privacy and posted a sign before his home: "No admittance on business." Of his domestic life he said:

> I live in a shabby stone house in the country where nothing is under one hundred years old except the plumbing, and that does not work. I collect books in an inexpensive desultory way. I have a fast emptying cellar of wine, and gardens reverting to jungle. I am very contentedly married. I have numerous children whom I see once a day for ten, I hope, awe-inspiring minutes.

Waugh frequented the best of London clubs, and his ambivalence about the English aristocracy and his moral critique are perhaps summed up by one of his famous aphorisms: "Manners are especially the need of the plain. The pretty can get away with anything."

From John A. O'Brien, ed., *The Road to Damascus: The Spiritual Pilgrimage of Fifteen Converts to Catholicism* (Garden City, N.Y.: Doubleday & Co., 1949), 17–21. Copyright © 1949 by John A. O'Brien.

I was born in England in 1903 with a strong hereditary predisposition toward the Established Church. My family tree burgeons on every twig with Anglican clergymen. My father was what was called a "sound churchman"; that is to say, he attended church regularly and led an exemplary life. He had no interest in theology. He had no interest in politics but always voted Tory as his father and grandfather had done. In the same spirit he was punctilious in his religious duties.

At the age of ten I composed a long and tedious poem about Purgatory in the meter of *Hiawatha* and to the dismay of my parents, who held a just estimate of my character, expressed my intention of becoming a clergyman. The enthusiasm which my little schoolfellows devoted to birds' eggs and model trains I turned on church affairs and spoke glibly of chasubles and Erastianism. I was accordingly sent to the school which was reputed to have the strongest ecclesiastical bent. At the age of sixteen I formally notified the school chaplain that there was no God. At the age of twenty-six I was received into the Catholic Church to which all subsequent experience has served to confirm my loyalty.

I am now invited to explain these vagaries to American readers.

First, of my early religiosity. I am reluctant to deny all reality to that precocious enthusiasm, but it was in the main a hobby like the birds' eggs and model trains of my schoolfellows. The appeal was part hereditary and part aesthetic. Many are drawn in this way throughout their lives. In my case it was a concomitant of puberty. But those who do not know my country should understand that the aesthetic appeal of the Church of England is unique and peculiar to those islands. Elsewhere a first interest in the Catholic Church is often kindled in the convert's imagination by the splendors of her worship in contrast with the bleakness and meanness of the Protestant sects. In England the pull is all the other way. The medieval cathedrals and churches, the rich ceremonies that surround the monarchy, the historic titles of Canterbury and York, the social organization of the country parishes, the traditional culture of Oxford and Cambridge, the liturgy composed in the heyday of English prose style—all these are the property of the Church of England, while Catholics meet in modern buildings, often of deplorable design, and are usually served by simple Irish missionaries.

The shallowness of my early piety is shown by the ease with which I abandoned it. There are, of course, countless Catholics who, for a part of their lives at least, lose their faith, but it is always after a bitter struggle—usually a moral struggle. I shed my inherited faith as lightheartedly as though it had been an out-grown coat. The circumstances were these: During the first World War many university dons patriotically volunteered to release young schoolmasters to serve in the army. Among these there came to my school a leading Oxford theologian, now a bishop. This learned and devout man inadvertently made me an atheist. He explained to his divinity class that none of the books of the Bible were by their supposed authors; he invited us to speculate, in the manner of the fourth century, on the nature of Christ. When he had removed the inherited axioms of my faith I found myself quite unable to follow him in the higher flights of logic by which he reconciled his own skepticism with his position as a clergyman.

At the same time I read Pope's *Essay on Man*; the notes led me to Leibnitz and I began an unguided and half-comprehended study of metaphysics. I advanced far enough to be thoroughly muddled about the nature of cognition. It seemed simplest to abandon the quest and assume that man was incapable of knowing anything. I have no doubt I was a prig and a bore but I think that if I had been a Catholic boy at a Catholic school I should have found among its teaching orders someone patient enough to examine with me my callow presumption. Also, if I had been fortified by the sacraments, I should have valued my faith too highly to abandon it so capriciously. At my school I was quite correctly regarded as "going through a phase" normal to all clever boys, and left to find my own way home.

The next ten years of my life are material more suitable to the novelist than the essayist. Those who have read my works will perhaps understand the character of the world into which I exuberantly launched myself. Ten years of that world sufficed to show me that life there, or anywhere, was unintelligible and unendurable without God. The conclusion was obvious; the question now arises: Why Rome? A Catholic who loses his faith and rediscovers the need of it returns inevitably to the church he left. Why did not I?

Here, I think, the European has some slight advantage over the American. It is possible, I conceive, for a man to grow up in parts of the

United States without ever being really aware of the Church's unique position. He sees Catholics as one out of a number of admirable societies,
each claiming his allegiance. That is not possible for a European. England
was Catholic for nine hundred years, then Protestant for three hundred,
then agnostic for a century. The Catholic structure still lies lightly buried
beneath every phase of English life; history, topography, law, archaeology
everywhere reveal Catholic origins. Foreign travel anywhere reveals the
local, temporary character of the heresies and schisms and the universal,
eternal character of the Church. It was self-evident to me that no heresy
or schism could be right and the Church wrong. It was possible that all
were wrong, that the whole Christian revelation was an imposture or a
misconception. But if the Christian revelation was true, then the Church
was the society founded by Christ and all other bodies were only good so
far as they had salvaged something from the wrecks of the Great Schism
and the Reformation. This proposition seemed so plain to me that it admitted of no discussion. It only remained to examine the historical and
philosophic grounds for supposing the Christian revelation to be genuine.
I was fortunate enough to be introduced to a brilliant and holy priest who
undertook to prove this to me, and so on firm intellectual conviction but
with little emotion I was admitted into the Church.

My life since then has been an endless delighted tour of discovery
in the huge territory of which I was made free. I have heard it said that
some converts in later life look back rather wistfully to the fervor of their
first months of faith. With me it is quite the opposite. I look back aghast
at the presumption with which I thought myself suitable for reception and
with wonder at the trust of the priest who saw the possibility of growth in
such a dry soul.

From time to time friends outside the Church consult me. They are
attracted by certain features, repelled or puzzled by others. To them I can
only say, from my own experience: "Come inside. You cannot know what
the Church is like from outside. However learned you are in theology,
nothing you know amounts to anything in comparison with the knowledge
of the simplest actual member of the Communion of Saints."

Dag Hammarskjöld
(1905–1961)

Many today think of Hammarskjöld as a deeply reflective and religiously motivated person. His intimate diary, known as *Markings*, which he did not want published until after his death, has become a minor classic of modern religious spirituality. He was also, of course, a distinguished Swedish civil servant, an international banker, and the highly respected, twice-elected Secretary-General of the United Nations (1953 – 1961).

Born in Sweden into a politically active family, he graduated from Stockholm University where, for a time, he taught political economy. During his UN tenure, Hammarskjöld was everywhere acclaimed for his political neutrality and his vigorous pursuit of world peace. While on a peace mission to the Congo in 1961, he was killed in a plane crash.

Not many knew that in the midst of his unrelenting schedule, he was all the time quietly recording his innermost thoughts about life and death in a series of aphorisms, queries, and scattered allusions to literature and the Bible. He was particularly fond of the book of Psalms and often quoted from the Anglican Psalter and from an early edition of the Book of Common Prayer.

Two of his interpreters, Henry P. Van Dusen, the theologian, and W. H. Auden, the poet, detect in his musings a radical change that came about between 1952 and 1953. Van Dusen notes that this was "at the peak of public achievement and at the nadir of private despondency." And in the midst of this crisis, Hammarskjöld experienced a breakthrough so that he could say "Yes" to God and to life.

While his diary is not always easy to follow, we must remember that Hammarskjöld was not writing for us but for himself. Sometimes we can only guess at what he was thinking or feeling. But to read these personal reflections is, as W. H. Auden says, to appreciate "the privilege of being in contact with a great, good, and lovable man."

The text of the excerpts is *Markings*, trans. Leif Sjöberg and W. H. Auden (New York: Alfred A. Knopf, 1964), 89-102. Copyright © 1964 by Alfred A. Knopf, Inc. and Faber and Faber, Ltd. Reprinted by permission of the publisher.

1953

"— Night is drawing nigh—"
For all that has been—Thanks!
To all that shall be—Yes!

Maturity: among other things—not to hide one's strength out of fear and, consequently, live below one's best.

Goodness is something so simple: always to live for others, never to seek one's own advantage.

When in decisive moments—as now—God acts, it is with a stern purposefulness, a Sophoclean irony. When the hour strikes, He takes what is His. What have *you* to say?—Your prayer has been answered, as you know. God has a use for you, even though what He asks doesn't happen to suit you at the moment. God, who "abases him whom He raises up."

Will it come, or will it not,
The day when the joy becomes great,
The day when the grief becomes small?
                                    (*Gunnar Ekelöf*)

It *did* come—the day when the grief became small. For what had befallen me and seemed so hard to bear became insignificant in the light of the demands which God was now making. But how difficult it is to feel that this was also, and for that very reason, the day when the joy became great.

Not I, but God in me.

Maturity: among other things, a new lack of self-consciousness—the kind you can only attain when you have become entirely indifferent to yourself through an absolute assent to your fate.

He who has placed himself in God's hand stands free vis-à-vis men: he is entirely at his ease with them, because he has granted them the right to judge.

"Their lives grounded in and sustained by God, they are incapable of any kind of pride; because they give back to God all the benefits He has bestowed on them, they do not glorify each other, but do all things to the Glory of God alone." (*Thomas Aquinas*)

I am the vessel. The draught is God's. And God is the thirsty one.

In the last analysis, what does the word "sacrifice" mean? Or even the word "gift"? He who has nothing can give nothing. The gift is God's— to God.

He who has surrendered himself to it knows that the Way ends on the Cross—even when it is leading him through the jubilation of Gennesaret or the triumphal entry into Jerusalem.

To be free, to be able to stand up and leave *everything* behind—
without looking back. To say *Yes*—

Except in faith, nobody is humble. The mask of weakness or of
Phariseeism is not the naked face of humility.

And, except in faith, nobody is proud. The vanity displayed in all
its varieties by the spiritually immature is not pride.

To be, in faith, both humble and proud: that is, to *live,* to know that
in God I am nothing, but that God is in me.

To say Yes to life is at one and the same time to say Yes to oneself.

Yes—even to that element in one which is most unwilling to let
itself be transformed from a temptation into a strength. . . .

1954

Thou who has created us free, Who seest all that happens—yet art
confident of victory,
Thou who at this time art the one among us who suffereth the
uttermost loneliness,
Thou—who art also in me,
May I bear Thy burden, when my hour comes,
May I—
. . . .

Thou who art over us,
Thou who art one of us,
Thou who *art*—
Also within us,
May all see Thee—in me also,
May I prepare the way for Thee,
May I thank Thee for all that shall fall to my lot,
May I also not forget the needs of others,
Keep me in Thy love
As Thou wouldest that all should be kept in mine.
May everything in this my being be directed to Thy glory
And may I never despair.
For I am under Thy hand,
And in Thee is all power and goodness.

Give me a pure heart—that I may see Thee,
A humble heart—that I may hear Thee,
A heart of love—that I may serve Thee,
A heart of faith—that I may abide in Thee.

The "unheard-of"—to be in the hands of God.

Once again a reminder that this is all that remains for you to live for—and once more the feeling of disappointment which shows how slow you are to learn. . . .

So long as you abide in the Unheard-of, you are beyond and above—to hold fast to this must be the First Commandment in your spiritual discipline. . . .

To have faith—not to hesitate!

"If I take the wings of the morning and remain in the uttermost parts of the sea;
even there also shall thy hand lead me." (*Psalm 139:8*)

Simone Weil

(1909–1943)

Simone Weil is one of the most provocative and yet perplexing thinkers of the twentieth century. She witnessed the horrors of Europe first-hand — the barbarism of industry, the rise of fascism, the brutality of war — and from her experience emerged a philosophy that was never systematized but spoke eloquently of the sanctity of the human spirit.

Born into an affluent Jewish family in Paris, she was an extremely intelligent child, despite the fact that she felt inferior to her brilliant brother. She also demonstrated very early the sensitivity to human need that marked her entire life; at the age of five she refused to eat sugar when French soldiers at the front had none. After studying philosophy, classical philology, and science, she held a number of positions teaching philosophy, but her conflict with school boards made each appointment short-lived.

In 1934 — 1935 she began work in an auto factory to experience first-hand the oppression of workers, but her delicate health failed. In 1936, she joined an anarchist unit training for battle in the Spanish Civil War, but since she was a pacifist, she would not carry a gun. Instead, she served as a cook for the soldiers until she suffered severe burns from boiling oil.

Recovering in Portugal, she visited a monastery at Solesmes where she had a deep and powerful religious experience in which, she said, "Christ himself came down and took possession of me." Despite her Jewish background, she said that she was born and grew up "within the Christian inspiration." She studied the Gospels avidly, but her commitment to Christianity did not include membership in the church. She refused baptism, for she argued that her faith was inclusive, embodying the truths of non-Christian and even heretical traditions. She centered this claim on the incarnation of Christ, emphasizing that in becoming human Christ took on the flesh of all peoples and all cultures.

The persecution of European Jewry forced Weil's parents to escape from France to New York with their daughter. Simone pleaded for an opportunity to return to France, and finally she did go to London in 1942 where she worked for the Free French Movement. Refusing to eat more than the daily French ration, she became sick again and died of pleurisy.

After her death, her writings were published, including *Waiting for God* (1951), her spiritual autobiography, and it is from this volume that the following account is taken. It is a letter written in 1942, addressed to the Roman Catholic priest, J. M. Perrin. Her philosophy and theology were spelled out in other volumes, including *Gravity and Grace* (1952), *Oppression and Liberty* (1958), and *Notebooks* (1956). For Simone Weil as for Søren Kierkegaard, suffering lay at the heart of Christian discipleship, and she could not endure society's inhumanity without protesting and taking suffering on herself.

Father,

Before leaving I want to speak to you again, it may be the last time perhaps, for over there I shall probably send you only my news from time to time just so as to have yours.

I told you that I owed you an enormous debt. I want to try to tell you exactly what it consists of. I think that if you could really understand what my spiritual state is you would not be at all sorry that you did not lead me to baptism. But I do not know if it is possible for you to understand this.

You neither brought me the Christian inspiration nor did you bring me to Christ; for when I met you there was no longer any need; it had been done without the intervention of any human being. If it had been otherwise, if I had not already been won, not only implicitly but consciously, you would have given me nothing, because I should have received nothing from you. My friendship for you would have been a reason for me to refuse your message, for I should have been afraid of the possibilities of error and illusion which human influence in the divine order is likely to involve.

I may say that never at any moment in my life have I "sought for God." For this reason, which is probably too subjective, I do not like this expression and it strikes me as false. As soon as I reached adolescence I saw the problem of God as a problem of which the data could not be obtained here below, and I decided that the only way of being sure not to reach a wrong solution, which seemed to me the greatest possible evil, was to leave it alone. So I left it alone. I neither affirmed nor denied anything. It seemed to me useless to solve the problem, for I thought that being in this world, our business was to adopt the best attitude with regard to the problems of this world, and that such an attitude did not depend upon the solution of the problem of God.

This held good as far as I was concerned at any rate, for I never hesitated in my choice of an attitude; I always adopted the Christian attitude as the only possible one. I might say that I was born, I grew up and I always remained within the Christian inspiration. Whilst the very name of God had no part in my thoughts, with regard to the problems of this world and this life I shared the Christian conception in an explicit and rigorous manner, with the most specific notions it involves. Some of these notions have been part of my outlook for as far back as I can remember. With others I know the time and manner of their coming and the form under which they imposed themselves upon me.

For instance I never allowed myself to think of a future state, but I always believed that the instant of death is the centre and object of life. I used to think that, for those who live as they should, it is the instant when, for an infinitesimal fraction of time, pure truth, naked, certain and eternal enters the soul. I may say that I never desired any other good for myself. I thought that the life which leads to this good is not only defined by a code of morals common to all, but that for each one it consists of a succession of acts and events which are strictly personal to him, and so essential that he who leaves them on one side never reaches the goal. The notion of vocation was like this for me. I saw the carrying out of a vocation differed from the actions dictated by reason or inclination in that it was due to an impulse of an essentially and manifestly different order; and not to follow such an impulse when it made itself felt, even if it demanded impossibilities, seemed to me the greatest of all ills. Hence my conception of obedience; and I put this conception to the test when I entered the factory and stayed on there, even when I was in that state of intense and uninterrupted misery about which I recently told you. The most beautiful life possible has always seemed to me to be one where everything is determined, either by the pressure of circumstances or by impulses such as I have just mentioned and where there is never any room for choice.

At fourteen I fell into one of those fits of bottomless despair which come with adolescence, and I seriously thought of dying because of the mediocrity of my natural faculties. The exceptional gifts of my brother, who had a childhood and youth comparable to those of Pascal, brought my own inferiority home to me. I did not mind having no visible successes, but what did grieve me was the idea of being excluded from that transcendent kingdom to which only the truly great have access and wherein truth abides. I preferred to die rather than live without that truth. After months of inward darkness, I suddenly had the everlasting conviction that no matter what human being, even though practically devoid of natural faculties, can penetrate to the kingdom of truth reserved for genius, if only he longs for truth and perpetually concentrates all his attention upon its attainment. He thus becomes a genius too, even though for lack of talent his genius cannot be visible from outside. Later on, when the strain of headaches caused the feeble faculties I possess to be invaded by a paralysis which I was quick to imagine was probably incurable, the same conviction led me to persevere for ten years in an effort of concentrated attention which was practically unsupported by any hope of results.

Under the name of truth I also included beauty, virtue and every kind of goodness, so that for me it was a question of a conception of the relationship between grace and desire. The conviction which had come to me was that when one hungers for bread one does not receive stones. But at that time I had not read the Gospel.

Just as I was certain that desire has in itself an efficacy in the realm of spiritual goodness whatever its form, I thought it was also possible that it might not be effective in any other realm.

As for the spirit of poverty, I do not remember any moment when it was not in me, although only to that unhappily small extent which is compatible with my imperfection. I fell in love with Saint Francis of Assisi as soon as I came to know about him. I always believed and hoped that one day Fate would force upon me the condition of a vagabond and a beggar which he embraced freely. Actually I felt the same way about prison.

From my earliest childhood I always had also the Christian idea of love for one's neighbour, to which I gave the name of justice; a name it bears in many passages of the Gospel and which is so beautiful. You know that on this point I have failed seriously several times.

The duty of acceptance in all that concerns the will of God, whatever it may be, was impressed upon my mind as the first and most necessary of all duties from the time when I found it set down in Marcus Aurelius under the form of the *amor fati* of the Stoics. I saw it as a duty we cannot fail in without dishonouring ourselves.

The idea of purity, with all that this word can imply for a Christian, took possession of me at the age of sixteen, after a period of several months during which I had been going through the emotional unrest natural in adolescence. This idea came to me when I was contemplating a mountain landscape and little by little it was imposed upon me in an irresistible manner.

Of course I knew quite well that my conception of life was Christian. That is why it never occurred to me that I could enter the Christian community. I had the idea that I was born inside. But to add dogma to this conception of life, without being forced to do so by indisputable evidence, would have seemed to me like a lack of honesty. I should even have thought I was lacking in honesty had I considered the question of the truth of dogma as a problem for myself, or even had I simply desired to reach a conclusion on this subject. I have an extremely severe standard for intellectual honesty, so severe that I never met anyone who did not seem to fall short of it in more than one respect; and I am always afraid of failing in it myself.

Keeping away from dogma in this way, I was prevented by a sort of shame from going into churches, though all the same I like being in them. Nevertheless I had three contacts with Catholicism which really counted.

After my year in the factory, before going back to teaching, I had
been taken by my parents to Portugal, and while there I left them to go
alone to a little village. I was, as it were, in pieces, soul and body. That
contact with affliction had killed my youth. Until then I had not had any
experience of affliction, unless we count my own, which, as it was my own,
seemed to me, to have little importance, and which moreover was only a
partial affliction, being biological and not social. I knew quite well that
there was a great deal of affliction in the world. I was obsessed with the
idea, but I had not had prolonged and first-hand experience of it. As I
worked in the factory, indistinguishable to all eyes, including my own, from
the anonymous mass, the affliction of others entered into my flesh and my
soul. Nothing separated me from it, for I had really forgotten my past and
I looked forward to no future, finding it difficult to imagine the possibility
of surviving all the fatigue. What I went through there marked me in so
lasting a manner that still today when any human being, whoever he may
be and in whatever circumstances, speaks to me without brutality, I cannot
help having the impression that there must be a mistake and that unfortunately the mistake will in all probability disappear. There I received for
ever the mark of a slave, like the branding of the red-hot iron which the
Romans put on the foreheads of their most despised slaves. Since then I
have always regarded myself as a slave.

In this state of mind then, and in a wretched condition physically,
I entered the little Portuguese village, which, alas, was very wretched too,
on the very day of its patronal festival. I was alone. It was the evening and
there was a full moon. It was by the sea. The wives of the fishermen were
going in procession to make a tour of all the ships, carrying candles and
singing what must certainly be very ancient hymns of a heart-rending sadness. Nothing can give any idea of it. I have never heard anything so
poignant unless it were the song of the boatmen on the Volga. There the
conviction was suddenly borne in upon me that Christianity is preeminently the religion of slaves, that slaves cannot help belonging to it, and
I among others.

In 1937 I had two marvellous days at Assisi. There, alone in the
little XIIth Century Romanesque chapel of Santa Maria degli Angeli, an
incomparable marvel of purity where Saint Francis often used to pray,
something stronger than I was compelled me for the first time in my life
to go down on my knees.

In 1938 I spent ten days at Solesmes, from Palm Sunday to Easter
Tuesday, following all the liturgical services. I was suffering from splitting
headaches; each sound hurt me like a blow; by an extreme effort of concentration I was able to rise above this wretched flesh, to leave it to suffer
by itself, heaped up in a corner, and to find a pure and perfect joy in the
unimaginable beauty of the chanting and the words. This experience enabled me by analogy to get a better understanding of the possibility of

loving divine love in the midst of affliction. It goes without saying that in the course of these services the thought of the Passion of Christ entered into my being once and for all. . . .

Christianity should contain all vocations without exception since it is catholic. In consequence the Church should also. But in my eyes Christianity is catholic by right but not in fact. So many things are outside it, so many things that I love and do not want to give up, so many things that God loves, otherwise they would not be in existence. All the immense stretches of past centuries, except the last twenty are among them; all the countries inhabited by coloured races; all secular life in the white peoples' countries; in the history of these countries, all the traditions banned as heretical, those of the Manicheans, and Albigenses for instance; all those things resulting from the Renaissance, too often degraded but not quite without value.

Christianity being catholic by right but not in fact, I regard it as legitimate on my part to be a member of the Church by right but not in fact, not only for a time, but for my whole life if need be.

But it is not merely legitimate. So long as God does not give me the certainty that he is ordering me to do anything else, I think it is my duty.

I think, and so do you, that our obligation for the next two or three years, an obligation so strict that we can scarcely fail in it without treason, is to show the public the possibility of a truly incarnated Christianity. In all the history now known there has never been a period in which souls have been in such peril as they are today in every part of the globe. The bronze serpent must be lifted up again so that whoever raises his eyes to it may be saved.

But everything is so closely bound up together that Christianity cannot be really incarnated unless it is catholic in the sense that I have just defined. How could it circulate through the flesh of all the nations of Europe if it did not contain absolutely everything in itself? Except of course falsehood. But in everything that exists there is most of the time more truth than falsehood.

Having so intense and so painful a sense of this urgency, I should betray the truth, that is to say the aspect of truth that I see, if I left the point, where I have been since my birth, at the intersection of Christianity and everything that is not Christianity.

I have always remained at this exact point, on the threshold of the Church, without moving, quite still ἐν ὑπομένῃ (it is so much more beautiful a word that *patiential* !); only now my heart has been transported, for ever, I hope, into the Blessed Sacrament exposed on the altar.

Thomas Merton
(1915–1968)

Poet, novelist, mystic, and theologian, Thomas Merton has become one of the most widely-read Catholic authors of the twentieth century. He was equally knowledgeable of both Western and Eastern spirituality, and he immersed himself in medieval piety, struggling to use the resources of the monastic tradition to address the religious and social issues of the modern world. He entered one of the strictest Catholic orders, the Trappists, which requires a vow of silence. Fortunately, the abbot encouraged this silent monk to speak through writing. The words flowed from his pen — a synthesis of the ancient and the contemporary, East and West.

Born in France, Merton was given a fine education there, in Bermuda, and the United States. Orphaned in his youth, his parents left him a generous trust fund, and he used it to live extravagantly. While studying in England, he fathered an illegitimate child, and his trustee arranged for a financial settlement with the mother. Both the mother and the child were killed in the bombing raids on London during World War II.

Migrating to America, Merton studied at Columbia University and received a master's degree in literature. He was invited to join the faculty, but his dissatisfaction with his life and the injustices of society immobilized him. He first turned to a young Communist group, and he also served in a Catholic settlement house in Harlem. Devouring Catholic writings of all kinds, he came to the conclusion that he must be baptized and enter "at last into the supernatural life of the Church."

He set out to climb "the high, seven-circled mountain of a Purgatory, steeper and more arduous than I was able to imagine," and climb it he did. In 1941, he entered the Trappist monastery of Gethsemani in Kentucky, and there he wrote his autobiography, The Seven-Storey Mountain, published in 1948 and an immediate best-seller. More books followed, and people flocked to Gethsemani on pilgrimage to learn from this person who had tasted the best of Western culture, rejecting it for silent, quiet contemplation.

Merton became a strong advocate of civil rights during the 1950s and 1960s and was critical of American foreign policy. Fame and controversy came to him in almost equal measure. His visitors increased and finally he withdrew to a hermitage on the abbey property so that he could be completely isolated. Yet even that extreme measure was unsuccessful,

and he left the abbey to find peace and anonymity in Asia. Agreeing to
attend a religious conference in Bangkok, he died in a hotel from a freak
accident, apparently the victim of electrocution when a fan fell into his
bathtub.

Merton believed that "the whole work of man in this life is to find
God," and he sought this goal with discipline and self-sacrifice. He concluded his autobiography with his own epitaph which he believed to be
the words of God:

> And when you have been praised a little and loved a little, I will
> take away all your gifts and all your love and all your praise and
> you will be utterly forgotten and abandoned and you will be noth-
> ing, a dead thing, a rejection. And in that day you shall begin to
> possess the solitude you have so long desired.

Excerpted from Thomas Merton, *The Seven-Storey Mountain* (New
York: Harcourt, Brace, and Co., 1948), 221-32. Reprinted by permission of
Harcourt Brace Jovanovich, New York, and Sheldon Press, London.

M y mind was taken up with this one thought: of getting baptized
and entering at last into the supernatural life of the Church. In spite of all
my studying and all my reading and all my talking, I was still infinitely poor
and wretched in my appreciation of what was about to take place within
me. I was about to set foot on the shore at the foot of the high, seven-
circled mountain of a Purgatory steeper and more arduous than I was able
to imagine, and I was not at all aware of the climbing I was about to have
to do.

The essential thing was to begin the climb. Baptism was that beginning, and a most generous one, on the part of God. For, although I was
baptized conditionally, I hope that His mercy swallowed up all the guilt
and temporal punishment of my twenty-three black years of sin in the
waters of the font, and allowed me a new start. But my human nature, my
weakness, and the cast of my evil habits still remained to be fought and
overcome.

Towards the end of the first week in November, Father Moore told
me I would be baptized on the sixteenth. I walked out of the rectory that
evening happier and more contented than I had ever been in my life. I
looked at a calendar to see what saint had that day for a feast, and it was
marked for St. Gertrude.

It was only in the last days before being liberated from my slavery
to death, that I had the grace to feel something of my own weakness and
helplessness. It was not a very vivid light that was given to me on the
subject: but I was really aware, at last, of what a poor and miserable thing
I was. On the night of the fifteenth of November, the eve of my Baptism
and First Communion, I lay in my bed awake and timorous for fear that

something might go wrong the next day. And to humiliate me still further, as I lay there, fear came over me that I might not be able to keep the eucharistic fast. It only meant going from midnight to ten o'clock without drinking any water or taking any food, yet all of a sudden this little act of self-denial which amounts to no more, in reality, than a sort of an abstract token, a gesture of good-will, grew in my imagination until it seemed to be utterly beyond my strength—as if I were about to go without food and drink for ten days, instead of ten hours. I had enough sense left to realize that this was one of those curious psychological reactions with which our nature, not without help from the devil, tries to confuse us and avoid what reason and our will demand of it, and so I forgot about it all and went to sleep.

In the morning, when I got up, having forgotten to ask Father Moore if washing your teeth was against the eucharistic fast or not, I did not wash them, and, facing a similar problem about cigarettes, I resisted the temptation to smoke.

I went downstairs and out into the street to go to my happy execution and rebirth.

The sky was bright and cold. The river glittered like steel. There was a clean wind in the street. It was one of those fall days full of life and triumph, made for great beginnings, and yet I was not altogether exalted: for there were still in my mind these vague, half animal apprehensions about the externals of what was to happen in the church—would my mouth be so dry that I could not swallow the Host? If that happened, what would I do? I did not know.

Gerdy joined me as I was turning in to Broadway. I do not remember whether Ed Rice caught up with us on Broadway or not. Lax and Seymour came after we were in church.

Ed Rice was my godfather. He was the only Catholic among us—the only Catholic among all my close friends. Lax, Seymour, and Gerdy were Jews. They were very quiet, and so was I. Rice was the only one who was not cowed or embarrassed or shy.

The whole thing was very simple. First of all, I knelt at the altar of Our Lady where Father Moore received my abjuration of heresy and schism. Then we went to the baptistery, in a little dark corner by the main door.

I stood at the threshold.

"*Quid Petis ab ecclesia Dei?*" asked Father Moore.

"*Fidem!*"

"*Fides quid tibi praestat?*"

"*Vitam aeternam.*"

Then the young priest began to pray in Latin, looking earnestly and calmly at the page of the *Rituale* through the lenses of his glasses. And I, who was asking for eternal life, stood and watched him, catching a word of the Latin here and there.

He turned to me:

"*Abrenuntias Satanae?*"

In a triple vow I renounced Satan and his pomps and his works.

"Dost thou believe in God the Father almighty, Creator of heaven and earth?"

"*Credo!*"

"Dost thou believe in Jesus Christ His only Son, Who was born, and suffered?"

"*Credo!*"

"Dost thou believe in the Holy Spirit, in the Holy Catholic Church, the Communion of saints, the remission of sins, the resurrection of the body and eternal life?"

"*Credo!*"

What mountains were falling from my shoulders! What scales of dark night were peeling off my intellect, to let in the inward vision of God and His truth! But I was absorbed in the liturgy, and waiting for the next ceremony. It had been one of the things that had rather frightened me— or rather, which frightened the legion that had been living in me for twenty-three years.

Now the priest blew into my face. He said: "*Exi ab eo, spiritus immunde*: Depart from him, thou impure spirit, and give place to the Holy Spirit, the Paraclete."

It was the exorcism. I did not see them leaving, but there must have been more than seven of them. I had never been able to count them. Would they ever come back? Would that terrible threat of Christ be fulfilled, that threat about the man whose house was clean and garnished, only to be reoccupied by the first devil and many others worse than himself?

The priest, and Christ in him—for it was Christ that was doing these things through his visible ministry, in the Sacrament of my purification— breathed again into my face.

"Thomas, receive the good Spirit through this breathing, and receive the Blessing of God. Peace be with thee."

Then he began again to pray, and sign me with Crosses, and presently came the salt which he put on my tongue—the salt of wisdom, that I might have the savor of divine things, and finally he poured the water on my head, and named me Thomas, "if thou be not already baptized."

After that, I went into the confessional, where one of the other assistants was waiting for me. I knelt in the shadows. Through the dark, close-meshed wire of the grille between us, I saw Father McGough, his head bowed, and resting on his hand, inclining his ear towards me. "Poor man," I thought. He seemed very young and he had always looked so innocent to me that I wondered how he was going to identify and understand the things I was about to tell him.

But one by one, that is, species by species, as best I could, I tore out all those sins by their roots, like teeth. Some of them were hard, but I did it quickly, doing the best I could to approximate the number of times all these things had happened—there was no counting them, only guessing.

I did not have any time to feel how relieved I was when I came stumbling out, as I had to go down to the front of the church where Father Moore would see me and come out to begin his—and my—Mass. But ever since that day, I have loved confessionals.

Now he was at the altar, in his white vestments, opening the book. I was kneeling right at the altar rail. The bright sanctuary was all mine. I could hear the murmur of the priest's voice, and the responses of the server, and it did not matter that I had no one to look at, so that I could tell when to stand up and kneel down again, for I was still not very sure of these ordinary ceremonies. But when the little bells were rung I knew what was happening. And I saw the raised Host—the silence and simplicity with which Christ once again triumphed, raised up, drawing all things to Himself—drawing me to Himself.

Presently the priest's voice was louder, saying the *Pater Noster.* Then, soon, the server was running through the *Confiteor* in a rapid murmur. That was for me. Father Moore turned around and made a big cross in absolution, and held up the little Host.

"Behold the Lamb of God: behold Him Who taketh away the sins of the world."

And my First Communion began to come towards me, down the steps. I was the only one at the altar rail. Heaven was entirely mine—that Heaven in which sharing makes no division or diminution. But this solitariness was a kind of reminder of the singleness with which this Christ, hidden in the small Host, was giving Himself for me, and to me, and, with Himself, the entire Godhead and Trinity—a great new increase of the power and grasp of their indwelling that had begun only a few minutes before at the font.

I left the altar rail and went back to the pew where the others were kneeling like four shadows, four unrealities, and I hid my face in my hands.

In the Temple of God that I had just become, the One Eternal and Pure Sacrifice was offered up to the God dwelling in me: the sacrifice of God to God, and me sacrificed together with God, incorporated in His Incarnation. Christ born in me, a new Bethlehem, and sacrificed in me, His new Calvary, and risen in me: offering me to the Father, in Himself, asking the Father, my Father and His, to receive me into His infinite and special love—not the love He has for all things that exist—for mere existence is a token of God's love, but the love of those creatures who are drawn to Him in and with the power of His own love for Himself.

For now I had entered into the everlasting movement of that gravitation which is the very life and spirit of God: God's own gravitation toward the depths of His own infinite nature, His goodness without end.

And God, that center Who is everywhere, and whose circumference is nowhere, finding me, through incorporation with Christ, incorporated into this immense and tremendous gravitational movement which is love, which is the Holy Spirit, loved me.

And He called out to me from His own immense depths.

John Cogley
(1916–1976)

Newspaper reporters and editors of journals are seldom taken as exemplars of Christian faith, even when their assignments include churches and religious events. But John Cogley was an exception. A professional in every way, he covered his stories with distinction, perhaps partly because he was himself a person of faith.

Born into a Catholic family and tradition, Cogley graduated from Loyola University, Chicago, and took further studies at the University of Fribourg, Switzerland. There followed for him a succession of prestigious positions, editor of *Today Magazine*, executive editor of *Commonweal*, religion editor of *The New York Times*, and editor of *The Center Magazine*.

Cogley served as a member of the Center for Study of Democratic Institutions, on the selection board of the Department of State, and as a trustee for the Council on Religion and International Affairs. He was the recipient of an award for his coverage of Vatican Council II. The author of numerous books on Catholicism and religion in America, he contributed articles to the *Encyclopaedia Britannica* and the *New Catholic Encyclopaedia*.

After having lived congenially with his Catholic faith for many years, Cogley began to worry about his tacit approval of Roman dogmas for which he had little intellectual liking. Through great agony of spirit, he decided to join the Episcopal Church and regarded his move as fulfilling rather than denying the classic Catholic heritage.

In 1973, shortly after he was received into the Episcopal Church, he suffered a severe illness but recovered sufficiently to write his autobiography and to apply for Episcopal ordination. "I am now an Episcopal cleric," he wrote. "My whole life, as I see it now, has led up to this move."

The account of his church conversion is taken from his autobiography, A *Canterbury Tale: Experiences and Reflections* (New York: Seabury Press, 1976), 122-25. Copyright © 1976 by The Seabury Press and reprinted by permission.

I was formally received into the Episcopal Church in September, 1973, by Bishop Crowther at Mount Calvary Retreat, a remote Anglican monastery of the Order of the Holy Cross in the mountains near Santa Barbara.

Theodora and our daughter Joan attended the regular monastic Mass with me. In the middle of the familiar Eucharist, Bishop Crowther accepted my pledge of obedience to the Episcopal ordinary of California. I stated that I accepted the Episcopal body as a part of Christ's Holy Catholic Church. I was not asked to forswear anything that had been sacramentalized in the past or to renounce any peculiarly Roman Catholic belief.

When it was over, before nine in the morning, I went to work a happy man. I felt relieved because I realized that never again could it be presumed that I believed certain dogmas that I wordlessly denied and certain others that I was totally indifferent to. I could deny the infallibility of ecclesiastical councils and the divine supremacy of the Bishop of Rome. I no longer professed to believe that the full Christian truth was entrusted solely to a small percentage of Christians, but that we all saw through a glass, darkly. My belief, now formal, was that all Christians were in possession of the basic Christian truths through the Scriptures; the residue of the remaining theological lore was interesting but did not ultimately matter. I was naturally pleased to be free of the moral discipline and regulations imposed in the name of Jesus Christ's "one true Church" by the Roman Curia.

The liturgy of the new Church was only slightly different from what I had known. Most of the peculiarities of Roman Catholic worship could now be practiced if I found them devotional, or ignored if I found them offensive. I no longer felt any guilt because I found that saying the rosary was a bore and Benediction of the Blessed Sacrament a stately but senseless exercise. There are Anglicans who practice both, of course, but there are others who feel free to march out of the church when they begin. (Of course there is no dogmatic character given to these practices in the Roman communion either; but they are highly valued "pious practices" and enjoy official commendation. To reject them out of hand would have required more daring than I had.)

The advantage in staying where I was would have been that I would not have had to turn my back on the religio-ethnic community in which I was reared and in which I had enjoyed a certain prestige. As I grew older, and as ancient controversies died out, that position might have mellowed into something like honor and respect. In late middle age, I was going into an alien community, one historically hostile to my forefathers, generally identified in America with a class into which I was not born. I was not leaving Roman Catholicism by mindless attrition, as so many were in those days, but by liturgized decision.

To make things worse, I felt no bitter sentiments toward the Church I was leaving. I knew that the antidemocratic charges made against American Catholics were baseless and that Catholics in this country were superbly acceptable in their American sentiments. They were, in fact, largely indifferent to the ancient canard that they had to choose between two masters: the pope and Uncle Sam. I did not personally feel that I was separating myself from the "ideal" Church that really already united Anglican and Roman Catholic. I knew that this idea was, sadly, not a present reality but only a hope for the future and that it probably would not be actualized in my lifetime.

If I were angry with the priests or hierarchy of Rome, if I had been seriously "hurt" by them (as one monk friend later suggested), or if I were without hope for Roman Catholicism, there might then be extenuating circumstances for my so-called "apostasy"; but there was no such evidence in my case.

After the ceremony at Mount Calvary, I informed the *National Catholic Reporter* by letter of what I had done. In the letter to the *NCR,* I did not elaborate on why I had left the Church of my birth for, of all things, Anglicanism. Theodora and I then went immediately to Mexico to remain incommunicado when the *Reporter* published the story on its front page. The item was thereafter taken up by the news services and *The New York Times.*

Reactions to my change of Churches were revealing. Most friends— Roman Catholic, Anglican, Protestant, Jewish, and agnostic—did not really care. Predictably, I received a small number of letters from old-style conservative Catholics, promising their prayers for my return to true Christianity. The outgoing Presiding Bishop of the Episcopal Church, John Hines, sent me a welcoming telegram. Some of the few Anglican divines I knew personally sent words of encouragement, with no hint of religious triumphalism. I received a few letters from Roman Catholics who were holding on for dear life, wondering whether they might also come to accept Anglicanism as valid Christianity. (I did not encourage them to change.) A prominent Roman Catholic priest inaccurately used my case as an example of the once-ardent Catholic who found the *aggiornamento* so disappointingly slow that he decided to move elsewhere and avoid the incessant internal turmoil in the Roman Church.

A few Catholics affected boredom and elaborate indifference to the case. Dan Herr, the lay publisher of *The Critic,* wrote that it was time the "John Cogleys of this world stop taking themselves so damn seriously and spare the rest of us their pompous pronouncements." I had tried to avoid pomposity in my announcement in *The National Catholic Reporter,* but I suppose the very fact that I wrote such a letter was an indication that Mr. Herr had hit pay dirt.

Later, the editor of *The New York Times'* Op Ed page requested a short article about my journey from Rome to Canterbury, which I obligingly and foolishly honored. I had hoped at the time that the article might inform some of my friends who did not keep up with *The National Catholic Reporter* about the big change in my life. The article seemed to enrage Andrew Greeley. He described its author in a subsequent column, not only as a clever "apostate," but as a "vain little man with an exaggerated notion of his own importance." The extent of my "vanity and shallowness," I took it, was clearly displayed to him in the *Times* piece. All in all, "we might be well rid of him," Father Greeley concluded.

It seems to me that the Churches must be united or disappear from the modern world. I now believe that the Anglican branch of the Church gives the best example for that future united Christian Church. One reason for this is the very antiquity of the Anglican communion. There were British bishops at the Council of Arles in the fourth century. Another reason is the present democratic structure which the Episcopal Church somehow manages to combine with episcopacy. Third, its freedom of theological investigation pays off in the long run; just as it did decades ago when the Church, contradicting an earlier position, gave its approval of birth control. I feel confident that it will continue in this tradition when it authorizes the ordination of women to the priesthood. Fourth, there is the Anglican insistence that every doctrine must be "proved" by the Scriptures before it may be enforced as a point of belief. The only Anglican certainty is its devotion to the Savior and his teachings; its only *Summa Theologica* is the Bible itself.

For that reason it has never excluded other Christian denominations from the Church of Christ, even Roman Catholics during a period when feelings against Rome were exacerbated by political loyalties. Today, one finds a carving of John Henry Newman in the elaborate pulpit of St. Thomas Episcopal Church in Manhattan and a window commemorating the beloved pontiff, John XXIII, in Grace Cathedral in San Francisco, where the Jesuit theologian Karl Rahner is also depicted in stained glass.

This kind of ecumenical gesture, forgetting bitter past history, has a tremendous appeal. I am convinced that I have found the right Church for me when I see the excellent relations the Episcopal Church enjoys with Greek Orthodoxy and Protestantism in general.

I used to hope that the Roman Catholic Church would take the lead in ecumenical endeavors. But that hope was lost some time after Vatican II. The will is there, of course; most Roman Catholics are ready for a greater communion of Churches. But I am afraid that the uncompromising Roman insistence on the God-given primacy of the pope and the residuum of the "one true Church" idea will stand as a blockade to Christian unity, at least for my lifetime.

Right now, everything concerned with ecclesiastical structure and doctrinal loyalty—the infallibility of the pope, the exact number of sacraments, the "validity" of Holy Orders, Baptism by immersion, for example—seems much more important to many churchpeople than Christian unity. This is how things will surely remain for a time.

I hope that the Episcopal Church continues to give example. But I certainly do not wish to convert any other Christian to Anglicanism. I only hope that belief in Christ remains a liberating rather than a confining fact of life for everyone. It is Jesus Christ who must remain the center of Christian lives; it was his cause that all the Churches were meant to serve, rather than impede. Christianity was supposed to bring mankind to unity.

Clare Boothe Luce
(1903–)

A gifted and creative person in many areas, Clare Boothe Luce achieved acclaim as a journalist, editor, war correspondent, playwright, author, and congresswoman. She served in various editorial positions on magazines such as *Vanity Fair*, *Life*, and *Vogue*. She was elected to Congress for two terms and was appointed U.S. Ambassador to Italy.

A prolific author, Clare Boothe Luce wrote, among other things, three highly successful plays — *The Women* (1936), *Kiss the Boys Goodbye* (1938), and *Margin for Error* (1939). All three were Broadway successes, and all three were later made into films. She also wrote and lectured on religious and humanitarian issues, and in 1948 she spoke before large audiences all across the country on "Christianity in the Atomic Age."

In 1935, she married Henry R. Luce, the well-known editor and publisher of *Time* magazine. Mr. Luce, born of Protestant missionary parents, was a staunch Presbyterian, but in 1946 Clare Boothe Luce converted to the Roman Catholic Church. She prepared several articles for *McCall's Magazine* under the title "The Real Reason," explaining the steps and arguments that seemed persuasive to her at the time.

In another connection, she reported an early visionary experience that much later came back to her as confirmation of her decision to become a Catholic. Her later reflective reasons were mostly intellectual and theological, but her early conversion experience was on a very different level of awareness. A portion of that mystical illumination is reprinted here.

The text is from *The Road to Damascus: The Spiritual Pilgrimage of Fifteen Converts to Catholicism*, ed. John A. O'Brien (Garden City, N.Y.: Doubleday, 1949), 223-25.

Let me give one example from my own experience of the honest difficulty in revealing all that seems important to a conversion.

It is an experience which occurred when I was perhaps sixteen or seventeen years old. I no longer remember where it took place, except that it was a summer day on an American beach. I seem to remember that it was early morning, and that I must have been standing on the sand for some time alone, for even now I distinctly remember that this experience was preceded by a sensation of utter aloneness. Not loneliness, but a sort of intense solitariness.

I remember that it was a cool, clean, fresh, calm, blue, radiant day, and that I stood by the shore, my feet not in the waves. And now—as then—I find it difficult to explain what did happen. I expect that the easiest thing is to say that suddenly SOMETHING WAS. My whole soul was cleft clean by it, as a silk veil slit by a shining sword. And I *knew*. I do not know now what I knew. I remember, I didn't know even then. That is, I didn't *know* with any "faculty." It was not in my mind or heart or blood stream. But whatever it was I knew, it was something that made ENORMOUS SENSE. And it was final. And yet that word could not be used, for it meant *end,* and there was no end to *this* finality. Then joy abounded in all of me. Or rather, I abounded in joy. I seemed to have no nature, and yet my whole nature was adrift in this immense joy, as a speck of dust is seen to dance in a great golden shaft of sunlight.

I don't know how long this experience lasted. It was, I should think, closer to a second than to an hour—though it might have been either. The memory of it possessed me for several months afterward. At first I marveled at it. Then I reveled in it. Then it began to obsess me and I tried to put it in some category of previous experience. I remember, I concluded that on that certain day the beauty of nature must have concorded with some unexpected flush of tremendous physical well-being. . . . Gradually I forgot it.

The memory of it never returned to me until one day several years after my conversion, during the first minute of the liturgy of the Mass, where the server says: *"Ad Deum qui laetificat juventutem meum . . ."*

My childhood had been an unusually unhappy and bitter one. I had brooded about it increasingly as I grew older. Indeed until the very day of my conversion, it was a source of deep melancholy and resentment.

"Unless the cup is clean, whatever you pour into it turns sour," said Plato. A conversion cleans the heart of much of its bitterness. Afterward I seldom remembered my marred childhood, except at one strange moment: at the very beginning of the Mass, during the prayers at the foot of the altar. The priest says: "I will go in unto the altar of God." And generally a small altar boy responds in a clear, shy, thin, little voice: "Unto God who giveth joy to my youth." This phrase, unhappily, always awakened faint echoes of bitter youth, and I would think: *Why* didn't God give joy to *my* youth! Why was joy withheld from *my* innocence?

One day, long months after I had been a convert, as these words were said, the bitterness did not come. Instead there suddenly flooded into my mind the experience of which I speak, and my heart was gently suffused with an afterglow of that incredible joy.

Then I knew that this strange occurrence had had an enormous part in my conversion, although I had *seemed* to forget it completely. Long ago, in its tremendous purity and simplicity, and now, in its far fainter evocation, I knew it had been, somehow, the most real experience of my whole life.

But how exactly did this affect my conversion? Why had I forgotten it? Why had I remembered it? God only knows! And what use is it to recount it to anyone interested in "Why I Became a Catholic"?

I mention it here partly to elucidate the real difficulty of "telling all," and partly lest anyone think the convert is not aware of the mysterious movements of his own soul, and that much of a conversion may take place on subconscious levels.

Malcolm Muggeridge
(1903–)

A maverick with a quick wit, a nimble intellect, and a prophetic conscience, Malcolm Muggeridge enjoys his self-appointed role as moral gadfly. A "vendor of words," as he calls himself, he has been associated all his long life with journalism, writing, editing, and publishing.

Most of the time he was moving from one place to another — from Cambridge to Cairo, back to the *Manchester Guardian*, then to Moscow as correspondent, to India, Africa, Italy, and France with the Intelligence Corps in World War II, later to Washington as a correspondent, and then to England as editor of *Punch*. During this incessant, 50-year pilgrimage, he was in addition to his journalistic assignments also writing books on a variety of topics.

Two deepening experiences began to absorb Muggeridge's full attention. One was his growing disillusionment with the programs and politics of modern society, whether communist, capitalist, or socialist, to bring in a kingdom of heaven on earth. As his custom was, he stated it bluntly:

> I disbelieve in progress, the pursuit of happiness, and all the concomitant notions and projects for creating a society in which human beings find ever greater contentment by being given in ever greater abundance the means to satisfy their material and bodily hopes and desires. . . . The half century in which I have been consciously alive seems to me to have been quite exceptionally destructive, murderous, and brutal. More people have been killed and terrorized, more driven from their homes and native places, more of the past's heritage has been destroyed, more lies propagated and base persuasion engaged in, with less compensatory achievement in art, literature, and imaginative understanding, than in any comparable period of history.

But Muggeridge's second compelling idea, as if to redeem his gloomy analysis of modern society, embraces classical Christianity as the only support, comfort, and hope in a time such as ours. He disclaims being a theologian or even a conventional church-goer. But he believes that the Christ figure enshrines the only sure and certain truth in an age of skepticism, shifting values, and gross materialism.

Muggeridge has written several books growing out of his Christian

251

convictions, but his conversion — as he tells it — was more in the nature of an intellectual self-persuasion than an emotional surrender before some dazzling light from heaven. In the excerpt reprinted here, Muggeridge allows us to relive with him his dawning awareness of the only alternative to ultimate despair. Addressed, as it were, to Jesus himself, he speaks informally yet with reverence of the Christ figure as "You."

The text is taken from the chapter "Jesus Rediscovered," in his book with the same title (New York: Doubleday & Co., 1969), 48-51. The chapter originally appeared in Esquire magazine, June 1969, under the title "On Rediscovering Jesus." Reprinted by permission by Doubleday & Co. and David Higham Associates, Ltd., London.

It was padding about the streets of Moscow that the other dream—the kingdom of heaven on earth—dissolved for me, never to be revived. Those gray, anonymous figures, likewise padding about the streets, seemed infinitely remote, withdrawn, forever strangers, yet somehow near and dear. The gray streets were paradise, the eyeless buildings the many mansions of which heaven is composed. I caught another glimpse of paradise in Berlin after it had been liberated—there the mansions made of rubble, and the heavenly hosts, the glow of liberation still upon them, bartering cigarettes for tins of Spam, and love for both. (Later, this paradise was transformed by means of mirrors into a shining, glowing one, running with *schlag* and fat cigars, with bartered love still plentifully available, but for paper money, not Spam.) So many paradises springing up all over the place, all with many mansions, mansions of light and love; the most majestic of all, the master paradise on which all the others were based—on Manhattan Island! Oh, what marvelous mansions there reaching into the sky! What heavenly Muzak overflowing the streets and buildings, what brilliant lights spelling out what delectable hopes and desires, what heavenly hosts pursuing what happiness on magic screens in living color!

And You? I never caught even a glimpse of You in any paradise—unless You were an old, colored shoeshine man on a windy corner in Chicago one February morning, smiling from ear to ear; or a little man with a lame leg in the Immigration Department in New York, whose smiling patience as he listened to one Puerto Rican after another seemed to reach from there to eternity. Oh, and whoever painted the front of the little church in the woods at Kliasma near Moscow—painted it in blues as bright as the sky and whites that outshone the snow? That might have been You. Or again at Kiev, at an Easter service when the collectivization famine was in full swing, and Bernard Shaw and newspaper correspondents were telling the world of the bursting granaries and apple-cheeked dairymaids in the Ukraine. What a congregation that was, packed in tight, squeezed together like sardines! I myself was pressed against a stone pillar, and scarcely able to breathe. Not that I wanted to, particularly. So many gray, hungry faces, all luminous like an El Greco painting; and all singing. How they sang—about how there was no help except in You, nowhere to turn except to You; nothing, nothing that could possibly bring any comfort except You. I could have touched You then, You were so near—not up at the altar, of course, where the bearded priests, crowned and bowing and chanting, swung their censers—one of the gray faces, the grayest and most luminous of all.

It was strange in a way that I should thus have found myself nearest to You in the land where for half a century past the practice of the Christian religion has been most ruthlessly suppressed; where the very printing of the Gospels is forbidden, and You are derided by all the organs of an all-powerful state as once You were by ribald Roman soldiers when they decked you out as King of the Jews. Yet, on reflection, not so strange. How infinitely preferable it is to be abhorred, rather than embraced, by those in authority. Where the distinction between God and Caesar is so abundantly clear, no one in his senses—or out of them, for that matter— is likely to suggest that any good purpose would be served by arranging a dialogue between the two of them. In the Communist countries an unmistakable and unbridgeable abyss divides the kingdoms on earth in the Devil's gift and Your kingdom, with no crazed clerics gibbering and grimacing in the intervening no man's land. It provides the perfect circumstances for the Christian faith to bloom anew—so uncannily like the circumstances in which it first bloomed at the beginning of the Christian era. I look eastwards, not westwards, for a new Star of Bethlehem.

It would be comforting to be able to say, Now I see! To recite with total satisfaction one of the Church's venerable creeds: "I believe in God, the Father Almighty. . . ." To point to such a moment of illumination when all became miraculously clear. To join with full identification in one of the varieties of Christian worship. Above all, to feel able to say to you, "Lord!" and confidently await Your command. Comforting—but, alas, it would not be true. The one thing above all others that You require of us is, surely, the truth. I have to confess, then, that I see only fitfully, believe no creed wholly, have had no all-sufficing moment of illumination.

And You? What do I know of You? A living presence in the world; the one who, of all the billions of our human family, came most immediately from God and went most immediately to God, while remaining most humanly and intimately here among us, today, as yesterday and tomorrow; for all time. Did You live and die and rise from the dead as they say? Who knows, or, for that matter, cares? History is for the dead, and You are alive. Similarly, all those churches raised and maintained in Your name, from the tiniest, weirdest conventicle to the great cathedrals rising so sublimely into the sky—they are for the dead, and must themselves die; are, indeed, dying fast. They belong to time, You to eternity. At the intersection of time and eternity—nailed there—You confront us; a perpetual reminder that living, we die, and dying, we live. An incarnation wonderful to contemplate; the light of the world, indeed.

Fiat lux! Let there be light! So everything began at God's majestic command; so it might have continued till the end of time—history unending—except that You intervened, shining another light into the innermost recesses of the human will, where the ego reigns and reaches out in tentacles of dark desire. Having seen this other light, I turn to it, striving and growing toward it as plants do toward the sun. The light of love, abolishing the darkness of hate; the light of peace, abolishing the darkness of strife and confusion; the light of life, abolishing the darkness of death; the light of creativity, abolishing the darkness of destruction. Though, in terms of history, the darkness falls, blacking out us and our world, You have overcome history. You came as light into the world in order that whoever believed in You should not remain in darkness. Your light shines in the darkness, and the darkness has not overcome it. Nor ever will.

Eldridge Cleaver
(1935–   )

The conversion of Eldridge Cleaver has been one of the most widely publicized stories of recent years. During the 1960s, Cleaver attained fame and notoriety as a black revolutionary and one of the leaders of the strongly militant Black Panther organization. From prison he published his best-selling autobiography, Soul on Ice (1966), and after his release he was involved in a shoot-out with Oakland police in 1968. He fled to Canada and then traveled to Cuba, Algeria, and France, securing asylum as a political refugee.

Although he was strongly influenced by Marxist thought during the 1960s and 1970s, he began to be disillusioned with its revolutionary implications, for as he wrote, "Communism had nothing to offer me but another chapter in tyranny. I had been trying to escape that all my life and ended up running headlong into its main centers." Gradually he began to want to return to the United States and tried to work out an arrangement with his lawyers to make that possible. All his friends told him that it was not possible; one friend said that even his former black political allies did not want to be bothered with him. "It was like a sentence," Cleaver wrote, "another era of serving time."

His conversion, described later in his book Soul on Fire (1978), came at this point of discouragement and despair in his life, and he decided to return to the United States to face trial. Various Christians came to see him in jail, and a group of Christian businessmen raised $100,000 for his bail. He was released in 1976 and pled guilty in 1980 to three assault charges. He was sentenced to probation and 2,000 hours of community service work.

Cleaver's turn to Christianity was not a rejection of his concern for social justice, for he said, "Socialism is in part based on the teachings of Jesus Christ. I find no conflict between [Christianity and socialism] until you get to revolutionary ideology." Theologically, Cleaver sampled many diverse trends — ranging from the charismatic movement, to Black Muslims, to the Moonies; he confessed, "I'm still getting to know what's going on in the Christian family. . . . I'm still naive enough to believe that Jesus is for everybody. It is us and not Jesus who make these distinctions."

Cleaver's conversion was greeted with skepticism and disbelief both within and outside the church. The Society of Separationists, an organization of atheists, gave Cleaver its Religious Hypocrite of the Year award in 1977, and Cleaver complained about some reactions from Christians as well. "There are some Christians who need to be more concerned with encouraging new Christians, instead of putting banana peels under their feet," he declared. "Some people don't want to accept me into the family of the church." Cleaver has established his own evangelistic organization and travels widely, speaking to religious groups.

Excerpted from *Soul on Fire* (Waco, Tex.: Word Books, 1978), 210-12. Copyright © Eldridge Cleaver, 1978. Reprinted by permission of Word Books.

That [hearing he could not return to the United States] was like a thread, I was suspended from, being cut. I began to experience a severe depression. Perhaps I have been crazy all my life, but I never went around depressed or brooding or tormented or anything like that. In this situation in France, I began to be terribly depressed. I began to feel completely, totally useless, burdened. I began to put a lot of pressure on my wife with the idea of driving her away and forcing her to go back to the United States and take the children. I was the obstacle. Kathleen had never been arrested in her life. My children had never been arrested. They were free. I was the fugitive and it was my fault we were locked out; and I began to feel guilty to the extent that I could hardly face them. To be around them I felt miserable, guilty, seeing the emptiness that had become our life.

In addition to our house in Paris, we had an apartment on the Mediterranean coast near Cannes and Nice. Here I had all of my books and filing cabinets, typewriter, manuscripts; and I could go there to be alone to write. I would go there and just sit and stare out in space with a blank mind—just miserable—becoming more and more miserable as if there were no end to misery—just becoming worse and worse and worse. I would return to Paris, and that didn't help. I'd go back down to the coast, and that didn't help. I was running back and forth—getting worse and worse.

Finally, one night in Paris I became aware of the hopelessness of our situation. We were sitting down to dinner and we had two candles on the table. All the lights in the house were out, and I was suddenly struck that this was a perfect metaphor for our life: our life was empty—there was no light in our life. We were going through an empty ritual, eating in the same spirit in which you might drive to a gas station and fill up the tank. It was meaningless, pointless, getting nowhere.

I returned to the Mediterranean Coast and began thinking of putting an end to it all by committing suicide. I really began to think about that. I was sitting up on my balcony, one night, on the thirteenth floor—just sitting there. It was a beautiful Mediterranean night—sky, stars, moon hanging there in a sable void. I was brooding, downcast, at the end of my rope. I looked up at the moon and saw certain shadows . . . and the shadows became a man in the moon, and I saw a profile of myself (a profile that we had used on posters for the Black Panther Party—something I had seen a thousand times). I was already upset and this scared me. When I saw that image, I started trembling. It was a shaking that came from deep inside, and it had a threat about it that this mood was getting worse, that I could possibly disintegrate on the scene and fall apart. As I stared at this image, it changed, and I saw my former heroes paraded before my eyes. Here were Fidel Castro, Mao Tse-tung, Karl Marx, Frederick Engels, passing in review—each one appearing for a moment of time, and then dropping out of sight, like fallen heroes. Finally, at the end of the procession, in dazzling, shimmering light, the image of Jesus Christ appeared. That was the last straw.

I just crumbled and started crying. I fell to my knees, grabbing hold of the banister; and in the midst of this shaking and crying the Lord's Prayer and the 23rd Psalm came into my mind. I hadn't thought about these prayers for years. I started repeating them, and after a time I gained some control over the trembling and crying. Then I jumped up and ran to my bookshelf and got the Bible. It was the family Bible my mother had given to me because I am the oldest boy—the oldest son. And this Bible . . . when Kathleen left the United States, she brought with her a very small bag, and instead of grabbing the Communist Manifesto or *Das Kapital,* she packed that Bible. That is the Bible that I grabbed from the shelf that night and in which I turned to the 23rd Psalm. I discovered that my memory really had not served me that well. I got lost somewhere between the Valley of the Shadow of Death and the overflowing cup. But it was the Bible in which I searched and found that psalm. I read through it. At that time I didn't even know where to find the Lord's Prayer. I looked for it desperately. Pretty soon the type started swimming before my eyes, and I lay down on the bed and went to sleep.

That night I slept the most peaceful sleep I have ever known in my life. I woke up the next morning with a start, as though someone had touched me, and I could see in my mind the way, all the way back home, just as clear as I've ever seen anything. I saw a path of light that ran through a prison cell. . . . This prison cell was a dark spot on this path of light, and the meaning, which was absolutely clear to me, was that I didn't have to wait on any politician to help me get back home. I had it within my power to get back home by taking that first step, by surrendering; and it was a certainty that everything was going to be all right. I just knew that—that was the solution, and I would be all right if I would take that step.

Charles W. Colson
(1931–   )

Known as "the hatchet man" for Richard Nixon, Charles Colson's name was implicated in the Watergate scandal in 1974. As Special Assistant to the President, he was at the top and in the center of the political intrigues during that famous and frenetic period of time. Sentenced to prison, Colson served a seven-month term until his release, January 31, 1975.

Two years earlier, in 1973, Colson made public his conversion, saying that he had "accepted Jesus Christ." His account of that experience, in the context of the political events of the time, is graphically set forth in his book *Born Again* (1976). Though not described in theological or doctrinal language, his conversion has the authentic mark of sincerity and honesty.

After his prison release, Colson became increasingly involved in helping prison inmates. With the encouragement of good friends in Washington, such as Harold Hughes, former senator from Iowa, himself a twice-born Christian, and several interested wardens, he established what became known as the Prison Fellowship. Colson has written about his work with this Christian evangelistic movement in a lively book entitled *Life Sentence* (1979).

Although some have questioned the genuineness of Colson's conversion, others, such as Billy Graham and Catharine Marshall, have testified in his favor, and many have been moved and inspired by his innovative and practical prison ministry.

As so often happens in conversion experiences, someone stands by to help and encourage. In Colson's case, it was his friend Tom Phillips, President of the Raytheon Company, who gave him a copy of C. S. Lewis's *Mere Christianity*.

The text of Charles Colson's conversion account is from *Born Again* (Old Tappan, N.J.: Chosen Books, Inc.; London: Hodder and Stoughton, 1976), 109-17. © 1976 by Charles Colson and reprinted by permission.

It was an unusually hot night for New England, the humidity like a heavy blanket wrapped around me. At Tom's insistence, first the dark gray business-suit jacket, then my tie came off. He pulled a wrought-iron ottoman close to the comfortable outdoor settee I sat on.

"Tell me, Chuck," he began, "are you okay?" It was the same question he had asked in March.

As the President's confidant and so-called big-shot Washington law-yer I was still keeping my guard up. "I'm not doing too badly, I guess. All of this Watergate business, all the accusations—I suppose it's wearing me down some. But I'd rather talk about you, Tom. You've changed and I'd like to know what happened."

Tom drank from his glass and sat back reflectively. Briefly he re-viewed his past, the rapid rise to power at Raytheon: executive vice-pres-ident at thirty-seven, president when he was only forty. He had done it with hard work, day and night, nonstop.

"The success came, all right, but something was missing," he mused. "I felt a terrible emptiness. Sometimes I would get up in the middle of the night and pace the floor of my bedroom or stare out into the darkness for hours at a time."

"I don't understand it," I interrupted. "I knew you in those days, Tom. You were a straight arrow, good family life, successful, everything in fact going your way."

"All that may be true, Chuck, but my life wasn't complete. I would go to the office each day and do my job, striving all the time to make the company succeed, but there was a big hole in my life. I began to read the Scriptures, looking for answers. Something made me realize I needed a personal relationship with God, forced me to search."

A prickly feeling ran down my spine. Maybe what I had gone through in the past several months wasn't so unusual after all—except I had not sought spiritual answers. I had not even been aware that finding a personal relationship with God was possible. I pressed him to explain the apparent contradiction between the emptiness inside while seeming to enjoy the affluent life.

"It may be hard to understand," Tom chuckled. "But I didn't seem to have anything that mattered. It was all on the surface. All the material things in life are meaningless if a man hasn't discovered what's underneath them."

We were both silent for a while as I groped for understanding. Outside, the first fireflies punctuated the mauve dusk. Tom got up and switched on two small lamps on end tables in the corners of the porch.

"One night I was in New York on business and noticed that Billy Graham was having a Crusade in Madison Square Garden," Tom continued. "I went—curious, I guess—hoping maybe I'd find some answers. What Graham said that night put it all into place for me. I saw what was missing, the personal relationship with Jesus Christ, the fact that I hadn't ever asked Him into my life, hadn't turned my life over to Him. So I did it—that very night at the Crusade."

Tom's tall, gangling frame leaned toward me, silhouetted by the yellow light behind him. Though his face was shaded, I could see his eyes begin to glisten and his voice became softer. "I asked Christ to come into my life and I could feel His presence with me, His peace within me. I could sense His Spirit there with me. Then I went out for a walk alone on the streets of New York. I never liked New York before, but this night it was beautiful. I walked for blocks and blocks, I guess. Everything seemed different to me. It was raining softly and the city lights created a golden glow. Something had happened to me and I knew it."

"That's what you mean by accepting Christ—you just ask?" I was more puzzled than ever.

"That's it, as simple as that," Tom replied. "Of course, you have to want Jesus in your life, really want Him. That's the way it starts. And let me tell you, things then begin to change. Since then I have found a satisfaction and a joy about living that I simply never knew was possible."

To me Jesus had always been an historical figure, but Tom explained that you could hardly invite Him into your life if you didn't believe that He is alive today and that His Spirit is a part of today's scene. I was moved by Tom's story even though I couldn't imagine how such a miraculous change could take place in such a simple way. Yet the excitement in Tom's voice as he described his experience was convincing and Tom was indeed different. More alive.

Then Tom turned the conversation again to my plight. I described some of the agonies of Watergate, the pressures I was under, how unfairly I thought the press was treating me. I was being defensive and when I ran out of explanations, Tom spoke gently but firmly.

"You know that I supported Nixon in this past election, but you guys made a serious mistake. You would have won the election without any of the hanky-panky. Watergate and the dirty tricks were so unnecessary. And it was wrong, just plain wrong. You didn't have to do it."

Tom was leaning forward, elbows on his knees, his hands stretched forward almost as if he was trying to reach out for me. There was an urgent appeal in his eyes. "Don't you understand that?" he asked with such genuine feeling that I couldn't take offense.

"If only you had believed in the rightness of your cause, none of this would have been necessary. None of this would have happened. The problem with all of you, including you, Chuck—you simply had to go for the other guy's jugular. You had to try to destroy your enemies. You had to destroy them because you couldn't trust in yourselves."

The heat at that moment seemed unbearable as I wiped away drops of perspiration over my lip. The iced tea was soothing as I sipped it, although with Tom's points hitting home so painfully, I longed for a Scotch and soda. To myself I admitted that Tom was on target: the world of *us* against *them* as we saw it from our insulated White House enclave—the Nixon White House against the world. Insecure about our cause, our overkill approach was a way to play it safe. And yet. . . .

"Tom, one thing you don't understand. In politics it's dog-eat-dog;

you simply can't survive otherwise. I've been in the political business for twenty years, including several campaigns right here in Massachusetts. I know how things are done. Politics is like war. If you don't keep the enemy on the defensive, you'll be on the defensive yourself. Tom, this man Nixon has been under constant attack all of his life. The only way he could make it was to fight back. Look at the criticism he took over Vietnam. Yet he was right. We never would have made it if we hadn't fought the way we did, hitting our critics, never letting them get the best of us. We didn't have any choice."

Even as I talked, the words sounded more and more empty to me. Tired old lines, I realized. I was describing the ways of the political world, all right, while suddenly wondering if there could be a better way.

Tom believed so, anyway. He was so gentle I couldn't resent what he said as he cut right through it all: "Chuck, I hate to say this, but you guys brought it on yourselves. If you had put your faith in God, and if your cause were just, He would have guided you. And His help would have been a thousand times more powerful than all your phony ads and shady schemes put together."

With any other man the notion of relying on God would have seemed to me pure Pollyanna. Yet I had to be impressed with the way this man ran his company in the equally competitive world of business: ignoring his enemies, trying to follow God's ways. Since his conversion Raytheon had never done better, sales and profits soaring. Maybe there was something to it; anyway it's tough to argue with success.

"Chuck, I don't think you will understand what I'm saying about God until you are willing to face yourself honestly and squarely. This is the first step." Tom reached to the corner table and picked up a small paperback book. I read the title: *Mere Christianity* by C. S. Lewis.

"I suggest you take this with you and read it while you are on vacation." Tom started to hand it to me, then paused. "Let me read you one chapter."

I leaned back, still on the defensive, my mind and emotions whirling.

There is one vice of which no man in the world is free; which every one in the world loathes when he sees it in someone else; and of which hardly any people, except Christians, ever imagine that they are guilty themselves. I have heard people admit that they are bad-tempered, or that they cannot keep their heads about girls or drink, or even that they are cowards. I do not think I have ever heard anyone who was not a Christian accuse himself of this vice. . . . There is no fault . . . which we are more unconscious of in ourselves. And the more we have it ourselves, the more we dislike it in others.

The vice I am talking of is Pride or Self-Conceit. . . . Pride leads to every other vice: it is the complete anti-God state of mind.

As he read, I could feel a flush coming into my face and a curious burning sensation that made the night seem even warmer. Lewis's words seemed to pound straight at me.

> ... it is Pride which has been the chief cause of misery in every nation and every family since the world began. Other vices may sometimes bring people together: you may find good fellowship and jokes and friendliness among drunken people or unchaste people. But Pride always means enmity—it *is* enmity. And not only enmity between man and man, but enmity to God.

> In God you come up against something which is in every respect immeasurably superior to yourself. Unless you know God as that— and, therefore, know yourself as nothing in comparison—you do not know God at all. As long as you are proud you cannot know God. A proud man is always looking down on things and people: and, of course, as long as you are looking down, you cannot see something that is above you.

Suddenly I felt naked and unclean, my bravado defenses gone. I was exposed, unprotected, for Lewis's words were describing me. As he continued, one passage in particular seemed to sum up what had happened to all of us at the White House:

> For Pride is spiritual cancer: it eats up the very possibility of love, or contentment, or even common sense.

Just as a man about to die is supposed to see flash before him, sequence by sequence, the high points of his life, so, as Tom's voice read on that August evening, key events in my life paraded before me as if projected on a screen. Things I hadn't thought about in years—my graduation speech at prep school—being "good enough" for the Marines—my first marriage, into the "right" family—sitting on the Jaycees' dais while civic leader after civic leader praised me as the outstanding young man of Boston—then to the White House—the clawing and straining for status and position—"Mr. Colson, the President is calling—Mr. Colson, the President wants to see you right away."

For some reason I thought of an incident after the 1972 election when a reporter, an old Nixon nemesis, came by my office and contritely asked what he could do to get in the good graces of the White House. I suggested that he try "slashing his wrists." I meant it as a joke, of course, but also to make him squirm. It was the arrogance of the victor over an enemy brought to submission.

Now, sitting there on the dimly lit porch, my self-centered past was washing over me in waves. It was painful. Agony. Desperately I tried to defend myself. What about my sacrifices for government service, the giving up of a big income, putting my stocks into a blind trust? The truth, I saw in an instant, was that I'd wanted the position in the White House more than I'd wanted money. There was no sacrifice. And the more I had talked about my own sacrifices, the more I was really trying to build myself up in the eyes of others. I would eagerly have given up everything I'd ever earned to prove myself at the mountaintop of government. It was pride—Lewis's "great sin"—that had propelled me through life.

Tom finished the chapter on pride and shut the book. I mumbled something noncommittal to the effect that "I'll look forward to reading that." But Lewis's torpedo had hit me amidships. I think Phillips knew it as he stared into my eyes. That one chapter ripped through the protective armor in which I had unknowingly encased myself for forty-two years. Of course, I had not known God. *How could I?* I had been concerned with myself. *I* had done this and that, *I* had achieved, *I* had succeeded and *I* had given God none of the credit, never once thanking Him for any of His gifts to me. I had never thought of anything being "immeasurably superior" to myself, or if I had in fleeting moments thought about the infinite power of God, I had not related Him to my life. In those brief moments while Tom read, I saw myself as I never had before. And the picture was ugly.

"How about it, Chuck?" Tom's question jarred me out of my trance. I knew precisely what he meant. Was I ready to make the leap of faith as he had in New York, to "accept" Christ?

"Tom, you've shaken me up. I'll admit that. That chapter describes me. But I can't tell you I'm ready to make the kind of commitment you did. I've got to be certain. I've got to learn a lot more, be sure all my reservations are satisfied. I've got a lot of intellectual hang-ups to get past."

For a moment Tom looked disappointed, then he smiled. "I understand, I understand."

"You see," I continued, "I saw men turn to God in the Marine Corps; I did once myself. Then afterwards it's all forgotten and everything is back to normal. Foxhole religion is just a way of using God. How can I make a commitment now? My whole world is crashing down around me. How can I be sure I'm not just running for shelter and that when the crisis is over I'll forget it? I've got to answer all the intellectual arguments first and if I can do that, I'll be sure."

"I understand," Tom repeated quietly.

I was relieved he did, yet deep inside of me something wanted to tell Tom to press on. He was making so much sense, the first time anyone ever had in talking about God.

But Tom did not press on. He handed me his copy of *Mere Christianity*. "Once you've read this, you might want to read the Book of John in the Bible." I scribbled notes on the key passages he quoted. "Also there's a man in Washington you should meet," he continued, "name of Doug Coe. He gets people together for Christian fellowship—prayer breakfasts and things like that. I'll ask him to contact you."

Tom then reached for his Bible and read a few of his favorite psalms. The comforting words were like a cold soothing ointment. For the first time in my life, familiar verses I'd heard chanted lifelessly in church came alive. "Trust in the Lord," I remember Tom reading, and I wanted to, right that moment I wanted to—if only I knew how, if only I could be sure.

"Would you like to pray together, Chuck?" Tom asked, closing his Bible and putting it on the table beside him.

Startled, I emerged from my deep thoughts. "Sure—I guess I would— Fine." I'd never prayed with anyone before except when someone said grace before a meal. Tom bowed his head, folded his hands, and leaned forward on the edge of his seat. "Lord," he began, "we pray for Chuck and his family, that You might open his heart and show him the light and the way. . . ."

As Tom prayed, something began to flow into me—a kind of energy. Then came a wave of emotion which nearly brought tears. I fought them back. It sounded as if Tom were speaking directly and personally to God, almost as if He were sitting beside us. The only prayers I'd ever heard were formal and stereotyped, sprinkled with *Thees* and *Thous*.

When he finished, there was a long silence. I knew he expected me to pray but I didn't know what to say and was too self-conscious to try. We walked to the kitchen together where Gert was still at the big table, reading. I thanked her and Tom for their hospitality.

"Come back, won't you?" she said. Her smile convinced me she meant it.

"Take care of yourself, Chuck, and let me know what you think of that book, will you?" With that, Tom put his hand on my shoulder and grinned. "I'll see you soon."

I didn't say much; I was afraid my voice would crack, but I had the strong feeling that I *would* see him soon. And I couldn't wait to read his little book.

Outside in the darkness, the iron grip I'd kept on my emotions began to relax. Tears welled up in my eyes as I groped in the darkness for the right key to start my car. Angrily I brushed them away and started the engine. "What kind of weakness is this?" I said to nobody.

The tears spilled over and suddenly I knew I had to go back into the house and pray with Tom. I turned off the motor, got out of the car. As I did, the kitchen light went out, then the light in the dining room. Through the hall window I saw Tom stand aside as Gert started up the stairs ahead of him. Now the hall was in darkness. It was too late. I stood for a moment staring at the darkened house, only one light burning now in an upstairs bedroom. Why hadn't I prayed when he gave me the chance? I wanted to so badly. Now I was alone, really alone.

As I drove out of Tom's driveway, the tears were flowing uncontrollably. There were no streetlights, no moonlight. The car headlights were flooding illumination before my eyes, but I was crying so hard it was like trying to swim underwater. I pulled to the side of the road not more than a hundred yards from the entrance to Tom's driveway, the tires sinking into soft mounds of pine needles.

I remember hoping that Tom and Gert wouldn't hear my sobbing, the only sound other than the chirping of crickets that penetrated the still of the night. With my face cupped in my hands, head leaning forward against the wheel, I forgot about machismo, about pretenses, about fears of being weak. And as I did, I began to experience a wonderful feeling of being released. Then came the strange sensation that water was not only running down my cheeks, but surging through my whole body as well, cleansing and cooling as it went. They weren't tears of sadness and remorse, nor of joy—but somehow, tears of relief.

And then I prayed my first real prayer. "God, I don't know how to find You, but I'm going to try! I'm not much the way I am now, but somehow I want to give myself to You." I didn't know how to say more, so I repeated over and over the words: *Take me.*

I had not "accepted" Christ—I still didn't know who He was. My mind told me it was important to find that out first, to be sure that I knew what I was doing, that I meant it and would stay with it. Only, that night, something inside me was urging me to surrender—to what or to whom I did not know.

I stayed there in the car, wet-eyed, praying, thinking, for perhaps half an hour, perhaps longer, alone in the quiet of the dark night. Yet for the first time in my life I was not alone at all.